Just The facts101

Textbook Key Facts

China Pharmaceutical Chemicals Producers Directory

by Cram101
Textbook NOT Included

Table of Contents

Title Page

Copyright

Foundations of Business

Management

Business law

Finance

Human resource management

Information systems

Marketing

Manufacturing

Commerce

Business ethics

Accounting

Index: Answers

Just The Facts101

Exam Prep for

China Pharmaceutical Chemicals Producers Directory

Just The Facts101 Exam Prep is your link from
the textbook and lecture to your exams.

**Just The Facts101 Exam Preps are unauthorized and comprehensive reviews
of your textbooks.**

All material provided by CTI Publications (c) 2019

Textbook publishers and textbook authors do not participate in or contribute to these reviews.

Just The Facts101 Exam Prep

Copyright © 2019 by CTI Publications. All rights reserved.

eAIN 449720

Foundations of Business

A business, also known as an enterprise, agency or a firm, is an entity involved in the provision of goods and/or services to consumers. Businesses are prevalent in capitalist economies, where most of them are privately owned and provide goods and services to customers in exchange for other goods, services, or money.

:: Management ::

_____ is the process of thinking about the activities required to achieve a desired goal. It is the first and foremost activity to achieve desired results. It involves the creation and maintenance of a plan, such as psychological aspects that require conceptual skills. There are even a couple of tests to measure someone's capability of _____ well. As such, _____ is a fundamental property of intelligent behavior. An important further meaning, often just called " _____ " is the legal context of permitted building developments.

Exam Probability: **Medium**

1. *Answer choices:*

(see index for correct answer)

- a. Management cockpit
- b. Allegiance
- c. Management entrenchment
- d. Planning

Guidance: level 1

:: ::

Business is the activity of making one's living or making money by producing or buying and selling products. Simply put, it is "any activity or enterprise entered into for profit. It does not mean it is a company, a corporation, partnership, or have any such formal organization, but it can range from a street peddler to General Motors."

Exam Probability: **Medium**

2. *Answer choices:*

(see index for correct answer)

- a. empathy
- b. Firm
- c. interpersonal communication
- d. corporate values

Guidance: level 1

:: Marketing ::

_____ comes from the Latin neg and otsia referring to businessmen who, unlike the patricians, had no leisure time in their industriousness; it held the meaning of business until the 17th century when it took on the diplomatic connotation as a dialogue between two or more people or parties intended to reach a beneficial outcome over one or more issues where a conflict exists with respect to at least one of these issues. Thus, _____ is a process of combining divergent positions into a joint agreement under a decision rule of unanimity.

Exam Probability: **Low**

3. *Answer choices:*

(see index for correct answer)

- a. Negotiation
- b. Customer to customer
- c. Product planning
- d. Alpha consumer

Guidance: level 1

:: Business models ::

A _____ is "an autonomous association of persons united voluntarily to meet their common economic, social, and cultural needs and aspirations through a jointly-owned and democratically-controlled enterprise". _____ s may include.

Exam Probability: **Medium**

4. *Answer choices:*

(see index for correct answer)

- a. Dependent growth business model
- b. Legacy carrier
- c. Interactive contract manufacturing
- d. Cooperative

Guidance: level 1

:: ::

_____ is the study and management of exchange relationships. _____ is the business process of creating relationships with and satisfying customers. With its focus on the customer, _____ is one of the premier components of business management.

Exam Probability: **High**

5. *Answer choices:*

(see index for correct answer)

- a. corporate values
- b. open system
- c. Marketing
- d. similarity-attraction theory

Guidance: level 1

:: Information systems ::

_____ are formal, sociotechnical, organizational systems designed to collect, process, store, and distribute information. In a sociotechnical perspective, _____ are composed by four components: task, people, structure, and technology.

Exam Probability: **High**

6. Answer choices:

(see index for correct answer)

- a. Manufacturing execution system
- b. Ucode system
- c. Information systems
- d. Feral information systems

Guidance: level 1

:: Business planning ::

_____ is an organization's process of defining its strategy, or direction, and making decisions on allocating its resources to pursue this strategy. It may also extend to control mechanisms for guiding the implementation of the strategy. _____ became prominent in corporations during the 1960s and remains an important aspect of strategic management. It is executed by strategic planners or strategists, who involve many parties and research sources in their analysis of the organization and its relationship to the environment in which it competes.

Exam Probability: **Low**

7. Answer choices:

(see index for correct answer)

- a. Stakeholder management
- b. Strategic planning

- c. Customer Demand Planning
- d. Open Options Corporation

Guidance: level 1

:: ::

Competition arises whenever at least two parties strive for a goal which cannot be shared: where one's gain is the other's loss .

Exam Probability: **Low**

8. *Answer choices:*

(see index for correct answer)

- a. co-culture
- b. Competitor
- c. functional perspective
- d. information systems assessment

Guidance: level 1

:: Foreign direct investment ::

A _____ is an investment in the form of a controlling ownership in a business in one country by an entity based in another country. It is thus distinguished from a foreign portfolio investment by a notion of direct control.

Exam Probability: **Low**

9. *Answer choices:*

(see index for correct answer)

- a. Foreign ownership
- b. Oligopolistic reaction
- c. Foreign direct investment
- d. FDi magazine

Guidance: level 1

:: Planning ::

_____ is a high level plan to achieve one or more goals under conditions of uncertainty. In the sense of the "art of the general," which included several subsets of skills including tactics, siegecraft, logistics etc., the term came into use in the 6th century C.E. in East Roman terminology, and was translated into Western vernacular languages only in the 18th century. From then until the 20th century, the word "_____" came to denote "a comprehensive way to try to pursue political ends, including the threat or actual use of force, in a dialectic of wills" in a military conflict, in which both adversaries interact.

Exam Probability: **High**

10. *Answer choices:*

(see index for correct answer)

- a. Cross-cultural differences in decision-making
- b. School timetable
- c. BLUF
- d. Strategy

Guidance: level 1

:: Health promotion ::

_____, as defined by the World _____ Organization, is "a state of complete physical, mental and social well-being and not merely the absence of disease or infirmity." This definition has been subject to controversy, as it may have limited value for implementation. _____ may be defined as the ability to adapt and manage physical, mental and social challenges throughout life.

Exam Probability: **Low**

11. *Answer choices:*

(see index for correct answer)

- a. Care Continuum Alliance
- b. United States Army Public Health Command

- c. Health
- d. Health impact assessment

Guidance: level 1

:: Cash flow ::

_____s are narrowly interconnected with the concepts of value, interest rate and liquidity. A _____ that shall happen on a future day tN can be transformed into a _____ of the same value in t0.

Exam Probability: **High**

12. *Answer choices:*
(see index for correct answer)

- a. Cash flow
- b. Cash flow statement
- c. Propequity
- d. First Chicago Method

Guidance: level 1

:: Television commercials ::

_____ is a characteristic that distinguishes physical entities that have biological processes, such as signaling and self-sustaining processes, from those that do not, either because such functions have ceased, or because they never had such functions and are classified as inanimate. Various forms of _____ exist, such as plants, animals, fungi, protists, archaea, and bacteria. The criteria can at times be ambiguous and may or may not define viruses, viroids, or potential synthetic _____ as "living". Biology is the science concerned with the study of _____ .

Exam Probability: **Low**

13. *Answer choices:*

(see index for correct answer)

- a. Robotskin
- b. Life
- c. Blue Velvet
- d. The Force

Guidance: level 1

:: Real estate ::

_____ s serve several societal needs – primarily as shelter from weather, security, living space, privacy, to store belongings, and to comfortably live and work. A _____ as a shelter represents a physical division of the human habitat and the outside .

Exam Probability: **Low**

14. *Answer choices:*

(see index for correct answer)

- a. Building
- b. Association law
- c. Bundle of rights
- d. RealtyCompass

Guidance: level 1

:: Majority–minority relations ::

_____ , also known as reservation in India and Nepal, positive discrimination / action in the United Kingdom, and employment equity in Canada and South Africa, is the policy of promoting the education and employment of members of groups that are known to have previously suffered from discrimination. Historically and internationally, support for _____ has sought to achieve goals such as bridging inequalities in employment and pay, increasing access to education, promoting diversity, and redressing apparent past wrongs, harms, or hindrances.

Exam Probability: **High**

15. *Answer choices:*

(see index for correct answer)

- a. cultural Relativism
- b. positive discrimination
- c. cultural dissonance

Guidance: level 1

:: ::

_____ is the administration of an organization, whether it is a business, a not-for-profit organization, or government body. _____ includes the activities of setting the strategy of an organization and coordinating the efforts of its employees to accomplish its objectives through the application of available resources, such as financial, natural, technological, and human resources. The term " _____ " may also refer to those people who manage an organization.

Exam Probability: **Low**

16. *Answer choices:*

(see index for correct answer)

- a. Management
- b. functional perspective
- c. interpersonal communication
- d. corporate values

Guidance: level 1

:: Critical thinking ::

An _____ is a set of statements usually constructed to describe a set of facts which clarifies the causes, context, and consequences of those facts. This description of the facts et cetera may establish rules or laws, and may clarify the existing rules or laws in relation to any objects, or phenomena examined. The components of an _____ can be implicit, and interwoven with one another.

Exam Probability: **High**

17. *Answer choices:*

(see index for correct answer)

- a. Explanation
- b. Adviser
- c. Attacking Faulty Reasoning
- d. Argument by example

Guidance: level 1

:: Debt ::

_____ is the trust which allows one party to provide money or resources to another party wherein the second party does not reimburse the first party immediately, but promises either to repay or return those resources at a later date. In other words, _____ is a method of making reciprocity formal, legally enforceable, and extensible to a large group of unrelated people.

Exam Probability: **Low**

18. *Answer choices:*

(see index for correct answer)

- a. Troubled Debt Restructuring
- b. Bad debt
- c. Floating charge
- d. Museum of Foreign Debt

Guidance: level 1

:: Decision theory ::

A _____ is a deliberate system of principles to guide decisions and achieve rational outcomes. A _____ is a statement of intent, and is implemented as a procedure or protocol. Policies are generally adopted by a governance body within an organization. Policies can assist in both subjective and objective decision making. Policies to assist in subjective decision making usually assist senior management with decisions that must be based on the relative merits of a number of factors, and as a result are often hard to test objectively, e.g. work-life balance _____ . In contrast policies to assist in objective decision making are usually operational in nature and can be objectively tested, e.g. password _____ .

Exam Probability: **Low**

19. *Answer choices:*

(see index for correct answer)

- a. Outcome primacy
- b. Emotional bias
- c. Subjective expected utility
- d. Policy

Guidance: level 1

:: Business ::

A _____ is a mathematical object used to count, measure, and label. The original examples are the natural _____ s 1, 2, 3, 4, and so forth. A written symbol like "5" that represents a _____ is called a numeral. A numeral system is an organized way to write and manipulate this type of symbol, for example the Hindu–Arabic numeral system allows combinations of numerical digits like "5" and "0" to represent larger _____ s like 50. A numeral in linguistics can refer to a symbol like 5, the words or phrase that names a _____ , like "five hundred", or other words that mean a specific _____ , like "dozen". In addition to their use in counting and measuring, numerals are often used for labels , for ordering , and for codes . In common usage, _____ may refer to a symbol, a word or phrase, or the mathematical object.

Exam Probability: **Low**

20. *Answer choices:*

(see index for correct answer)

- a. Mavis Amankwah
- b. Number
- c. Business interaction networks
- d. Local multiplier effect

Guidance: level 1

:: Business law ::

_____ is where a person's financial liability is limited to a fixed sum, most commonly the value of a person's investment in a company or partnership. If a company with _____ is sued, then the claimants are suing the company, not its owners or investors. A shareholder in a limited company is not personally liable for any of the debts of the company, other than for the amount already invested in the company and for any unpaid amount on the shares in the company, if any. The same is true for the members of a _____ partnership and the limited partners in a limited partnership. By contrast, sole proprietors and partners in general partnerships are each liable for all the debts of the business.

Exam Probability: **Medium**

21. *Answer choices:*

(see index for correct answer)

- a. Limited liability
- b. Family and Medical Leave Act of 1993
- c. Limited liability limited partnership
- d. Starting a Business Index

Guidance: level 1

:: Finance ::

_____ is a field that is concerned with the allocation of assets and liabilities over space and time, often under conditions of risk or uncertainty. _____ can also be defined as the art of money management. Participants in the market aim to price assets based on their risk level, fundamental value, and their expected rate of return. _____ can be split into three sub-categories: public _____, corporate _____ and personal _____.

Exam Probability: **Medium**

22. *Answer choices:*

(see index for correct answer)

- a. AzeriCard
- b. Finance
- c. Universal default
- d. Participation certificate

Guidance: level 1

:: Legal terms ::

An _____ is an action which is inaccurate or incorrect. In some usages, an _____ is synonymous with a mistake. In statistics, "_____" refers to the difference between the value which has been computed and the correct value. An _____ could result in failure or in a deviation from the intended performance or behaviour.

Exam Probability: **High**

23. *Answer choices:*

(see index for correct answer)

- a. Officious intermeddler
- b. Legal recourse
- c. Culpability
- d. Public Order Act 1986

Guidance: level 1

:: Security compliance ::

A _____ is a communicated intent to inflict harm or loss on another person. A _____ is considered an act of coercion. _____ s are widely observed in animal behavior, particularly in a ritualized form, chiefly in order to avoid the unnecessary physical violence that can lead to physical damage or the death of both conflicting parties.

Exam Probability: **Low**

24. *Answer choices:*

(see index for correct answer)

- a. Nikto Web Scanner
- b. Threat

- c. Month of bugs
- d. North American Electric Reliability Corporation

Guidance: level 1

:: ::

> _____ is the production of products for use or sale using labour and machines, tools, chemical and biological processing, or formulation. The term may refer to a range of human activity, from handicraft to high tech, but is most commonly applied to industrial design, in which raw materials are transformed into finished goods on a large scale. Such finished goods may be sold to other manufacturers for the production of other, more complex products, such as aircraft, household appliances, furniture, sports equipment or automobiles, or sold to wholesalers, who in turn sell them to retailers, who then sell them to end users and consumers.

Exam Probability: **Low**

25. *Answer choices:*

(see index for correct answer)

- a. Character
- b. Manufacturing
- c. hierarchical perspective
- d. surface-level diversity

Guidance: level 1

:: Stock market ::

The _____ of a corporation is all of the shares into which ownership of the corporation is divided. In American English, the shares are commonly known as "_____ s". A single share of the _____ represents fractional ownership of the corporation in proportion to the total number of shares. This typically entitles the _____ holder to that fraction of the company's earnings, proceeds from liquidation of assets, or voting power, often dividing these up in proportion to the amount of money each _____ holder has invested. Not all _____ is necessarily equal, as certain classes of _____ may be issued for example without voting rights, with enhanced voting rights, or with a certain priority to receive profits or liquidation proceeds before or after other classes of shareholders.

Exam Probability: **High**

26. *Answer choices:*

(see index for correct answer)

- a. Piqqem
- b. P chip
- c. Securities offering
- d. Sector rotation

Guidance: level 1

:: Production economics ::

In microeconomics, _____ are the cost advantages that enterprises obtain due to their scale of operation, with cost per unit of output decreasing with increasing scale.

Exam Probability: **Medium**

27. *Answer choices:*

(see index for correct answer)

- a. Robinson Crusoe economy
- b. Economies of scale
- c. Marginal product of labor
- d. Cost-of-production theory of value

Guidance: level 1

:: Auditing ::

_____, as defined by accounting and auditing, is a process for assuring of an organization's objectives in operational effectiveness and efficiency, reliable financial reporting, and compliance with laws, regulations and policies. A broad concept, _____ involves everything that controls risks to an organization.

Exam Probability: **High**

28. *Answer choices:*

(see index for correct answer)

- a. Walk-through test
- b. Assurance services
- c. Detection risk
- d. Sales tax audit

Guidance: level 1

:: Contract law ::

A _____ is a legally-binding agreement which recognises and governs the rights and duties of the parties to the agreement. A _____ is legally enforceable because it meets the requirements and approval of the law. An agreement typically involves the exchange of goods, services, money, or promises of any of those. In the event of breach of _____ , the law awards the injured party access to legal remedies such as damages and cancellation.

Exam Probability: **Medium**

29. *Answer choices:*

(see index for correct answer)

- a. Implied authority
- b. Tertius
- c. Contract B
- d. Exceptio non adimpleti contractus

Guidance: level 1

:: Management ::

The term _____ refers to measures designed to increase the degree of autonomy and self-determination in people and in communities in order to enable them to represent their interests in a responsible and self-determined way, acting on their own authority. It is the process of becoming stronger and more confident, especially in controlling one's life and claiming one's rights. _____ as action refers both to the process of self-_____ and to professional support of people, which enables them to overcome their sense of powerlessness and lack of influence, and to recognize and use their resources. To do work with power.

Exam Probability: **High**

30. *Answer choices:*

(see index for correct answer)

- a. Product breakdown structure
- b. Stewardship theory
- c. Empowerment
- d. Critical path method

Guidance: level 1

:: Organizational theory ::

_____ is the process of groups of organisms working or acting together for common, mutual, or some underlying benefit, as opposed to working in competition for selfish benefit. Many animal and plant species cooperate both with other members of their own species and with members of other species.

Exam Probability: **High**

31. *Answer choices:*
(see index for correct answer)

- a. Cooperation
- b. Mimetic isomorphism
- c. City Protocol
- d. Staff augmentation

Guidance: level 1

:: Stock market ::

A _____, equity market or share market is the aggregation of buyers and sellers of stocks, which represent ownership claims on businesses; these may include securities listed on a public stock exchange, as well as stock that is only traded privately. Examples of the latter include shares of private companies which are sold to investors through equity crowdfunding platforms. Stock exchanges list shares of common equity as well as other security types, e.g. corporate bonds and convertible bonds.

Exam Probability: **High**

32. Answer choices:

(see index for correct answer)

- a. Registered share
- b. Accelerated share repurchase
- c. Stock market
- d. Follow-on offering

Guidance: level 1

:: Analysis ::

> _____ is the process of breaking a complex topic or substance into smaller parts in order to gain a better understanding of it. The technique has been applied in the study of mathematics and logic since before Aristotle, though _____ as a formal concept is a relatively recent development.

Exam Probability: **High**

33. Answer choices:

(see index for correct answer)

- a. Paradox of analysis
- b. Analysis
- c. Psychopolitical validity
- d. SWOQe

Guidance: level 1

:: Data management ::

_____ is a form of intellectual property that grants the creator of an original creative work an exclusive legal right to determine whether and under what conditions this original work may be copied and used by others, usually for a limited term of years. The exclusive rights are not absolute but limited by limitations and exceptions to _____ law, including fair use. A major limitation on _____ on ideas is that _____ protects only the original expression of ideas, and not the underlying ideas themselves.

Exam Probability: **High**

34. *Answer choices:*

(see index for correct answer)

- a. Mobile content management system
- b. Master data management
- c. Reactive business intelligence
- d. Copyright

Guidance: level 1

:: Actuarial science ::

_____ is the possibility of losing something of value. Values can be gained or lost when taking _____ resulting from a given action or inaction, foreseen or unforeseen. _____ can also be defined as the intentional interaction with uncertainty. Uncertainty is a potential, unpredictable, and uncontrollable outcome; _____ is a consequence of action taken in spite of uncertainty.

Exam Probability: **High**

35. *Answer choices:*

(see index for correct answer)

- a. Risk
- b. Compound annual growth rate
- c. Insurable risk
- d. Actuarial present value

Guidance: level 1

:: Stochastic processes ::

_____ is a system of rules that are created and enforced through social or governmental institutions to regulate behavior. It has been defined both as "the Science of Justice" and "the Art of Justice". _____ is a system that regulates and ensures that individuals or a community adhere to the will of the state. State-enforced _____ s can be made by a collective legislature or by a single legislator, resulting in statutes, by the executive through decrees and regulations, or established by judges through precedent, normally in common _____ jurisdictions. Private individuals can create legally binding contracts, including arbitration agreements that may elect to accept alternative arbitration to the normal court process. The formation of _____ s themselves may be influenced by a constitution, written or tacit, and the rights encoded therein. The _____ shapes politics, economics, history and society in various ways and serves as a mediator of relations between people.

Exam Probability: **High**

36. *Answer choices:*

(see index for correct answer)

- a. Narrow escape problem
- b. Bernoulli process
- c. Law
- d. Kolmogorov continuity theorem

Guidance: level 1

:: Costs ::

In microeconomic theory, the _____, or alternative cost, of making a particular choice is the value of the most valuable choice out of those that were not taken. In other words, opportunity that will require sacrifices.

Exam Probability: **Low**

37. *Answer choices:*
(see index for correct answer)

- a. Travel and subsistence
- b. Opportunity cost
- c. Social cost
- d. Psychic cost

Guidance: level 1

:: Problem solving ::

In other words, _____ is a situation where a group of people meet to generate new ideas and solutions around a specific domain of interest by removing inhibitions. People are able to think more freely and they suggest as many spontaneous new ideas as possible. All the ideas are noted down and those ideas are not criticized and after _____ session the ideas are evaluated. The term was popularized by Alex Faickney Osborn in the 1953 book Applied Imagination.

Exam Probability: **Low**

38. *Answer choices:*

(see index for correct answer)

- a. Community method
- b. Brainstorming
- c. Heuristic
- d. Spider mapping

Guidance: level 1

:: International trade ::

> The law or principle of _____ holds that under free trade, an agent will produce more of and consume less of a good for which they have a _____. _____ is the economic reality describing the work gains from trade for individuals, firms, or nations, which arise from differences in their factor endowments or technological progress. In an economic model, agents have a _____ over others in producing a particular good if they can produce that good at a lower relative opportunity cost or autarky price, i.e. at a lower relative marginal cost prior to trade. One shouldn't compare the monetary costs of production or even the resource costs of production. Instead, one must compare the opportunity costs of producing goods across countries.

Exam Probability: **High**

39. *Answer choices:*

(see index for correct answer)

- a. Harberger-Laursen-Metzler effect

- b. Team Canada Mission
- c. Comparative advantage
- d. Balanced trade

Guidance: level 1

:: ::

Some scenarios associate "this kind of planning" with learning "life skills". Schedules are necessary, or at least useful, in situations where individuals need to know what time they must be at a specific location to receive a specific service, and where people need to accomplish a set of goals within a set time period.

Exam Probability: **Medium**

40. *Answer choices:*

(see index for correct answer)

- a. Scheduling
- b. empathy
- c. deep-level diversity
- d. hierarchical perspective

Guidance: level 1

:: Financial accounting ::

_____ is a financial metric which represents operating liquidity available to a business, organisation or other entity, including governmental entities. Along with fixed assets such as plant and equipment, _____ is considered a part of operating capital. Gross _____ is equal to current assets. _____ is calculated as current assets minus current liabilities. If current assets are less than current liabilities, an entity has a _____ deficiency, also called a _____ deficit.

Exam Probability: **Low**

41. *Answer choices:*

(see index for correct answer)

- a. Valuation
- b. Working capital
- c. Deferred Acquisition Costs
- d. Accounting identity

Guidance: level 1

:: ::

_____ is the means to see, hear, or become aware of something or someone through our fundamental senses. The term _____ derives from the Latin word perceptio, and is the organization, identification, and interpretation of sensory information in order to represent and understand the presented information, or the environment.

Exam Probability: **Medium**

42. *Answer choices:*

(see index for correct answer)

- a. Perception
- b. deep-level diversity
- c. information systems assessment
- d. cultural

Guidance: level 1

:: Data collection ::

A _____ is an utterance which typically functions as a request for information. _____ s can thus be understood as a kind of illocutionary act in the field of pragmatics or as special kinds of propositions in frameworks of formal semantics such as alternative semantics or inquisitive semantics. The information requested is expected to be provided in the form of an answer. _____ s are often conflated with interrogatives, which are the grammatical forms typically used to achieve them. Rhetorical _____ s, for example, are interrogative in form but may not be considered true _____ s as they are not expected to be answered. Conversely, non-interrogative grammatical structures may be considered _____ s as in the case of the imperative sentence "tell me your name".

Exam Probability: **High**

43. *Answer choices:*

(see index for correct answer)

- a. Paradata
- b. Question
- c. Datalogix
- d. PowerLab

Guidance: level 1

:: Management ::

In business, a _____ is the attribute that allows an organization to outperform its competitors. A _____ may include access to natural resources, such as high-grade ores or a low-cost power source, highly skilled labor, geographic location, high entry barriers, and access to new technology.

Exam Probability: **Medium**

44. *Answer choices:*

(see index for correct answer)

- a. Knowledge ecosystem
- b. Organizational hologram
- c. Enterprise planning system
- d. Competitive advantage

Guidance: level 1

:: Identity management ::

_____ is the ability of an individual or group to seclude themselves, or information about themselves, and thereby express themselves selectively. The boundaries and content of what is considered private differ among cultures and individuals, but share common themes. When something is private to a person, it usually means that something is inherently special or sensitive to them. The domain of _____ partially overlaps with security, which can include the concepts of appropriate use, as well as protection of information. _____ may also take the form of bodily integrity.

Exam Probability: **Low**

45. *Answer choices:*

(see index for correct answer)

- a. Identity management theory
- b. Identity 3.0
- c. DigiD
- d. Trombinoscope

Guidance: level 1

:: Human resource management ::

_____ are the people who make up the workforce of an organization, business sector, or economy. "Human capital" is sometimes used synonymously with "_____", although human capital typically refers to a narrower effect. Likewise, other terms sometimes used include manpower, talent, labor, personnel, or simply people.

Exam Probability: **Medium**

46. *Answer choices:*

(see index for correct answer)

- a. Simultaneous recruiting of new graduates
- b. Appreciative inquiry

- c. Employeeship
- d. Human resources

Guidance: level 1

:: ::

An _____ is an area of the production, distribution, or trade, and consumption of goods and services by different agents. Understood in its broadest sense, 'The _____ is defined as a social domain that emphasize the practices, discourses, and material expressions associated with the production, use, and management of resources'. Economic agents can be individuals, businesses, organizations, or governments. Economic transactions occur when two parties agree to the value or price of the transacted good or service, commonly expressed in a certain currency. However, monetary transactions only account for a small part of the economic domain.

Exam Probability: **Low**

47. *Answer choices:*
(see index for correct answer)

- a. functional perspective
- b. Economy
- c. interpersonal communication
- d. hierarchical

Guidance: level 1

:: Monopoly (economics) ::

A _____ is a form of intellectual property that gives its owner the legal right to exclude others from making, using, selling, and importing an invention for a limited period of years, in exchange for publishing an enabling public disclosure of the invention. In most countries _____ rights fall under civil law and the _____ holder needs to sue someone infringing the _____ in order to enforce his or her rights. In some industries _____ s are an essential form of competitive advantage; in others they are irrelevant.

Exam Probability: **Medium**

48. *Answer choices:*

(see index for correct answer)

- a. Average cost pricing
- b. Tesco Town
- c. Municipalization
- d. National Competition Policy

Guidance: level 1

:: ::

A _____ is any person who contracts to acquire an asset in return for some form of consideration.

Exam Probability: **High**

49. *Answer choices:*
(see index for correct answer)

- a. Buyer
- b. open system
- c. Character
- d. co-culture

Guidance: level 1

:: Generally Accepted Accounting Principles ::

In business and accounting, _____ is an entity's income minus cost of goods sold, expenses and taxes for an accounting period. It is computed as the residual of all revenues and gains over all expenses and losses for the period, and has also been defined as the net increase in shareholders' equity that results from a company's operations. In the context of the presentation of financial statements, the IFRS Foundation defines _____ as synonymous with profit and loss. The difference between revenue and the cost of making a product or providing a service, before deducting overheads, payroll, taxation, and interest payments. This is different from operating income .

Exam Probability: **High**

50. *Answer choices:*

(see index for correct answer)

- a. Engagement letter
- b. Deferral
- c. Insurance asset management
- d. Net income

Guidance: level 1

:: Marketing ::

A _____ is the quantity of payment or compensation given by one party to another in return for one unit of goods or services.. A _____ is influenced by both production costs and demand for the product. A _____ may be determined by a monopolist or may be imposed on the firm by market conditions.

Exam Probability: **Medium**

51. *Answer choices:*

(see index for correct answer)

- a. Marketing supply chain
- b. Markup
- c. Processing fluency
- d. Exploratory research

Guidance: level 1

:: Economic globalization ::

_____ is an agreement in which one company hires another company to be responsible for a planned or existing activity that is or could be done internally, and sometimes involves transferring employees and assets from one firm to another.

Exam Probability: **Low**

52. *Answer choices:*
(see index for correct answer)

- a. global financial
- b. reshoring

Guidance: level 1

:: Business ::

The seller, or the provider of the goods or services, completes a sale in response to an acquisition, appropriation, requisition or a direct interaction with the buyer at the point of sale. There is a passing of title of the item, and the settlement of a price, in which agreement is reached on a price for which transfer of ownership of the item will occur. The seller, not the purchaser typically executes the sale and it may be completed prior to the obligation of payment. In the case of indirect interaction, a person who sells goods or service on behalf of the owner is known as a _____ man or _____ woman or _____ person, but this often refers to someone selling goods in a store/shop, in which case other terms are also common, including _____ clerk, shop assistant, and retail clerk.

Exam Probability: **Medium**

53. *Answer choices:*

(see index for correct answer)

- a. Corporate services
- b. Casengo
- c. Relationship Science
- d. EPG Model

Guidance: level 1

:: Management ::

In organizational studies, _____ is the efficient and effective development of an organization's resources when they are needed. Such resources may include financial resources, inventory, human skills, production resources, or information technology and natural resources.

Exam Probability: **High**

54. *Answer choices:*

(see index for correct answer)

- a. Lead scoring
- b. Management by exception
- c. Task-oriented and relationship-oriented leadership
- d. Resource management

Guidance: level 1

:: Organizational structure ::

An _____ defines how activities such as task allocation, coordination, and supervision are directed toward the achievement of organizational aims.

Exam Probability: **Medium**

55. *Answer choices:*

(see index for correct answer)

- a. Organization of the New York City Police Department
- b. Followership
- c. The Starfish and the Spider
- d. Organizational structure

Guidance: level 1

:: Casting (manufacturing) ::

A _____ is a regularity in the world, man-made design, or abstract ideas. As such, the elements of a _____ repeat in a predictable manner. A geometric _____ is a kind of _____ formed of geometric shapes and typically repeated like a wallpaper design.

Exam Probability: **High**

56. *Answer choices:*

(see index for correct answer)

- a. Foundry sand testing
- b. Chill
- c. Pattern
- d. Vacuum casting

Guidance: level 1

:: Loans ::

In finance, a _____ is the lending of money by one or more individuals, organizations, or other entities to other individuals, organizations etc. The recipient incurs a debt, and is usually liable to pay interest on that debt until it is repaid, and also to repay the principal amount borrowed.

Exam Probability: **High**

57. *Answer choices:*
(see index for correct answer)

- a. Loan
- b. Home equity loan
- c. Farm operating loans
- d. Loan-to-value

Guidance: level 1

:: Management occupations ::

_____ ship is the process of designing, launching and running a new business, which is often initially a small business. The people who create these businesses are called _____ s.

Exam Probability: **Medium**

58. *Answer choices:*

(see index for correct answer)

- a. entrepreneurial
- b. Faculty consulting
- c. Comprador
- d. Female entrepreneur

Guidance: level 1

:: Currency ::

A _____ , in the most specific sense is money in any form when in use or circulation as a medium of exchange, especially circulating banknotes and coins. A more general definition is that a _____ is a system of money in common use, especially for people in a nation. Under this definition, US dollars , pounds sterling , Australian dollars , European euros , Russian rubles and Indian Rupees are examples of currencies. These various currencies are recognized as stores of value and are traded between nations in foreign exchange markets, which determine the relative values of the different currencies. Currencies in this sense are defined by governments, and each type has limited boundaries of acceptance.

Exam Probability: **Medium**

59. *Answer choices:*

(see index for correct answer)

- a. Remonetisation

- b. Currency intervention
- c. Medium of exchange
- d. Cross currency swap

Guidance: level 1

Management

Management is the administration of an organization, whether it is a business, a not-for-profit organization, or government body. Management includes the activities of setting the strategy of an organization and coordinating the efforts of its employees (or of volunteers) to accomplish its objectives through the application of available resources, such as financial, natural, technological, and human resources.

:: ::

The _____ is an agreement signed by Canada, Mexico, and the United States, creating a trilateral trade bloc in North America. The agreement came into force on January 1, 1994, and superseded the 1988 Canada–United States Free Trade Agreement between the United States and Canada. The NAFTA trade bloc is one of the largest trade blocs in the world by gross domestic product.

Exam Probability: **High**

1. *Answer choices:*

(see index for correct answer)

- a. Sarbanes-Oxley act of 2002
- b. levels of analysis
- c. surface-level diversity
- d. corporate values

Guidance: level 1

:: Personality tests ::

The Myers–Briggs Type Indicator is an introspective self-report questionnaire with the purpose of indicating differing psychological preferences in how people perceive the world around them and make decisions. . Though the test superficially resembles some psychological theories it is commonly classified as pseudoscience, especially as pertains to its supposed predictive abilities.

Exam Probability: **Medium**

2. *Answer choices:*

(see index for correct answer)

- a. Myers-Briggs Type Indicator
- b. Johari window

- c. personality quiz
- d. Keirsey Temperament Sorter

Guidance: level 1

:: Project management ::

_____ is a process of setting goals, planning and/or controlling the organizing and leading the execution of any type of activity, such as.

Exam Probability: **Low**

3. *Answer choices:*

(see index for correct answer)

- a. Iteration
- b. Identifying and Managing Project Risk
- c. Project management 2.0
- d. Responsibility assignment matrix

Guidance: level 1

:: Statistical terminology ::

_____ es can be learned implicitly within cultural contexts. People may develop _____ es toward or against an individual, an ethnic group, a sexual or gender identity, a nation, a religion, a social class, a political party, theoretical paradigms and ideologies within academic domains, or a species. _____ ed means one-sided, lacking a neutral viewpoint, or not having an open mind. _____ can come in many forms and is related to prejudice and intuition.

Exam Probability: **Medium**

4. *Answer choices:*

(see index for correct answer)

- a. Efficient estimator
- b. Bias
- c. Probable error
- d. Endogeneity

Guidance: level 1

:: Reputation management ::

_____ or image of a social entity is an opinion about that entity, typically as a result of social evaluation on a set of criteria.

Exam Probability: **High**

5. *Answer choices:*

(see index for correct answer)

- a. EigenTrust
- b. Reputation
- c. Star
- d. ClaimID

Guidance: level 1

:: ::

In business strategy, _____ is establishing a competitive advantage by having the lowest cost of operation in the industry. _____ is often driven by company efficiency, size, scale, scope and cumulative experience. A _____ strategy aims to exploit scale of production, well-defined scope and other economies, producing highly standardized products, using advanced technology. In recent years, more and more companies have chosen a strategic mix to achieve market leadership. These patterns consist of simultaneous _____, superior customer service and product leadership. Walmart has succeeded across the world due to its _____ strategy. The company has cut down on exesses at every point of production and thus are able to provide the consumers with quality products at low prices.

Exam Probability: **Low**

6. *Answer choices:*

(see index for correct answer)

- a. functional perspective
- b. Cost leadership
- c. interpersonal communication
- d. imperative

Guidance: level 1

:: ::

_____ Corporation was an American energy, commodities, and services company based in Houston, Texas. It was founded in 1985 as a merger between Houston Natural Gas and InterNorth, both relatively small regional companies. Before its bankruptcy on December 3, 2001, _____ employed approximately 29,000 staff and was a major electricity, natural gas, communications and pulp and paper company, with claimed revenues of nearly $101 billion during 2000. Fortune named _____ "America's Most Innovative Company" for six consecutive years.

Exam Probability: **Low**

7. *Answer choices:*

(see index for correct answer)

- a. Enron
- b. information systems assessment
- c. hierarchical perspective
- d. open system

Guidance: level 1

:: ::

A _____ is an approximate imitation of the operation of a process or system; the act of simulating first requires a model is developed. This model is a well-defined description of the simulated subject, and represents its key characteristics, such as its behaviour, functions and abstract or physical properties. The model represents the system itself, whereas the _____ represents its operation over time.

Exam Probability: **High**

8. *Answer choices:*

(see index for correct answer)

- a. Character
- b. interpersonal communication
- c. imperative
- d. Simulation

Guidance: level 1

:: ::

A _____ or GM is an executive who has overall responsibility for managing both the revenue and cost elements of a company's income statement, known as profit & loss responsibility. A _____ usually oversees most or all of the firm's marketing and sales functions as well as the day-to-day operations of the business. Frequently, the _____ is responsible for effective planning, delegating, coordinating, staffing, organizing, and decision making to attain desirable profit making results for an organization .

Exam Probability: **Medium**

9. *Answer choices:*

(see index for correct answer)

- a. surface-level diversity
- b. General manager
- c. similarity-attraction theory
- d. hierarchical perspective

Guidance: level 1

:: Business law ::

A _____ is an arrangement where parties, known as partners, agree to cooperate to advance their mutual interests. The partners in a _____ may be individuals, businesses, interest-based organizations, schools, governments or combinations. Organizations may partner to increase the likelihood of each achieving their mission and to amplify their reach. A _____ may result in issuing and holding equity or may be only governed by a contract.

Exam Probability: **Low**

10. *Answer choices:*

(see index for correct answer)

- a. Security interest
- b. Examinership
- c. Retained interest
- d. Partnership

Guidance: level 1

:: Mereology ::

_____ , in the abstract, is what belongs to or with something, whether as an attribute or as a component of said thing. In the context of this article, it is one or more components , whether physical or incorporeal, of a person's estate; or so belonging to, as in being owned by, a person or jointly a group of people or a legal entity like a corporation or even a society. Depending on the nature of the _____ , an owner of _____ has the right to consume, alter, share, redefine, rent, mortgage, pawn, sell, exchange, transfer, give away or destroy it, or to exclude others from doing these things, as well as to perhaps abandon it; whereas regardless of the nature of the _____ , the owner thereof has the right to properly use it , or at the very least exclusively keep it.

Exam Probability: **Medium**

11. *Answer choices:*

(see index for correct answer)

- a. Gunk
- b. Meronomy
- c. Mereology
- d. Property

Guidance: level 1

:: Management ::

In business, a _____ is the attribute that allows an organization to outperform its competitors. A _____ may include access to natural resources, such as high-grade ores or a low-cost power source, highly skilled labor, geographic location, high entry barriers, and access to new technology.

Exam Probability: **Medium**

12. *Answer choices:*
(see index for correct answer)

- a. Competitive advantage
- b. Business rule mining
- c. Decentralized decision-making
- d. Management by exception

Guidance: level 1

:: Management ::

_____ is the identification, evaluation, and prioritization of risks followed by coordinated and economical application of resources to minimize, monitor, and control the probability or impact of unfortunate events or to maximize the realization of opportunities.

Exam Probability: **Low**

13. *Answer choices:*

(see index for correct answer)

- a. Risk management
- b. Data Item Descriptions
- c. Event management
- d. Information excellence

Guidance: level 1

:: Production economics ::

In microeconomics, _____ are the cost advantages that enterprises obtain due to their scale of operation, with cost per unit of output decreasing with increasing scale.

Exam Probability: **High**

14. *Answer choices:*

(see index for correct answer)

- a. Returns to scale
- b. Marginal cost of capital schedule
- c. HMI quality
- d. Economies of scale

Guidance: level 1

:: Lean manufacturing ::

_____ is the Sino-Japanese word for "improvement". In business, _____ refers to activities that continuously improve all functions and involve all employees from the CEO to the assembly line workers. It also applies to processes, such as purchasing and logistics, that cross organizational boundaries into the supply chain. It has been applied in healthcare, psychotherapy, life-coaching, government, and banking.

Exam Probability: **Low**

15. *Answer choices:*

(see index for correct answer)

- a. Agent-assisted automation
- b. Kaizen

- c. Setsuban Kanri
- d. Lean construction

Guidance: level 1

:: Income ::

In business and accounting, net income is an entity's income minus cost of goods sold, expenses and taxes for an accounting period. It is computed as the residual of all revenues and gains over all expenses and losses for the period, and has also been defined as the net increase in shareholders' equity that results from a company's operations. In the context of the presentation of financial statements, the IFRS Foundation defines net income as synonymous with profit and loss. The difference between revenue and the cost of making a product or providing a service, before deducting overheads, payroll, taxation, and interest payments. This is different from operating income.

Exam Probability: **Low**

16. *Answer choices:*

(see index for correct answer)

- a. Signing bonus
- b. Mandatory tipping
- c. Bottom line
- d. Family income

Guidance: level 1

:: Critical thinking ::

In psychology, _____ is regarded as the cognitive process resulting in the selection of a belief or a course of action among several alternative possibilities. Every _____ process produces a final choice, which may or may not prompt action.

Exam Probability: **High**

17. *Answer choices:*

(see index for correct answer)

- a. Critical-Creative Thinking and Behavioral Research Laboratory
- b. Decision-making
- c. Precising definition
- d. Scholarly method

Guidance: level 1

:: ::

An _____ is a process where candidates are examined to determine their suitability for specific types of employment, especially management or military command. The candidates' personality and aptitudes are determined by techniques including interviews, group exercises, presentations, examinations and psychometric testing.

Exam Probability: **Medium**

18. *Answer choices:*

(see index for correct answer)

- a. cultural
- b. levels of analysis
- c. corporate values
- d. similarity-attraction theory

Guidance: level 1

:: Income ::

_____ is a ratio between the net profit and cost of investment resulting from an investment of some resources. A high ROI means the investment's gains favorably to its cost. As a performance measure, ROI is used to evaluate the efficiency of an investment or to compare the efficiencies of several different investments. In purely economic terms, it is one way of relating profits to capital invested. _____ is a performance measure used by businesses to identify the efficiency of an investment or number of different investments.

Exam Probability: **Low**

19. *Answer choices:*

(see index for correct answer)

- a. Stipend
- b. Private income
- c. Return on investment
- d. Per capita income

Guidance: level 1

:: Project management ::

A _____ is a professional in the field of project management. _____ s have the responsibility of the planning, procurement and execution of a project, in any undertaking that has a defined scope, defined start and a defined finish; regardless of industry. _____ s are first point of contact for any issues or discrepancies arising from within the heads of various departments in an organization before the problem escalates to higher authorities. Project management is the responsibility of a _____ . This individual seldom participates directly in the activities that produce the end result, but rather strives to maintain the progress, mutual interaction and tasks of various parties in such a way that reduces the risk of overall failure, maximizes benefits, and minimizes costs.

Exam Probability: **Medium**

20. *Answer choices:*

(see index for correct answer)

- a. ISO 31000
- b. Risk management plan
- c. Project initiation document

- d. Project manager

Guidance: level 1

:: Leadership ::

_____ Theory, or the _____ Model, is a model created by Paul Hersey and Ken Blanchard, developed while working on Management of Organizational Behavior. The theory was first introduced in 1969 as "life cycle theory of leadership". During the mid-1970s, life cycle theory of leadership was renamed "_____ Theory."

Exam Probability: **Low**

21. *Answer choices:*

(see index for correct answer)

- a. Authentic leadership
- b. The Leadership Council
- c. Sex differences in leadership
- d. Situational leadership

Guidance: level 1

:: Economic globalization ::

_____ is an agreement in which one company hires another company to be responsible for a planned or existing activity that is or could be done internally, and sometimes involves transferring employees and assets from one firm to another.

Exam Probability: **Low**

22. *Answer choices:*

(see index for correct answer)

- a. Outsourcing
- b. reshoring

Guidance: level 1

:: Telecommuting ::

_____, also called telework, teleworking, working from home, mobile work, remote work, and flexible workplace, is a work arrangement in which employees do not commute or travel to a central place of work, such as an office building, warehouse, or store. Teleworkers in the 21st century often use mobile telecommunications technology such as Wi-Fi-equipped laptop or tablet computers and smartphones to work from coffee shops; others may use a desktop computer and a landline phone at their home. According to a Reuters poll, approximately "one in five workers around the globe, particularly employees in the Middle East, Latin America and Asia, telecommute frequently and nearly 10 percent work from home every day." In the 2000s, annual leave or vacation in some organizations was seen as absence from the workplace rather than ceasing work, and some office employees used telework to continue to check work e-mails while on vacation.

Exam Probability: **High**

23. *Answer choices:*

(see index for correct answer)

- a. contracting out
- b. TalkPoint
- c. The Conference Group
- d. Collaborative working environment

Guidance: level 1

:: ::

_____ is the consumption and saving opportunity gained by an entity within a specified timeframe, which is generally expressed in monetary terms. For households and individuals, "_____ is the sum of all the wages, salaries, profits, interest payments, rents, and other forms of earnings received in a given period of time."

Exam Probability: **Medium**

24. *Answer choices:*

(see index for correct answer)

- a. Income
- b. hierarchical

- c. surface-level diversity
- d. functional perspective

Guidance: level 1

:: Employment ::

_____ is a relationship between two parties, usually based on a contract where work is paid for, where one party, which may be a corporation, for profit, not-for-profit organization, co-operative or other entity is the employer and the other is the employee. Employees work in return for payment, which may be in the form of an hourly wage, by piecework or an annual salary, depending on the type of work an employee does or which sector she or he is working in. Employees in some fields or sectors may receive gratuities, bonus payment or stock options. In some types of _____ , employees may receive benefits in addition to payment. Benefits can include health insurance, housing, disability insurance or use of a gym. _____ is typically governed by _____ laws, regulations or legal contracts.

Exam Probability: **Medium**

25. *Answer choices:*
(see index for correct answer)

- a. Intra-company transfer
- b. Legal working age
- c. Job shadow
- d. Make-work job

Guidance: level 1

:: ::

_____ involves the development of an action plan designed to motivate and guide a person or group toward a goal. _____ can be guided by goal-setting criteria such as SMART criteria. _____ is a major component of personal-development and management literature.

Exam Probability: **Low**

26. *Answer choices:*

(see index for correct answer)

- a. Sarbanes-Oxley act of 2002
- b. interpersonal communication
- c. Goal setting
- d. functional perspective

Guidance: level 1

:: ::

_____ is the collection of mechanisms, processes and relations by which corporations are controlled and operated. Governance structures and principles identify the distribution of rights and responsibilities among different participants in the corporation and include the rules and procedures for making decisions in corporate affairs. _____ is necessary because of the possibility of conflicts of interests between stakeholders, primarily between shareholders and upper management or among shareholders.

Exam Probability: **Medium**

27. *Answer choices:*

(see index for correct answer)

- a. Corporate governance
- b. imperative
- c. hierarchical perspective
- d. deep-level diversity

Guidance: level 1

:: Lean manufacturing ::

A continual improvement process, also often called a _____ process, is an ongoing effort to improve products, services, or processes. These efforts can seek "incremental" improvement over time or "breakthrough" improvement all at once. Delivery processes are constantly evaluated and improved in the light of their efficiency, effectiveness and flexibility.

Exam Probability: **Medium**

28. *Answer choices:*

(see index for correct answer)

- a. Lean services
- b. Continuous improvement
- c. Overall Labor Effectiveness
- d. JobShopLean

Guidance: level 1

:: Human resource management ::

_____ involves improving the effectiveness of organizations and the individuals and teams within them. Training may be viewed as related to immediate changes in organizational effectiveness via organized instruction, while development is related to the progress of longer-term organizational and employee goals. While _____ technically have differing definitions, the two are oftentimes used interchangeably and/or together. _____ has historically been a topic within applied psychology but has within the last two decades become closely associated with human resources management, talent management, human resources development, instructional design, human factors, and knowledge management.

Exam Probability: **Medium**

29. *Answer choices:*

(see index for correct answer)

- a. The Giving of Orders
- b. Autonomous work group
- c. Multiculturalism
- d. Human resource accounting

Guidance: level 1

:: ::

The business environment is a marketing term and refers to factors and forces that affect a firm's ability to build and maintain successful customer relationships. The business environment has been defined as "the totality of physical and social factors that are taken directly into consideration in the decision-making behaviour of individuals in the organisation."

Exam Probability: **Medium**

30. *Answer choices:*

(see index for correct answer)

- a. surface-level diversity
- b. Environmental scanning
- c. Sarbanes-Oxley act of 2002
- d. corporate values

Guidance: level 1

:: Generally Accepted Accounting Principles ::

In accounting, _____ is the income that a business have from its normal business activities, usually from the sale of goods and services to customers. _____ is also referred to as sales or turnover. Some companies receive _____ from interest, royalties, or other fees. _____ may refer to business income in general, or it may refer to the amount, in a monetary unit, earned during a period of time, as in "Last year, Company X had _____ of $42 million". Profits or net income generally imply total _____ minus total expenses in a given period. In accounting, in the balance statement it is a subsection of the Equity section and _____ increases equity, it is often referred to as the "top line" due to its position on the income statement at the very top. This is to be contrasted with the "bottom line" which denotes net income.

Exam Probability: **High**

31. *Answer choices:*
(see index for correct answer)

- a. Write-off
- b. Indian Accounting Standards
- c. Gross sales
- d. Pro forma

Guidance: level 1

:: ::

A _____, or also known as foreman, overseer, facilitator, monitor, area coordinator, or sometimes gaffer, is the job title of a low level management position that is primarily based on authority over a worker or charge of a workplace. A _____ can also be one of the most senior in the staff at the place of work, such as a Professor who oversees a PhD dissertation. Supervision, on the other hand, can be performed by people without this formal title, for example by parents. The term _____ itself can be used to refer to any personnel who have this task as part of their job description.

Exam Probability: **High**

32. *Answer choices:*

(see index for correct answer)

- a. empathy
- b. hierarchical perspective
- c. deep-level diversity
- d. surface-level diversity

Guidance: level 1

:: Decision theory ::

A _____ is a decision support tool that uses a tree-like model of decisions and their possible consequences, including chance event outcomes, resource costs, and utility. It is one way to display an algorithm that only contains conditional control statements.

Exam Probability: **Medium**

33. *Answer choices:*

(see index for correct answer)

- a. Aggregated indices randomization method
- b. Superiority and inferiority ranking method
- c. Analysis paralysis
- d. Mental accounting

Guidance: level 1

:: Asset ::

In financial accounting, an _____ is any resource owned by the business. Anything tangible or intangible that can be owned or controlled to produce value and that is held by a company to produce positive economic value is an _____ . Simply stated, _____ s represent value of ownership that can be converted into cash . The balance sheet of a firm records the monetary value of the _____ s owned by that firm. It covers money and other valuables belonging to an individual or to a business.

Exam Probability: **High**

34. *Answer choices:*

(see index for correct answer)

- a. Current asset

- b. Asset

Guidance: level 1

:: Training ::

_____ is action or inaction that is regulated to be in accordance with a particular system of governance. _____ is commonly applied to regulating human and animal behavior, and furthermore, it is applied to each activity-branch in all branches of organized activity, knowledge, and other fields of study and observation. _____ can be a set of expectations that are required by any governing entity including the self, groups, classes, fields, industries, or societies.

Exam Probability: **Low**

35. *Answer choices:*
(see index for correct answer)

- a. Large Group Capacitation
- b. Screencast
- c. Training camp
- d. Discipline

Guidance: level 1

:: Business law ::

A _____ is a group of people who jointly supervise the activities of an organization, which can be either a for-profit business, nonprofit organization, or a government agency. Such a board's powers, duties, and responsibilities are determined by government regulations and the organization's own constitution and bylaws. These authorities may specify the number of members of the board, how they are to be chosen, and how often they are to meet.

Exam Probability: **Medium**

36. *Answer choices:*

(see index for correct answer)

- a. Leave of absence
- b. Bulk sale
- c. Finance lease
- d. Negative option billing

Guidance: level 1

:: Human resource management ::

_____ expands the capacity of individuals to perform in leadership roles within organizations. Leadership roles are those that facilitate execution of a company's strategy through building alignment, winning mindshare and growing the capabilities of others. Leadership roles may be formal, with the corresponding authority to make decisions and take responsibility, or they may be informal roles with little official authority.

Exam Probability: **Low**

37. *Answer choices:*

(see index for correct answer)

- a. Contractor management
- b. Leadership development
- c. Organization chart
- d. Four-day week

Guidance: level 1

:: Human resource management ::

_____ means increasing the scope of a job through extending the range of its job duties and responsibilities generally within the same level and periphery. _____ involves combining various activities at the same level in the organization and adding them to the existing job. It is also called the horizontal expansion of job activities. This contradicts the principles of specialisation and the division of labour whereby work is divided into small units, each of which is performed repetitively by an individual worker and the responsibilities are always clear. Some motivational theories suggest that the boredom and alienation caused by the division of labour can actually cause efficiency to fall. Thus, _____ seeks to motivate workers through reversing the process of specialisation. A typical approach might be to replace assembly lines with modular work; instead of an employee repeating the same step on each product, they perform several tasks on a single item. In order for employees to be provided with _____ they will need to be retrained in new fields to understand how each field works.

Exam Probability: **High**

38. *Answer choices:*

(see index for correct answer)

- a. Talascend
- b. Service record
- c. Income bracket
- d. Job enlargement

Guidance: level 1

:: ::

_____ , known in Europe as research and technological development , refers to innovative activities undertaken by corporations or governments in developing new services or products, or improving existing services or products. _____ constitutes the first stage of development of a potential new service or the production process.

Exam Probability: **High**

39. *Answer choices:*

(see index for correct answer)

- a. empathy
- b. interpersonal communication

- c. Research and development
- d. similarity-attraction theory

Guidance: level 1

:: Marketing ::

_____ is the percentage of a market accounted for by a specific entity. In a survey of nearly 200 senior marketing managers, 67% responded that they found the revenue- "dollar _____" metric very useful, while 61% found "unit _____" very useful.

Exam Probability: **Medium**

40. *Answer choices:*

(see index for correct answer)

- a. Corporate capabilities package
- b. MWW
- c. Market share
- d. Pink money

Guidance: level 1

:: Workplace ::

A _____ , also referred to as a performance review, performance evaluation, development discussion, or employee appraisal is a method by which the job performance of an employee is documented and evaluated. _____ s are a part of career development and consist of regular reviews of employee performance within organizations.

Exam Probability: **High**

41. *Answer choices:*

(see index for correct answer)

- a. Workplace aggression
- b. Performance appraisal
- c. Workplace strategy
- d. Hostile environment sexual harassment

Guidance: level 1

:: ::

_____ is a kind of action that occur as two or more objects have an effect upon one another. The idea of a two-way effect is essential in the concept of _____ , as opposed to a one-way causal effect. A closely related term is interconnectivity, which deals with the _____ s of _____ s within systems: combinations of many simple _____ s can lead to surprising emergent phenomena. _____ has different tailored meanings in various sciences. Changes can also involve _____ .

Exam Probability: **Low**

42. *Answer choices:*

(see index for correct answer)

- a. surface-level diversity
- b. co-culture
- c. cultural
- d. Interaction

Guidance: level 1

:: Human resource management ::

_____ is a core function of human resource management and it is related to the specification of contents, methods and relationship of jobs in order to satisfy technological and organizational requirements as well as the social and personal requirements of the job holder or the employee. Its principles are geared towards how the nature of a person's job affects their attitudes and behavior at work, particularly relating to characteristics such as skill variety and autonomy. The aim of a _____ is to improve job satisfaction, to improve through-put, to improve quality and to reduce employee problems.

Exam Probability: **Medium**

43. *Answer choices:*

(see index for correct answer)

- a. Job design
- b. Job knowledge
- c. Organizational chart
- d. Inclusion

Guidance: level 1

:: Project management ::

In political science, an _____ is a means by which a petition signed by a certain minimum number of registered voters can force a government to choose to either enact a law or hold a public vote in parliament in what is called indirect _____ , or under direct _____ , the proposition is immediately put to a plebiscite or referendum, in what is called a Popular initiated Referendum or citizen-initiated referendum).

Exam Probability: **High**

44. *Answer choices:*
(see index for correct answer)

- a. The Transformation Project
- b. Initiative
- c. Defense Acquisition Workforce Improvement Act
- d. Cost-benefit

Guidance: level 1

:: ::

_____ is the amount of time someone works beyond normal working hours. The term is also used for the pay received for this time. Normal hours may be determined in several ways.

Exam Probability: **Low**

45. *Answer choices:*

(see index for correct answer)

- a. deep-level diversity
- b. cultural
- c. co-culture
- d. surface-level diversity

Guidance: level 1

:: ::

_____ refers to the overall process of attracting, shortlisting, selecting and appointing suitable candidates for jobs within an organization. _____ can also refer to processes involved in choosing individuals for unpaid roles. Managers, human resource generalists and _____ specialists may be tasked with carrying out _____, but in some cases public-sector employment agencies, commercial _____ agencies, or specialist search consultancies are used to undertake parts of the process. Internet-based technologies which support all aspects of _____ have become widespread.

Exam Probability: **Low**

46. *Answer choices:*

(see index for correct answer)

- a. empathy
- b. imperative
- c. Recruitment
- d. open system

Guidance: level 1

:: Game theory ::

_____ is the idea that rationality is limited when individuals make decisions: by the tractability of the decision problem, the cognitive limitations of the mind, and the time available to make the decision. Decision-makers, in this view, act as satisficers, seeking a satisfactory solution rather than an optimal one.

Exam Probability: **Medium**

47. *Answer choices:*

(see index for correct answer)

- a. Bounded rationality
- b. Quasi-perfect equilibrium

- c. Social value orientations
- d. Stromquist moving-knife procedure

Guidance: level 1

:: Monopoly (economics) ::

_____ is a category of property that includes intangible creations of the human intellect. _____ encompasses two types of rights: industrial property rights and copyright. It was not until the 19th century that the term " _____ " began to be used, and not until the late 20th century that it became commonplace in the majority of the world.

Exam Probability: **Low**

48. *Answer choices:*
(see index for correct answer)

- a. Patent
- b. Intellectual property
- c. Ownership unbundling
- d. Natural monopoly

Guidance: level 1

:: Management ::

_____ is an area of management concerned with designing and controlling the process of production and redesigning business operations in the production of goods or services. It involves the responsibility of ensuring that business operations are efficient in terms of using as few resources as needed and effective in terms of meeting customer requirements. _____ is primarily concerned with planning, organizing and supervising in the contexts of production, manufacturing or the provision of services.

Exam Probability: **High**

49. *Answer choices:*

(see index for correct answer)

- a. Context analysis
- b. Shrinkage
- c. DMSMS
- d. Operations management

Guidance: level 1

:: Marketing ::

_____ or stock control can be broadly defined as "the activity of checking a shop's stock." However, a more focused definition takes into account the more science-based, methodical practice of not only verifying a business' inventory but also focusing on the many related facets of inventory management "within an organisation to meet the demand placed upon that business economically." Other facets of _____ include supply chain management, production control, financial flexibility, and customer satisfaction. At the root of _____ , however, is the _____ problem, which involves determining when to order, how much to order, and the logistics of those decisions.

Exam Probability: **High**

50. *Answer choices:*

(see index for correct answer)

- a. Inventory control
- b. Discounting
- c. Consumer complaint
- d. Price on application

Guidance: level 1

:: Belief ::

_____ is the study of general and fundamental questions about existence, knowledge, values, reason, mind, and language. Such questions are often posed as problems to be studied or resolved. The term was probably coined by Pythagoras . Philosophical methods include questioning, critical discussion, rational argument, and systematic presentation. Classic philosophical questions include: Is it possible to know anything and to prove it What is most real Philosophers also pose more practical and concrete questions such as: Is there a best way to live Is it better to be just or unjust Do humans have free will

Exam Probability: **Low**

51. *Answer choices:*

(see index for correct answer)

- a. Philosophy
- b. Anthropocentrism
- c. Leap of faith
- d. Availability cascade

Guidance: level 1

:: Outsourcing ::

_____ is the relocation of a business process from one country to another—typically an operational process, such as manufacturing, or supporting processes, such as accounting. Typically this refers to a company business, although state governments may also employ _____ . More recently, technical and administrative services have been offshored.

Exam Probability: **High**

52. *Answer choices:*

(see index for correct answer)

- a. Talentica Software
- b. Service review
- c. Virtual Staff Finder
- d. Offshoring

Guidance: level 1

:: Customs duties ::

A _____ is a tax on imports or exports between sovereign states. It is a form of regulation of foreign trade and a policy that taxes foreign products to encourage or safeguard domestic industry. _____ s are the simplest and oldest instrument of trade policy. Traditionally, states have used them as a source of income. Now, they are among the most widely used instruments of protection, along with import and export quotas.

Exam Probability: **High**

53. *Answer choices:*

(see index for correct answer)

- a. Court of Exchequer
- b. World Customs Organization

- c. Import Surtaxes
- d. Specific rate duty

Guidance: level 1

:: Behavior modification ::

In psychotherapy and mental health, _____ has a positive sense of empowering individuals, or a negative sense of encouraging dysfunctional behavior.

Exam Probability: **Low**

54. *Answer choices:*

(see index for correct answer)

- a. Thought stopping
- b. behavioural change

Guidance: level 1

:: Product design ::

_____ as a verb is to create a new product to be sold by a business to its customers. A very broad coefficient and effective generation and development of ideas through a process that leads to new products. Thus, it is a major aspect of new product development.

Exam Probability: **High**

55. *Answer choices:*

(see index for correct answer)

- a. Product design
- b. Studio Job
- c. Marcus Notley
- d. Nottingham Spirk

Guidance: level 1

:: Organizational structure ::

An _____ defines how activities such as task allocation, coordination, and supervision are directed toward the achievement of organizational aims.

Exam Probability: **High**

56. *Answer choices:*

(see index for correct answer)

- a. Unorganisation
- b. Organization of the New York City Police Department
- c. Followership
- d. Organizational structure

Guidance: level 1

:: Labour relations ::

_____ is a field of study that can have different meanings depending on the context in which it is used. In an international context, it is a subfield of labor history that studies the human relations with regard to work – in its broadest sense – and how this connects to questions of social inequality. It explicitly encompasses unregulated, historical, and non-Western forms of labor. Here, _____ define "for or with whom one works and under what rules. These rules determine the type of work, type and amount of remuneration, working hours, degrees of physical and psychological strain, as well as the degree of freedom and autonomy associated with the work."

Exam Probability: **Medium**

57. *Answer choices:*

(see index for correct answer)

- a. Jesse Simons
- b. Labor relations
- c. Union representative
- d. Whipsaw strike

Guidance: level 1

:: Industrial Revolution ::

The _____, now also known as the First _____, was the transition to new manufacturing processes in Europe and the US, in the period from about 1760 to sometime between 1820 and 1840. This transition included going from hand production methods to machines, new chemical manufacturing and iron production processes, the increasing use of steam power and water power, the development of machine tools and the rise of the mechanized factory system. The _____ also led to an unprecedented rise in the rate of population growth.

Exam Probability: **Low**

58. *Answer choices:*
(see index for correct answer)

- a. Grubb Family Iron Dynasty
- b. Lancashire Loom
- c. Hulett
- d. Ironbridge Gorge

Guidance: level 1

:: ::

_____s and acquisitions are transactions in which the ownership of companies, other business organizations, or their operating units are transferred or consolidated with other entities. As an aspect of strategic management, M&A can allow enterprises to grow or downsize, and change the nature of their business or competitive position.

Exam Probability: **High**

59. *Answer choices:*

(see index for correct answer)

- a. interpersonal communication
- b. Merger
- c. open system
- d. imperative

Guidance: level 1

Business law

Corporate law (also known as business law) is the body of law governing the rights, relations, and conduct of persons, companies, organizations and businesses. It refers to the legal practice relating to, or the theory of corporations. Corporate law often describes the law relating to matters which derive directly from the life-cycle of a corporation. It thus encompasses the formation, funding, governance, and death of a corporation.

:: Commercial crimes ::

_____ is the process of concealing the origins of money obtained illegally by passing it through a complex sequence of banking transfers or commercial transactions. The overall scheme of this process returns the money to the launderer in an obscure and indirect way.

Exam Probability: **High**

1. *Answer choices:*

(see index for correct answer)

- a. Fence
- b. Money laundering
- c. FATF blacklist
- d. Offshore leaks

Guidance: level 1

:: Sexual harassment in the United States ::

In law, a _____, reasonable man, or the man on the Clapham omnibus is a hypothetical person of legal fiction crafted by the courts and communicated through case law and jury instructions.

Exam Probability: **Medium**

2. *Answer choices:*

(see index for correct answer)

- a. Fitzgerald v. Barnstable School Committee
- b. Alexander v. Yale
- c. Sexual harassment in education in the United States
- d. Reasonable person

Guidance: level 1

:: ::

According to the philosopher Piyush Mathur , "Tangibility is the property that a phenomenon exhibits if it has and/or transports mass and/or energy and/or momentum".

Exam Probability: **High**

3. *Answer choices:*

(see index for correct answer)

- a. personal values
- b. interpersonal communication
- c. deep-level diversity
- d. process perspective

Guidance: level 1

:: American legal terms ::

The phrase "by _____ " is a legal term that indicates that a right or liability has been created for a party, irrespective of the intent of that party, because it is dictated by existing legal principles. For example, if a person dies without a will, his or her heirs are determined by _____ . Similarly, if a person marries or has a child after his or her will has been executed, the law writes this pretermitted spouse or pretermitted heir into the will if no provision for this situation was specifically included. Adverse possession, in which title to land passes because non-owners have occupied it for a certain period of time, is another important right that vests by _____ .

Exam Probability: **Medium**

4. *Answer choices:*

(see index for correct answer)

- a. Operation of law
- b. Reasonable time

Guidance: level 1

:: ::

Competition arises whenever at least two parties strive for a goal which cannot be shared: where one's gain is the other's loss .

Exam Probability: **High**

5. *Answer choices:*

(see index for correct answer)

- a. corporate values
- b. Competitor
- c. cultural
- d. interpersonal communication

Guidance: level 1

:: Real estate ::

_____ , real estate, realty, or immovable property In English common law refers to landed properties belonging to some person. It include all structures, crops, buildings, machinery, wells, dams, ponds, mines, canals, and roads, among other things. The term is historic, arising from the now-discontinued form of action, which distinguish between _____ disputes and personal property disputes. Personal property was, and continues to refer to all properties that are not real properties.

Exam Probability: **Low**

6. *Answer choices:*

(see index for correct answer)

- a. Foreclosure Stripping
- b. Burgage
- c. Real property
- d. Premises

Guidance: level 1

:: Contract law ::

An _____ is a contract, the terms of which have been agreed by spoken communication. This is in contrast to a written contract, where the contract is a written document. There may be written, or other physical evidence, of an _____ – for example where the parties write down what they have agreed – but the contract itself is not a written one.

Exam Probability: **High**

7. *Answer choices:*

(see index for correct answer)

- a. The Death of Contract
- b. Per minas
- c. Formal contract
- d. Oral contract

Guidance: level 1

:: False advertising law ::

The Lanham Act is the primary federal trademark statute of law in the United States. The Act prohibits a number of activities, including trademark infringement, trademark dilution, and false advertising.

Exam Probability: **High**

8. *Answer choices:*

(see index for correct answer)

- a. POM Wonderful LLC v. Coca-Cola Co.
- b. Rebecca Tushnet

Guidance: level 1

:: Contract law ::

A _____ is a legally-binding agreement which recognises and governs the rights and duties of the parties to the agreement. A _____ is legally enforceable because it meets the requirements and approval of the law. An agreement typically involves the exchange of goods, services, money, or promises of any of those. In the event of breach of _____ , the law awards the injured party access to legal remedies such as damages and cancellation.

Exam Probability: **High**

9. *Answer choices:*

(see index for correct answer)

- a. Time is of the essence
- b. Implied-in-fact contract
- c. Third-party beneficiary
- d. Contract

Guidance: level 1

:: Business models ::

A _____, _____ company or daughter company is a company that is owned or controlled by another company, which is called the parent company, parent, or holding company. The _____ can be a company, corporation, or limited liability company. In some cases it is a government or state-owned enterprise. In some cases, particularly in the music and book publishing industries, subsidiaries are referred to as imprints.

Exam Probability: **Low**

10. *Answer choices:*
(see index for correct answer)

- a. Sailing Ship Effect
- b. Co-operative Wholesale Society
- c. Business model pattern
- d. Independent business

Guidance: level 1

:: Legal terms ::

_____s may be governments, corporations or investment trusts. _____s are legally responsible for the obligations of the issue and for reporting financial conditions, material developments and any other operational activities as required by the regulations of their jurisdictions.

Exam Probability: **Low**

11. *Answer choices:*

(see index for correct answer)

- a. Objection
- b. Abuse of process
- c. Commandeering
- d. Issuer

Guidance: level 1

:: Progressive Era in the United States ::

The Clayton Antitrust Act of 1914 , was a part of United States antitrust law with the goal of adding further substance to the U.S. antitrust law regime; the _____ sought to prevent anticompetitive practices in their incipiency. That regime started with the Sherman Antitrust Act of 1890, the first Federal law outlawing practices considered harmful to consumers . The _____ specified particular prohibited conduct, the three-level enforcement scheme, the exemptions, and the remedial measures.

Exam Probability: **Medium**

12. *Answer choices:*

(see index for correct answer)

- a. Clayton Antitrust Act

- b. Clayton Act
- c. pragmatism

Guidance: level 1

:: Asset ::

In financial accounting, an _____ is any resource owned by the business. Anything tangible or intangible that can be owned or controlled to produce value and that is held by a company to produce positive economic value is an _____ . Simply stated, _____ s represent value of ownership that can be converted into cash . The balance sheet of a firm records the monetary value of the _____ s owned by that firm. It covers money and other valuables belonging to an individual or to a business.

Exam Probability: **High**

13. *Answer choices:*
(see index for correct answer)

- a. Fixed asset
- b. Current asset

Guidance: level 1

:: Debt ::

A _____ is a party that has a claim on the services of a second party. It is a person or institution to whom money is owed. The first party, in general, has provided some property or service to the second party under the assumption that the second party will return an equivalent property and service. The second party is frequently called a debtor or borrower. The first party is called the _____ , which is the lender of property, service, or money.

Exam Probability: **Medium**

14. *Answer choices:*

(see index for correct answer)

- a. Debtors Anonymous
- b. Creditor
- c. Recourse debt
- d. Rule of 72

Guidance: level 1

:: ::

In the law of evidence, a _____ of a particular fact can be made without the aid of proof in some situations. The invocation of a _____ shifts the burden of proof from one party to the opposing party in a court trial.

Exam Probability: **Medium**

15. Answer choices:

(see index for correct answer)

- a. information systems assessment
- b. Presumption
- c. surface-level diversity
- d. Sarbanes-Oxley act of 2002

Guidance: level 1

:: Contract law ::

In common law jurisdictions, an _____ is a contract law term for certain assurances that are presumed to be made in the sale of products or real property, due to the circumstances of the sale. These assurances are characterized as warranties irrespective of whether the seller has expressly promised them orally or in writing. They include an _____ of fitness for a particular purpose, an _____ of merchantability for products, _____ of workmanlike quality for services, and an _____ of habitability for a home.

Exam Probability: **Medium**

16. Answer choices:

(see index for correct answer)

- a. Extinguishment
- b. Implied warranty

- c. Title-transfer theory of contract
- d. Executory contract

Guidance: level 1

:: Legal doctrines and principles ::

In the common law of torts, _____ loquitur is a doctrine that infers negligence from the very nature of an accident or injury in the absence of direct evidence on how any defendant behaved. Although modern formulations differ by jurisdiction, common law originally stated that the accident must satisfy the necessary elements of negligence: duty, breach of duty, causation, and injury. In _____ loquitur, the elements of duty of care, breach, and causation are inferred from an injury that does not ordinarily occur without negligence.

Exam Probability: **Low**

17. *Answer choices:*

(see index for correct answer)

- a. Unilateral mistake
- b. Res ipsa
- c. Abstention doctrine
- d. Proximate cause

Guidance: level 1

:: Investment ::

In finance, the benefit from an _____ is called a return. The return may consist of a gain realised from the sale of property or an _____, unrealised capital appreciation, or _____ income such as dividends, interest, rental income etc., or a combination of capital gain and income. The return may also include currency gains or losses due to changes in foreign currency exchange rates.

Exam Probability: **Low**

18. *Answer choices:*
_(see index for correct answer)

- a. Value Research
- b. Investment
- c. Miraclebet
- d. Philatelic investment

Guidance: level 1

:: ::

In law, a _____ is a coming together of parties to a dispute, to present information in a tribunal, a formal setting with the authority to adjudicate claims or disputes. One form of tribunal is a court. The tribunal, which may occur before a judge, jury, or other designated trier of fact, aims to achieve a resolution to their dispute.

Exam Probability: **Low**

19. *Answer choices:*

(see index for correct answer)

- a. similarity-attraction theory
- b. Character
- c. deep-level diversity
- d. Trial

Guidance: level 1

:: Contract law ::

_____ is a legal cause of action and a type of civil wrong, in which a binding agreement or bargained-for exchange is not honored by one or more of the parties to the contract by non-performance or interference with the other party's performance. Breach occurs when a party to a contract fails to fulfill its obligation as described in the contract, or communicates an intent to fail the obligation or otherwise appears not to be able to perform its obligation under the contract. Where there is _____ , the resulting damages will have to be paid by the party breaching the contract to the aggrieved party.

Exam Probability: **High**

20. *Answer choices:*

(see index for correct answer)

- a. Option contract
- b. Service plan
- c. Breach of contract
- d. Franchisor

Guidance: level 1

:: ::

A contract is a legally-binding agreement which recognises and governs the rights and duties of the parties to the agreement. A contract is legally enforceable because it meets the requirements and approval of the law. An agreement typically involves the exchange of goods, services, money, or promises of any of those. In the event of breach of contract, the law awards the injured party access to legal remedies such as damages and cancellation.

Exam Probability: **Low**

21. *Answer choices:*

(see index for correct answer)

- a. cultural
- b. co-culture
- c. surface-level diversity
- d. process perspective

Guidance: level 1

A _____ is the party who initiates a lawsuit before a court. By doing so, the _____ seeks a legal remedy; if this search is successful, the court will issue judgment in favor of the _____ and make the appropriate court order. "_____" is the term used in civil cases in most English-speaking jurisdictions, the notable exception being England and Wales, where a _____ has, since the introduction of the Civil Procedure Rules in 1999, been known as a "claimant", but that term also has other meanings. In criminal cases, the prosecutor brings the case against the defendant, but the key complaining party is often called the "complainant".

Exam Probability: **Medium**

22. *Answer choices:*

(see index for correct answer)

- a. information systems assessment
- b. cultural
- c. open system
- d. deep-level diversity

Guidance: level 1

_____ is a concept of English common law and is a necessity for simple contracts but not for special contracts. The concept has been adopted by other common law jurisdictions, including the US.

Exam Probability: **Low**

23. *Answer choices:*

(see index for correct answer)

- a. hierarchical perspective
- b. process perspective
- c. personal values
- d. cultural

Guidance: level 1

:: Anti-competitive behaviour ::

Restraints of trade is a common law doctrine relating to the enforceability of contractual restrictions on freedom to conduct business. It is a precursor of modern competition law. In an old leading case of Mitchel v Reynolds Lord Smith LC said,

Exam Probability: **High**

24. *Answer choices:*

(see index for correct answer)

- a. SK Hynix
- b. Restraint of trade
- c. Byrd Amendment
- d. Lang Law

Guidance: level 1

:: Psychometrics ::

_____ is a dynamic, structured, interactive process where a neutral third party assists disputing parties in resolving conflict through the use of specialized communication and negotiation techniques. All participants in _____ are encouraged to actively participate in the process. _____ is a "party-centered" process in that it is focused primarily upon the needs, rights, and interests of the parties. The mediator uses a wide variety of techniques to guide the process in a constructive direction and to help the parties find their optimal solution. A mediator is facilitative in that she/he manages the interaction between parties and facilitates open communication. _____ is also evaluative in that the mediator analyzes issues and relevant norms , while refraining from providing prescriptive advice to the parties .

Exam Probability: **Medium**

25. *Answer choices:*
(see index for correct answer)

- a. Pairwise comparison
- b. Statistical inference

- c. Mediation
- d. Reaction time

Guidance: level 1

:: ::

_____ is the principled guide to action taken by the administrative executive branches of the state with regard to a class of issues, in a manner consistent with law and institutional customs.

Exam Probability: **High**

26. *Answer choices:*
(see index for correct answer)

- a. Public policy
- b. hierarchical
- c. personal values
- d. functional perspective

Guidance: level 1

:: ::

In legal terminology, a _____ is any formal legal document that sets out the facts and legal reasons that the filing party or parties believes are sufficient to support a claim against the party or parties against whom the claim is brought that entitles the plaintiff to a remedy. For example, the Federal Rules of Civil Procedure that govern civil litigation in United States courts provide that a civil action is commenced with the filing or service of a pleading called a _____. Civil court rules in states that have incorporated the Federal Rules of Civil Procedure use the same term for the same pleading.

Exam Probability: **Low**

27. *Answer choices:*

(see index for correct answer)

- a. Complaint
- b. empathy
- c. process perspective
- d. imperative

Guidance: level 1

:: Legal doctrines and principles ::

In the United States, the _____ is a legal rule, based on constitutional law, that prevents evidence collected or analyzed in violation of the defendant's constitutional rights from being used in a court of law. This may be considered an example of a prophylactic rule formulated by the judiciary in order to protect a constitutional right. The _____ may also, in some circumstances at least, be considered to follow directly from the constitutional language, such as the Fifth Amendment's command that no person "shall be compelled in any criminal case to be a witness against himself" and that no person "shall be deprived of life, liberty or property without due process of law".

Exam Probability: **High**

28. *Answer choices:*

(see index for correct answer)

- a. Assumption of risk
- b. Mutual mistake
- c. Duty to rescue
- d. Res ipsa

Guidance: level 1

:: Criminal procedure ::

_____ is the adjudication process of the criminal law. While _____ differs dramatically by jurisdiction, the process generally begins with a formal criminal charge with the person on trial either being free on bail or incarcerated, and results in the conviction or acquittal of the defendant. _____ can be either in form of inquisitorial or adversarial _____ .

Exam Probability: **High**

29. *Answer choices:*

(see index for correct answer)

- a. directed verdict
- b. Exoneration

Guidance: level 1

:: Insolvency ::

_____ is a legal process through which people or other entities who cannot repay debts to creditors may seek relief from some or all of their debts. In most jurisdictions, _____ is imposed by a court order, often initiated by the debtor.

Exam Probability: **High**

30. *Answer choices:*

(see index for correct answer)

- a. Bankruptcy
- b. Debt consolidation
- c. Liquidator
- d. Insolvency law of Russia

Guidance: level 1

:: Real property law ::

A _____ is the grant of authority or rights, stating that the granter formally recognizes the prerogative of the recipient to exercise the rights specified. It is implicit that the granter retains superiority, and that the recipient admits a limited status within the relationship, and it is within that sense that _____ s were historically granted, and that sense is retained in modern usage of the term.

Exam Probability: **Low**

31. *Answer choices:*
(see index for correct answer)

- a. Deed in lieu of foreclosure
- b. Abstractor of title
- c. Catasto
- d. Charter

Guidance: level 1

:: ::

_____ is that part of a civil law legal system which is part of the jus commune that involves relationships between individuals, such as the law of contracts or torts , and the law of obligations . It is to be distinguished from public law, which deals with relationships between both natural and artificial persons and the state, including regulatory statutes, penal law and other law that affects the public order. In general terms, _____ involves interactions between private citizens, whereas public law involves interrelations between the state and the general population.

Exam Probability: **High**

32. *Answer choices:*

(see index for correct answer)

- a. surface-level diversity
- b. Character
- c. interpersonal communication
- d. personal values

Guidance: level 1

:: Contract law ::

_____ is a legal process for collecting a monetary judgment on behalf of a plaintiff from a defendant. _____ allows the plaintiff to take the money or property of the debtor from the person or institution that holds that property. A similar legal mechanism called execution allows the seizure of money or property held directly by the debtor.

Exam Probability: **Low**

33. *Answer choices:*

(see index for correct answer)

- a. Lease purchase contract
- b. Beneficial interest
- c. Community Benefits Agreement
- d. Garnishment

Guidance: level 1

:: ::

The _____ is the central philosophical concept in the deontological moral philosophy of Immanuel Kant. Introduced in Kant's 1785 Groundwork of the Metaphysics of Morals, it may be defined as a way of evaluating motivations for action.

Exam Probability: **Low**

34. Answer choices:

(see index for correct answer)

- a. hierarchical
- b. Categorical imperative
- c. personal values
- d. Sarbanes-Oxley act of 2002

Guidance: level 1

:: Auctioneering ::

An _____ is a process of buying and selling goods or services by offering them up for bid, taking bids, and then selling the item to the highest bidder. The open ascending price _____ is arguably the most common form of _____ in use today. Participants bid openly against one another, with each subsequent bid required to be higher than the previous bid. An _____ eer may announce prices, bidders may call out their bids themselves, or bids may be submitted electronically with the highest current bid publicly displayed. In a Dutch _____, the _____ eer begins with a high asking price for some quantity of like items; the price is lowered until a participant is willing to accept the _____ eer's price for some quantity of the goods in the lot or until the seller's reserve price is met. While _____ s are most associated in the public imagination with the sale of antiques, paintings, rare collectibles and expensive wines, _____ s are also used for commodities, livestock, radio spectrum and used cars. In economic theory, an _____ may refer to any mechanism or set of trading rules for exchange.

Exam Probability: **High**

35. *Answer choices:*

(see index for correct answer)

- a. Proxy bid
- b. Auction
- c. Auction school
- d. Camden auction

Guidance: level 1

:: Contract law ::

A _____ is a contract in which one party agrees to supply as much of a good or service as is required by the other party, and in exchange the other party expressly or implicitly promises that it will obtain its goods or services exclusively from the first party. For example, a grocery store might enter into a contract with the farmer who grows oranges under which the farmer would supply the grocery store with as many oranges as the store could sell. The farmer could sue for breach of contract if the store were thereafter to purchase oranges for this purpose from any other party. The converse of this situation is an output contract, in which one buyer agrees to purchase however much of a good or service the seller is able to produce.

Exam Probability: **High**

36. *Answer choices:*

(see index for correct answer)

- a. Warranty

- b. Material transfer agreement
- c. Requirements contract
- d. Severable contract

Guidance: level 1

:: ::

An _____, for United States federal income tax, is a closely held corporation that makes a valid election to be taxed under Subchapter S of Chapter 1 of the Internal Revenue Code. In general, _____ s do not pay any income taxes. Instead, the corporation's income or losses are divided among and passed through to its shareholders. The shareholders must then report the income or loss on their own individual income tax returns.

Exam Probability: **High**

37. *Answer choices:*

(see index for correct answer)

- a. hierarchical perspective
- b. functional perspective
- c. empathy
- d. Sarbanes-Oxley act of 2002

Guidance: level 1

:: Contract law ::

Offer and acceptance analysis is a traditional approach in contract law. The offer and acceptance formula, developed in the 19th century, identifies a moment of formation when the parties are of one mind. This classical approach to contract formation has been modified by developments in the law of estoppel, misleading conduct, misrepresentation and unjust enrichment.

Exam Probability: **Medium**

38. *Answer choices:*

(see index for correct answer)

- a. Mirror image rule
- b. Offeree
- c. Contract B
- d. Severable contract

Guidance: level 1

:: ::

_____, often abbreviated cert. in the United States, is a process for seeking judicial review and a writ issued by a court that agrees to review. A _____ is issued by a superior court, directing an inferior court, tribunal, or other public authority to send the record of a proceeding for review.

Exam Probability: **High**

39. *Answer choices:*

(see index for correct answer)

- a. similarity-attraction theory
- b. levels of analysis
- c. personal values
- d. Certiorari

Guidance: level 1

:: ::

A _____ is a law passed by a legislative body in a common law system to set the maximum time after an event within which legal proceedings may be initiated.

Exam Probability: **High**

40. *Answer choices:*

(see index for correct answer)

- a. surface-level diversity
- b. cultural
- c. Sarbanes-Oxley act of 2002
- d. empathy

Guidance: level 1

:: Treaties ::

A _____ is an agreement under international law entered into by actors in international law, namely sovereign states and international organizations. A _____ may also be known as an agreement, protocol, covenant, convention, pact, or exchange of letters, among other terms. Regardless of terminology, all of these forms of agreements are, under international law, equally considered treaties and the rules are the same.

Exam Probability: **High**

41. *Answer choices:*

(see index for correct answer)

- a. Investor state dispute settlement
- b. Guillotine clause
- c. Quasi alliance
- d. Clausula rebus sic stantibus

Guidance: level 1

:: Insurance law ::

_____ exists when an insured person derives a financial or other kind of benefit from the continuous existence, without repairment or damage, of the insured object. A person has an _____ in something when loss of or damage to that thing would cause the person to suffer a financial or other kind of loss. Normally, _____ is established by ownership, possession, or direct relationship. For example, people have _____ s in their own homes and vehicles, but not in their neighbors' homes and vehicles, and almost certainly not those of strangers.

Exam Probability: **Medium**

42. *Answer choices:*

(see index for correct answer)

- a. Uberrima fides
- b. Insurance regulatory law
- c. Commissioner v. First Security Bank of Utah, N.A.
- d. Motor vehicle insurance law in India

Guidance: level 1

:: Business law ::

A _____ is a contractual arrangement calling for the lessee to pay the lessor for use of an asset. Property, buildings and vehicles are common assets that are _____ d. Industrial or business equipment is also _____ d.

Exam Probability: **High**

43. *Answer choices:*

(see index for correct answer)

- a. Apparent authority
- b. Power harassment
- c. Lease
- d. Whitewash waiver

Guidance: level 1

:: ::

An _____ , commonly called an appeals court, court of appeals , appeal court , court of second instance or second instance court, is any court of law that is empowered to hear an appeal of a trial court or other lower tribunal. In most jurisdictions, the court system is divided into at least three levels: the trial court, which initially hears cases and reviews evidence and testimony to determine the facts of the case; at least one intermediate _____ ; and a supreme court which primarily reviews the decisions of the intermediate courts. A jurisdiction's supreme court is that jurisdiction's highest _____ . _____ s nationwide can operate under varying rules.

Exam Probability: **High**

44. *Answer choices:*

(see index for correct answer)

- a. Character
- b. interpersonal communication

- c. deep-level diversity
- d. functional perspective

Guidance: level 1

:: Debt ::

_____ , in finance and economics, is payment from a borrower or deposit-taking financial institution to a lender or depositor of an amount above repayment of the principal sum , at a particular rate. It is distinct from a fee which the borrower may pay the lender or some third party. It is also distinct from dividend which is paid by a company to its shareholders from its profit or reserve, but not at a particular rate decided beforehand, rather on a pro rata basis as a share in the reward gained by risk taking entrepreneurs when the revenue earned exceeds the total costs.

Exam Probability: **High**

45. *Answer choices:*

(see index for correct answer)

- a. Rule of 72
- b. Debt-lag
- c. Interest
- d. Household debt

Guidance: level 1

:: Trade secrets ::

The _____ of 1996 was a 6 title Act of Congress dealing with a wide range of issues, including not only industrial espionage, but the insanity defense, matters regarding the Boys & Girls Clubs of America, requirements for presentence investigation reports, and the United States Sentencing Commission reports regarding encryption or scrambling technology, and other technical and minor amendments.

Exam Probability: **Low**

46. *Answer choices:*

(see index for correct answer)

- a. Economic Espionage Act
- b. Old Bay Seasoning
- c. DVD Copy Control Association, Inc. v. Bunner
- d. Angostura bitters

Guidance: level 1

:: Services management and marketing ::

A _____ or servicemark is a trademark used in the United States and several other countries to identify a service rather than a product.

Exam Probability: **Medium**

47. *Answer choices:*

(see index for correct answer)

- a. Automated attendant
- b. Service mark
- c. The Experience Economy
- d. Brandlive

Guidance: level 1

:: Business law ::

A _____ is a form of partnership similar to a general partnership except that while a general partnership must have at least two general partners, a _____ must have at least one GP and at least one limited partner.

Exam Probability: **Medium**

48. *Answer choices:*

(see index for correct answer)

- a. Court auction
- b. Business.gov
- c. Whitewash waiver
- d. Security interest

Guidance: level 1

:: Business ::

An _____ is a key document used by limited liability companies to outline the business' financial and functional decisions including rules, regulations and provisions. The purpose of the document is to govern the internal operations of the business in a way that suits the specific needs of the business owners. Once the document is signed by the members of the limited liability company, it acts as an official contract binding them to its terms. _____ is mandatory as per laws only in 5 states - California, Delaware, Maine, Missouri, and New York LLCs operating without an _____ are governed by the state's default rules contained in the relevant statute and developed through state court decisions. An _____ is similar in function to corporate by-laws, or analogous to a partnership agreement in multi-member LLCs. In single-member LLCs, an _____ is a declaration of the structure that the member has chosen for the company and sometimes used to prove in court that the LLC structure is separate from that of the individual owner and thus necessary so that the owner has documentation to prove that he or she is indeed separate from the entity itself.

Exam Probability: **Low**

49. *Answer choices:*

(see index for correct answer)

- a. Ansoff Matrix
- b. Kingdomality
- c. Corporate housing
- d. Service recovery

Guidance: level 1

:: Business law ::

A _____ is a business entity created by two or more parties, generally characterized by shared ownership, shared returns and risks, and shared governance. Companies typically pursue _____ s for one of four reasons: to access a new market, particularly emerging markets; to gain scale efficiencies by combining assets and operations; to share risk for major investments or projects; or to access skills and capabilities.

Exam Probability: **Low**

50. *Answer choices:*
(see index for correct answer)

- a. Family and Medical Leave Act of 1993
- b. Business courts
- c. Joint venture
- d. Fraudulent trading

Guidance: level 1

:: ::

An _____ is a formal or official change made to a law, contract, constitution, or other legal document. It is based on the verb to amend, which means to change for better. _____ s can add, remove, or update parts of these agreements. They are often used when it is better to change the document than to write a new one.

Exam Probability: **Medium**

51. *Answer choices:*

(see index for correct answer)

- a. deep-level diversity
- b. surface-level diversity
- c. Amendment
- d. open system

Guidance: level 1

:: Meetings ::

A _____ is a body of one or more persons that is subordinate to a deliberative assembly. Usually, the assembly sends matters into a _____ as a way to explore them more fully than would be possible if the assembly itself were considering them. _____ s may have different functions and their type of work differ depending on the type of the organization and its needs.

Exam Probability: **Low**

52. *Answer choices:*

(see index for correct answer)

- a. AEI World Forum
- b. Committee

- c. W00tstock
- d. Unconference

Guidance: level 1

:: Project management ::

_____ is the right to exercise power, which can be formalized by a state and exercised by way of judges, appointed executives of government, or the ecclesiastical or priestly appointed representatives of a God or other deities.

Exam Probability: **Medium**

53. *Answer choices:*

(see index for correct answer)

- a. 10,000ft
- b. Project plan
- c. Theory Z of Ouchi
- d. Authority

Guidance: level 1

:: ::

_____ is the act or practice of forbidding something by law; more particularly the term refers to the banning of the manufacture, storage, transportation, sale, possession, and consumption of alcoholic beverages. The word is also used to refer to a period of time during which such bans are enforced.

Exam Probability: **High**

54. *Answer choices:*

(see index for correct answer)

- a. Prohibition
- b. similarity-attraction theory
- c. cultural
- d. functional perspective

Guidance: level 1

:: Contract law ::

_____ of Contract is a legal term. In contract law, it is the implied ability of an individual to make a legally binding contract on behalf of an organization, by way of uniform or interaction with the public on behalf of that organization. When a person is wearing a uniform or nametag bearing the logo or trademark of a business or organization; or if that person is functioning in an obviously authorized capacity on behalf of a business or organization, that person carries an _____ of Contract. _____ is authority that is not express or written into the contract, but which the agent is assumed to have in order to transact the business of insurance for the principal. _____ is incidental to express authority since not every single detail of an agent's authority can be spelled out in the written contract.

Exam Probability: **Medium**

55. *Answer choices:*

(see index for correct answer)

- a. Indian contract law
- b. Peppercorn
- c. first refusal
- d. Retainer agreement

Guidance: level 1

:: Business ::

_____ is a trade policy that does not restrict imports or exports; it can also be understood as the free market idea applied to international trade. In government, _____ is predominantly advocated by political parties that hold liberal economic positions while economically left-wing and nationalist political parties generally support protectionism, the opposite of _____.

Exam Probability: **Low**

56. *Answer choices:*

(see index for correct answer)

- a. Free trade
- b. Student@Home
- c. SONGZIO
- d. Business analysis

Guidance: level 1

:: ::

_____ is a means of protection from financial loss. It is a form of risk management, primarily used to hedge against the risk of a contingent or uncertain loss

Exam Probability: **Medium**

57. *Answer choices:*

(see index for correct answer)

- a. levels of analysis
- b. empathy
- c. similarity-attraction theory
- d. information systems assessment

Guidance: level 1

:: Law ::

_____ is a body of law which defines the role, powers, and structure of different entities within a state, namely, the executive, the parliament or legislature, and the judiciary; as well as the basic rights of citizens and, in federal countries such as the United States and Canada, the relationship between the central government and state, provincial, or territorial governments.

Exam Probability: **High**

58. *Answer choices:*

(see index for correct answer)

- a. Legal case
- b. Constitutional law

Guidance: level 1

:: ::

_____ Motor Company is an American multinational automaker that has its main headquarter in Dearborn, Michigan, a suburb of Detroit. It was founded by Henry _____ and incorporated on June 16, 1903. The company sells automobiles and commercial vehicles under the _____ brand and most luxury cars under the Lincoln brand. _____ also owns Brazilian SUV manufacturer Troller, an 8% stake in Aston Martin of the United Kingdom and a 32% stake in Jiangling Motors. It also has joint-ventures in China, Taiwan, Thailand, Turkey, and Russia. The company is listed on the New York Stock Exchange and is controlled by the _____ family; they have minority ownership but the majority of the voting power.

Exam Probability: **High**

59. *Answer choices:*

(see index for correct answer)

- a. cultural
- b. levels of analysis
- c. Ford
- d. imperative

Guidance: level 1

Finance

Finance is a field that is concerned with the allocation (investment) of assets and liabilities over space and time, often under conditions of risk or uncertainty. Finance can also be defined as the science of money management. Participants in the market aim to price assets based on their risk level, fundamental value, and their expected rate of return. Finance can be split into three sub-categories: public finance, corporate finance and personal finance.

:: Financial ratios ::

The _____ shows the percentage of how profitable a company's assets are in generating revenue.

Exam Probability: **High**

1. *Answer choices:*

(see index for correct answer)

- a. Diluted earnings per share
- b. Return on assets
- c. Cash flow return on investment
- d. Current ratio

Guidance: level 1

:: Financial accounting ::

_____ refers to any one of several methods by which a company, for 'financial accounting' or tax purposes, depreciates a fixed asset in such a way that the amount of depreciation taken each year is higher during the earlier years of an asset's life. For financial accounting purposes, _____ is expected to be much more productive during its early years, so that depreciation expense will more accurately represent how much of an asset's usefulness is being used up each year. For tax purposes, _____ provides a way of deferring corporate income taxes by reducing taxable income in current years, in exchange for increased taxable income in future years. This is a valuable tax incentive that encourages businesses to purchase new assets.

Exam Probability: **Medium**

2. *Answer choices:*

(see index for correct answer)

- a. Authorised capital
- b. Fixed asset register
- c. Accelerated depreciation
- d. Net worth

Guidance: level 1

:: Financial risk ::

_____ is any of various types of risk associated with financing, including financial transactions that include company loans in risk of default. Often it is understood to include only downside risk, meaning the potential for financial loss and uncertainty about its extent.

Exam Probability: **Medium**

3. *Answer choices:*
(see index for correct answer)

- a. Financial risk
- b. Active risk
- c. Foreign exchange risk
- d. Risk-free rate

Guidance: level 1

:: Generally Accepted Accounting Principles ::

A _____ or reacquired stock is stock which is bought back by the issuing company, reducing the amount of outstanding stock on the open market.

Exam Probability: **Medium**

4. *Answer choices:*
(see index for correct answer)

- a. Goodwill
- b. Access to finance
- c. deferred revenue
- d. Gross income

Guidance: level 1

:: Real estate ::

Amortisation is paying off an amount owed over time by making planned, incremental payments of principal and interest. To amortise a loan means "to kill it off". In accounting, amortisation refers to charging or writing off an intangible asset's cost as an operational expense over its estimated useful life to reduce a company's taxable income.

Exam Probability: **Medium**

5. *Answer choices:*

(see index for correct answer)

- a. Amortization
- b. Assignment
- c. Real estate investment club
- d. E-Pro

Guidance: level 1

:: Accounting terminology ::

A _____ contains all the accounts for recording transactions relating to a company's assets, liabilities, owners' equity, revenue, and expenses. In modern accounting software or ERP, the _____ works as a central repository for accounting data transferred from all subledgers or modules like accounts payable, accounts receivable, cash management, fixed assets, purchasing and projects. The _____ is the backbone of any accounting system which holds financial and non-financial data for an organization. The collection of all accounts is known as the _____ . Each account is known as a ledger account. In a manual or non-computerized system this may be a large book. The statement of financial position and the statement of income and comprehensive income are both derived from the _____ . Each account in the _____ consists of one or more pages. The _____ is where posting to the accounts occurs. Posting is the process of recording amounts as credits , and amounts as debits , in the pages of the _____ . Additional columns to the right hold a running activity total .

Exam Probability: **Medium**

6. *Answer choices:*

(see index for correct answer)

- a. Accounts receivable
- b. Record to report
- c. Double-entry accounting
- d. outstanding balance

Guidance: level 1

:: Generally Accepted Accounting Principles ::

In accounting, an economic item's _____ is the original nominal monetary value of that item. _____ accounting involves reporting assets and liabilities at their _____ s, which are not updated for changes in the items' values. Consequently, the amounts reported for these balance sheet items often differ from their current economic or market values.

Exam Probability: **Medium**

7. *Answer choices:*

(see index for correct answer)

- a. Matching principle
- b. Historical cost
- c. Normal balance
- d. Fixed investment

Guidance: level 1

:: Financial markets ::

For an individual, a _____ is the minimum amount of money by which the expected return on a risky asset must exceed the known return on a risk-free asset in order to induce an individual to hold the risky asset rather than the risk-free asset. It is positive if the person is risk averse. Thus it is the minimum willingness to accept compensation for the risk.

Exam Probability: **Low**

8. *Answer choices:*

(see index for correct answer)

- a. Electronic trade matching
- b. Fourth market
- c. Public offering
- d. Risk premium

Guidance: level 1

:: Land value taxation ::

_____, sometimes referred to as dry _____, is the solid surface of Earth that is not permanently covered by water. The vast majority of human activity throughout history has occurred in _____ areas that support agriculture, habitat, and various natural resources. Some life forms have developed from predecessor species that lived in bodies of water.

Exam Probability: **High**

9. *Answer choices:*

(see index for correct answer)

- a. Prosper Australia
- b. Land
- c. Georgism
- d. Harry Gunnison Brown

Guidance: level 1

:: Investment ::

In finance, the benefit from an _____ is called a return. The return may consist of a gain realised from the sale of property or an _____, unrealised capital appreciation, or _____ income such as dividends, interest, rental income etc., or a combination of capital gain and income. The return may also include currency gains or losses due to changes in foreign currency exchange rates.

Exam Probability: **High**

10. Answer choices:

(see index for correct answer)

- a. Security market line
- b. Acertus Market Sentiment Indicator
- c. Investment
- d. Traditional investments

Guidance: level 1

:: Capital gains taxes ::

> A _____ refers to profit that results from a sale of a capital asset, such as stock, bond or real estate, where the sale price exceeds the purchase price. The gain is the difference between a higher selling price and a lower purchase price. Conversely, a capital loss arises if the proceeds from the sale of a capital asset are less than the purchase price.

Exam Probability: **High**

11. Answer choices:

(see index for correct answer)

- a. Capital gains tax
- b. Capital gain
- c. Capital cost tax factor

Guidance: level 1

:: Retirement ::

An _____ is a series of payments made at equal intervals. Examples of annuities are regular deposits to a savings account, monthly home mortgage payments, monthly insurance payments and pension payments. Annuities can be classified by the frequency of payment dates. The payments may be made weekly, monthly, quarterly, yearly, or at any other regular interval of time.

Exam Probability: **Low**

12. *Answer choices:*

(see index for correct answer)

- a. Annuity
- b. Retirement spend-down
- c. Mortality drag
- d. Elder Village

Guidance: level 1

:: Business economics ::

In finance, _____ is the risk of losses caused by interest rate changes. The prices of most financial instruments, such as stocks and bonds move inversely with interest rates, so investors are subject to capital loss when rates rise.

Exam Probability: **High**

13. *Answer choices:*

(see index for correct answer)

- a. Financial risk modeling
- b. Rate risk
- c. Units of transportation measurement
- d. Kaizen costing

Guidance: level 1

:: Government bonds ::

A _____ or sovereign bond is a bond issued by a national government, generally with a promise to pay periodic interest payments called coupon payments and to repay the face value on the maturity date. The aim of a _____ is to support government spending. _____ s are usually denominated in the country's own currency, in which case the government cannot be forced to default, although it may choose to do so. If a government is close to default on its debt the media often refer to this as a sovereign debt crisis.

14. *Answer choices:*

(see index for correct answer)

- a. Direct operations
- b. Bond vigilante
- c. Sovereign bond
- d. Government bond

Guidance: level 1

:: Actuarial science ::

The _____ is the greater benefit of receiving money now rather than an identical sum later. It is founded on time preference.

Exam Probability: **Low**

15. *Answer choices:*

(see index for correct answer)

- a. Time value of money
- b. Actuarial exam
- c. Mortality forecasting
- d. Risk parity

Guidance: level 1

:: Real estate valuation ::

_____ or OMV is the price at which an asset would trade in a competitive auction setting. _____ is often used interchangeably with open _____, fair value or fair _____, although these terms have distinct definitions in different standards, and may or may not differ in some circumstances.

Exam Probability: **Low**

16. *Answer choices:*
(see index for correct answer)

- a. ZipRealty
- b. Days on market
- c. Market value
- d. Appraisal Standards Board

Guidance: level 1

:: Accounting journals and ledgers ::

The subledger, or _____, provides details behind entries in the general ledger used in accounting. The subledger shows detail for part of the accounting records such as property and equipment, prepaid expenses, etc. The detail would include such items as date the item was purchased or expense incurred, a description of the item, the original balance, and the net book value. The total of the subledger would match the line item amount on the general ledger. This corresponding line item in the general ledger is referred to as the controlling account. The _____ balance is compared with its controlling account balance as part of the process of preparing a trial balance.

Exam Probability: **High**

17. *Answer choices:*

(see index for correct answer)

- a. Cash receipts journal
- b. Subledger
- c. Subsidiary ledger
- d. Check register

Guidance: level 1

:: Actuarial science ::

_____ is the possibility of losing something of value. Values can be gained or lost when taking _____ resulting from a given action or inaction, foreseen or unforeseen. _____ can also be defined as the intentional interaction with uncertainty. Uncertainty is a potential, unpredictable, and uncontrollable outcome; _____ is a consequence of action taken in spite of uncertainty.

Exam Probability: **Low**

18. *Answer choices:*

(see index for correct answer)

- a. Value at risk
- b. John Graunt
- c. Risk
- d. Insurable risk

Guidance: level 1

:: Generally Accepted Accounting Principles ::

A _____ is a reduction of the recognized value of something. In accounting, this is a recognition of the reduced or zero value of an asset. In income tax statements, this is a reduction of taxable income, as a recognition of certain expenses required to produce the income.

Exam Probability: **Low**

19. *Answer choices:*

(see index for correct answer)

- a. Pro forma
- b. Net profit
- c. Income statement
- d. Reserve

Guidance: level 1

:: Subprime mortgage crisis ::

The _____ Group, Inc., is an American multinational investment bank and financial services company headquartered in New York City. It offers services in investment management, securities, asset management, prime brokerage, and securities underwriting.

Exam Probability: **Medium**

20. *Answer choices:*

(see index for correct answer)

- a. Foreclosure rescue
- b. Chris Dodd
- c. Goldman Sachs
- d. Subprime mortgage crisis solutions debate

Guidance: level 1

:: Management accounting ::

In finance, the _____ or net present worth applies to a series of cash flows occurring at different times. The present value of a cash flow depends on the interval of time between now and the cash flow. It also depends on the discount rate. NPV accounts for the time value of money. It provides a method for evaluating and comparing capital projects or financial products with cash flows spread over time, as in loans, investments, payouts from insurance contracts plus many other applications.

Exam Probability: **Low**

21. *Answer choices:*

(see index for correct answer)

- a. Grenzplankostenrechnung
- b. Managerial risk accounting
- c. Owner earnings
- d. Revenue center

Guidance: level 1

:: Cash flow ::

_____s are narrowly interconnected with the concepts of value, interest rate and liquidity. A _____ that shall happen on a future day tN can be transformed into a _____ of the same value in t0.

Exam Probability: **Low**

22. *Answer choices:*

(see index for correct answer)

- a. Factoring
- b. Cash carrier
- c. Operating cash flow
- d. Cash flow

Guidance: level 1

:: Financial accounting ::

_____ in accounting is the process of treating investments in associate companies. Equity accounting is usually applied where an investor entity holds 20–50% of the voting stock of the associate company. The investor records such investments as an asset on its balance sheet. The investor's proportional share of the associate company's net income increases the investment, and proportional payments of dividends decrease it. In the investor's income statement, the proportional share of the investor's net income or net loss is reported as a single-line item.

Exam Probability: **Low**

23. Answer choices:

(see index for correct answer)

- a. Carry
- b. Holding gains
- c. Net worth
- d. Equity method

Guidance: level 1

:: ::

An _____ is an area of the production, distribution, or trade, and consumption of goods and services by different agents. Understood in its broadest sense, 'The _____ is defined as a social domain that emphasize the practices, discourses, and material expressions associated with the production, use, and management of resources'. Economic agents can be individuals, businesses, organizations, or governments. Economic transactions occur when two parties agree to the value or price of the transacted good or service, commonly expressed in a certain currency. However, monetary transactions only account for a small part of the economic domain.

Exam Probability: **Medium**

24. Answer choices:

(see index for correct answer)

- a. Character
- b. co-culture

- c. corporate values
- d. Economy

Guidance: level 1

:: ::

_____ is the consumption and saving opportunity gained by an entity within a specified timeframe, which is generally expressed in monetary terms. For households and individuals, " _____ is the sum of all the wages, salaries, profits, interest payments, rents, and other forms of earnings received in a given period of time."

Exam Probability: **Low**

25. *Answer choices:*

(see index for correct answer)

- a. cultural
- b. deep-level diversity
- c. surface-level diversity
- d. Income

Guidance: level 1

:: Bonds (finance) ::

In finance, a _____ or convertible note or convertible debt is a type of bond that the holder can convert into a specified number of shares of common stock in the issuing company or cash of equal value. It is a hybrid security with debt- and equity-like features. It originated in the mid-19th century, and was used by early speculators such as Jacob Little and Daniel Drew to counter market cornering.

Exam Probability: **Low**

26. *Answer choices:*

(see index for correct answer)

- a. Luxembourg Depositary Receipt
- b. Bond Tender Offer
- c. Samurai bond
- d. Alternative risk transfer

Guidance: level 1

:: ::

A _____ is a fund into which a sum of money is added during an employee's employment years, and from which payments are drawn to support the person's retirement from work in the form of periodic payments. A _____ may be a "defined benefit plan" where a fixed sum is paid regularly to a person, or a "defined contribution plan" under which a fixed sum is invested and then becomes available at retirement age. _____ s should not be confused with severance pay; the former is usually paid in regular installments for life after retirement, while the latter is typically paid as a fixed amount after involuntary termination of employment prior to retirement.

Exam Probability: **Low**

27. *Answer choices:*

(see index for correct answer)

- a. interpersonal communication
- b. open system
- c. deep-level diversity
- d. information systems assessment

Guidance: level 1

:: Valuation (finance) ::

_____ refers to an assessment of the viability, stability, and profitability of a business, sub-business or project.

Exam Probability: **Low**

28. *Answer choices:*

(see index for correct answer)

- a. Stock valuation
- b. Dividend puzzle
- c. Diminution in value
- d. Financial analysis

Guidance: level 1

:: Pharmaceutical industry ::

A _____ is a document in which data collected for a clinical trial is first recorded. This data is usually later entered in the case report form. The International Conference on Harmonisation of Technical Requirements for Registration of Pharmaceuticals for Human Use guidelines define _____ s as "original documents, data, and records." _____ s contain source data, which is defined as "all information in original records and certified copies of original records of clinical findings, observations, or other activities in a clinical trial necessary for the reconstruction and evaluation of the trial."

Exam Probability: **High**

29. *Answer choices:*

(see index for correct answer)

- a. Source document
- b. Mexican barbasco trade

- c. Healthy Skepticism
- d. Cost of HIV treatment

Guidance: level 1

:: Debt ::

_____ , in finance and economics, is payment from a borrower or deposit-taking financial institution to a lender or depositor of an amount above repayment of the principal sum , at a particular rate. It is distinct from a fee which the borrower may pay the lender or some third party. It is also distinct from dividend which is paid by a company to its shareholders from its profit or reserve, but not at a particular rate decided beforehand, rather on a pro rata basis as a share in the reward gained by risk taking entrepreneurs when the revenue earned exceeds the total costs.

Exam Probability: **Low**

30. *Answer choices:*
(see index for correct answer)

- a. Interest
- b. Internal debt
- c. Debt adjustment
- d. Perpetual subordinated debt

Guidance: level 1

:: Fixed income analysis ::

The _____, book yield or redemption yield of a bond or other fixed-interest security, such as gilts, is the internal rate of return earned by an investor who buys the bond today at the market price, assuming that the bond is held until maturity, and that all coupon and principal payments are made on schedule. _____ is the discount rate at which the sum of all future cash flows from the bond is equal to the current price of the bond. The YTM is often given in terms of Annual Percentage Rate, but more often market convention is followed. In a number of major markets the convention is to quote annualized yields with semi-annual compounding; thus, for example, an annual effective yield of 10.25% would be quoted as 10.00%, because $1.05 \times 1.05 = 1.1025$ and $2 \times 5 = 10$.

Exam Probability: **Medium**

31. *Answer choices:*
(see index for correct answer)

- a. Chen model
- b. Bond equivalent yield
- c. Yield spread
- d. Yield to maturity

Guidance: level 1

:: ::

_____ refers to a business or organization attempting to acquire goods or services to accomplish its goals. Although there are several organizations that attempt to set standards in the _____ process, processes can vary greatly between organizations. Typically the word "_____" is not used interchangeably with the word "procurement", since procurement typically includes expediting, supplier quality, and transportation and logistics in addition to _____ .

Exam Probability: **Medium**

32. *Answer choices:*

(see index for correct answer)

- a. personal values
- b. Character
- c. Purchasing
- d. cultural

Guidance: level 1

:: ::

A _____ is the period used by governments for accounting and budget purposes, which varies between countries. It is also used for financial reporting by business and other organizations. Laws in many jurisdictions require company financial reports to be prepared and published on an annual basis, but generally do not require the reporting period to align with the calendar year. Taxation laws generally require accounting records to be maintained and taxes calculated on an annual basis, which usually corresponds to the _____ used for government purposes. The calculation of tax on an annual basis is especially relevant for direct taxation, such as income tax. Many annual government fees—such as Council rates, licence fees, etc.—are also levied on a _____ basis, while others are charged on an anniversary basis.

Exam Probability: **High**

33. *Answer choices:*

(see index for correct answer)

- a. Fiscal year
- b. surface-level diversity
- c. co-culture
- d. personal values

Guidance: level 1

The _____ of a function of a real variable measures the sensitivity to change of the function value with respect to a change in its argument.
_____ s are a fundamental tool of calculus. For example, the _____ of the position of a moving object with respect to time is the object's velocity: this measures how quickly the position of the object changes when time advances.

Exam Probability: **Medium**

34. *Answer choices:*

(see index for correct answer)

- a. personal values
- b. co-culture
- c. surface-level diversity
- d. Derivative

Guidance: level 1

:: E-commerce ::

A _____ is a plastic payment card that can be used instead of cash when making purchases. It is similar to a credit card, but unlike a credit card, the money is immediately transferred directly from the cardholder's bank account when performing a transaction.

Exam Probability: **Low**

35. Answer choices:

(see index for correct answer)

- a. Mobimoneybox
- b. Cleaning card
- c. Piano Media
- d. Debit card

Guidance: level 1

:: Financial crises ::

> A _____ is any of a broad variety of situations in which some financial assets suddenly lose a large part of their nominal value. In the 19th and early 20th centuries, many financial crises were associated with banking panics, and many recessions coincided with these panics. Other situations that are often called financial crises include stock market crashes and the bursting of other financial bubbles, currency crises, and sovereign defaults. Financial crises directly result in a loss of paper wealth but do not necessarily result in significant changes in the real economy .

Exam Probability: **Low**

36. Answer choices:

(see index for correct answer)

- a. Arendal crash
- b. Global saving glut

- c. Financial crisis
- d. Wreck of the Tennessee Gravy Train

Guidance: level 1

:: Inventory ::

_____ is a system of inventory in which updates are made on a periodic basis. This differs from perpetual inventory systems, where updates are made as seen fit.

Exam Probability: **High**

37. *Answer choices:*

(see index for correct answer)

- a. Safety stock
- b. Stock control
- c. Periodic inventory
- d. Item-level tagging

Guidance: level 1

:: Marketing ::

_____ is a financial mechanism in which a debtor obtains the right to delay payments to a creditor, for a defined period of time, in exchange for a charge or fee. Essentially, the party that owes money in the present purchases the right to delay the payment until some future date. The discount, or charge, is the difference between the original amount owed in the present and the amount that has to be paid in the future to settle the debt.

Exam Probability: **High**

38. *Answer choices:*

(see index for correct answer)

- a. Point of difference
- b. Medical science liaison
- c. Online marketing platform
- d. Discounting

Guidance: level 1

:: ::

In sales, commerce and economics, a _____ is the recipient of a good, service, product or an idea - obtained from a seller, vendor, or supplier via a financial transaction or exchange for money or some other valuable consideration.

Exam Probability: **Medium**

39. *Answer choices:*

(see index for correct answer)

- a. cultural
- b. hierarchical
- c. interpersonal communication
- d. Customer

Guidance: level 1

:: Financial economics ::

_____ , Inc. is an independent investment research and financial publishing firm based in New York City, New York, United States, founded in 1931 by Arnold Bernhard. _____ is best known for publishing The _____ Investment Survey, a stock analysis newsletter that is among the most highly regarded and widely used independent investment research resources in global investment and trading markets, tracking approximately 1,700 publicly traded stocks in over 99 industries.

Exam Probability: **Medium**

40. *Answer choices:*

(see index for correct answer)

- a. Value Line
- b. Single-index model
- c. Implementation shortfall

- d. Solvency

Guidance: level 1

:: ::

_____ is the concept of one topic being connected to another topic in a way that makes it useful to consider the second topic when considering the first. The concept of _____ is studied in many different fields, including cognitive sciences, logic, and library and information science. Most fundamentally, however, it is studied in epistemology. Different theories of knowledge have different implications for what is considered relevant and these fundamental views have implications for all other fields as well.

Exam Probability: **Low**

41. *Answer choices:*

(see index for correct answer)

- a. Character
- b. co-culture
- c. Relevance
- d. process perspective

Guidance: level 1

:: Stock market ::

The _____ of a corporation is all of the shares into which ownership of the corporation is divided. In American English, the shares are commonly known as "_____s". A single share of the _____ represents fractional ownership of the corporation in proportion to the total number of shares. This typically entitles the _____ holder to that fraction of the company's earnings, proceeds from liquidation of assets, or voting power, often dividing these up in proportion to the amount of money each _____ holder has invested. Not all _____ is necessarily equal, as certain classes of _____ may be issued for example without voting rights, with enhanced voting rights, or with a certain priority to receive profits or liquidation proceeds before or after other classes of shareholders.

Exam Probability: **Low**

42. *Answer choices:*

(see index for correct answer)

- a. Voting interest
- b. stock price
- c. Stock
- d. Tech Buzz

Guidance: level 1

:: Management accounting ::

In _____ or managerial accounting, managers use the provisions of accounting information in order to better inform themselves before they decide matters within their organizations, which aids their management and performance of control functions.

Exam Probability: **Low**

43. *Answer choices:*

(see index for correct answer)

- a. Constraints accounting
- b. Process costing
- c. Cost driver
- d. Direct material total variance

Guidance: level 1

:: Asset ::

In financial accounting, an _____ is any resource owned by the business. Anything tangible or intangible that can be owned or controlled to produce value and that is held by a company to produce positive economic value is an _____ . Simply stated, _____ s represent value of ownership that can be converted into cash . The balance sheet of a firm records the monetary value of the _____ s owned by that firm. It covers money and other valuables belonging to an individual or to a business.

Exam Probability: **Low**

44. *Answer choices:*

(see index for correct answer)

- a. Current asset
- b. Asset

Guidance: level 1

:: Business law ::

A _____ is a group of people who jointly supervise the activities of an organization, which can be either a for-profit business, nonprofit organization, or a government agency. Such a board's powers, duties, and responsibilities are determined by government regulations and the organization's own constitution and bylaws. These authorities may specify the number of members of the board, how they are to be chosen, and how often they are to meet.

Exam Probability: **Low**

45. *Answer choices:*

(see index for correct answer)

- a. Industrial relations
- b. Statutory liability
- c. Board of directors
- d. Arbitration award

Guidance: level 1

:: Debt ::

_____ is the trust which allows one party to provide money or resources to another party wherein the second party does not reimburse the first party immediately , but promises either to repay or return those resources at a later date. In other words, _____ is a method of making reciprocity formal, legally enforceable, and extensible to a large group of unrelated people.

Exam Probability: **Medium**

46. *Answer choices:*

(see index for correct answer)

- a. Perpetual subordinated debt
- b. Extendible bond
- c. Credit
- d. Crown debt

Guidance: level 1

:: Investment ::

The _____ is a measure of an investment's rate of return. The term internal refers to the fact that the calculation excludes external factors, such as the risk-free rate, inflation, the cost of capital, or various financial risks.

Exam Probability: **Medium**

47. *Answer choices:*

(see index for correct answer)

- a. Acertus Market Sentiment Indicator
- b. Diamonds as an investment
- c. Internal rate of return
- d. Master-KAG

Guidance: level 1

:: Occupations ::

An _____ is a practitioner of accounting or accountancy, which is the measurement, disclosure or provision of assurance about financial information that helps managers, investors, tax authorities and others make decisions about allocating resource.

Exam Probability: **Low**

48. *Answer choices:*

(see index for correct answer)

- a. Sanitary engineering
- b. Master arborist
- c. Nuclear gypsy
- d. Expeditor

Guidance: level 1

:: Marketing terminology ::

_____ in capital budgeting refers to the period of time required to recoup the funds expended in an investment, or to reach the break-even point. For example, a $1000 investment made at the start of year 1 which returned $500 at the end of year 1 and year 2 respectively would have a two-year _____. _____ is usually expressed in years. Starting from investment year by calculating Net Cash Flow for each year: Net Cash Flow Year 1 = Cash Inflow Year 1 - Cash Outflow Year 1. Then Cumulative Cash Flow = Accumulate by year until Cumulative Cash Flow is a positive number: that year is the payback year.

Exam Probability: **Low**

49. *Answer choices:*
(see index for correct answer)

- a. Promoter
- b. Business to many
- c. Payback period

- d. Numeric distribution

Guidance: level 1

:: Generally Accepted Accounting Principles ::

_____ , or non-current liabilities, are liabilities that are due beyond a year or the normal operation period of the company. The normal operation period is the amount of time it takes for a company to turn inventory into cash. On a classified balance sheet, liabilities are separated between current and _____ to help users assess the company's financial standing in short-term and long-term periods. _____ give users more information about the long-term prosperity of the company, while current liabilities inform the user of debt that the company owes in the current period. On a balance sheet, accounts are listed in order of liquidity, so _____ come after current liabilities. In addition, the specific long-term liability accounts are listed on the balance sheet in order of liquidity. Therefore, an account due within eighteen months would be listed before an account due within twenty-four months. Examples of _____ are bonds payable, long-term loans, capital leases, pension liabilities, post-retirement healthcare liabilities, deferred compensation, deferred revenues, deferred income taxes, and derivative liabilities.

Exam Probability: **High**

50. *Answer choices:*
(see index for correct answer)

- a. Cash method of accounting
- b. Liability
- c. Management accounting principles

- d. Deferral

Guidance: level 1

:: Financial ratios ::

The _____ is a liquidity ratio that measures whether a firm has enough resources to meet its short-term obligations. It compares a firm's current assets to its current liabilities, and is expressed as follows.

Exam Probability: **Low**

51. *Answer choices:*
(see index for correct answer)

- a. Fixed-asset turnover
- b. Statutory liquidity ratio
- c. Debt service ratio
- d. Current ratio

Guidance: level 1

:: Separation of investment and commercial banking ::

A _____ is a type of bank that provides services such as accepting deposits, making business loans, and offering basic investment products that is operated as a business for profit.

Exam Probability: **High**

52. *Answer choices:*

(see index for correct answer)

- a. Commercial bank
- b. Depository institution
- c. Bank Holding Company Act
- d. Bank holding company

Guidance: level 1

:: Financial ratios ::

_____ is the difference between revenue and cost of goods sold divided by revenue. _____ is expressed as a percentage. Generally, it is calculated as the selling price of an item, less the cost of goods sold . _____ is often used interchangeably with Gross Profit, but the terms are different. When speaking about a monetary amount, it is technically correct to use the term Gross Profit; when referring to a percentage or ratio, it is correct to use _____ . In other words, _____ is a percentage value, while Gross Profit is a monetary value.

Exam Probability: **High**

53. *Answer choices:*

(see index for correct answer)

- a. Gross margin
- b. Statutory liquidity ratio
- c. Average collection period
- d. Return on tangible equity

Guidance: level 1

:: Financial economics ::

A _____ is defined to include property of any kind held by an assessee, whether connected with their business or profession or not connected with their business or profession. It includes all kinds of property, movable or immovable, tangible or intangible, fixed or circulating. Thus, land and building, plant and machinery, motorcar, furniture, jewellery, route permits, goodwill, tenancy rights, patents, trademarks, shares, debentures, securities, units, mutual funds, zero-coupon bonds etc. are _____ s.

Exam Probability: **Medium**

54. *Answer choices:*

(see index for correct answer)

- a. Consumer leverage ratio
- b. Deutsche Bank Prize in Financial Economics
- c. Market correction

- d. Constant proportion portfolio insurance

Guidance: level 1

:: ::

MCI, Inc. was an American telecommunication corporation, currently a subsidiary of Verizon Communications, with its main office in Ashburn, Virginia. The corporation was formed originally as a result of the merger of _____ and MCI Communications corporations, and used the name MCI _____, succeeded by _____, before changing its name to the present version on April 12, 2003, as part of the corporation's ending of its bankruptcy status. The company traded on NASDAQ as WCOM and MCIP. The corporation was purchased by Verizon Communications with the deal finalizing on January 6, 2006, and is now identified as that company's Verizon Enterprise Solutions division with the local residential divisions being integrated slowly into local Verizon subsidiaries.

Exam Probability: **High**

55. *Answer choices:*

(see index for correct answer)

- a. WorldCom
- b. Sarbanes-Oxley act of 2002
- c. similarity-attraction theory
- d. information systems assessment

Guidance: level 1

:: Income taxes ::

An _____ is a tax imposed on individuals or entities that varies with respective income or profits. _____ generally is computed as the product of a tax rate times taxable income. Taxation rates may vary by type or characteristics of the taxpayer.

Exam Probability: **High**

56. *Answer choices:*

(see index for correct answer)

- a. Income tax
- b. Rouanet Law
- c. Income Tax Act 2007
- d. Personal allowance

Guidance: level 1

:: Accounting in the United States ::

The _____ is a private-sector, nonprofit corporation created by the Sarbanes–Oxley Act of 2002 to oversee the audits of public companies and other issuers in order to protect the interests of investors and further the public interest in the preparation of informative, accurate and independent audit reports. The PCAOB also oversees the audits of broker-dealers, including compliance reports filed pursuant to federal securities laws, to promote investor protection. All PCAOB rules and standards must be approved by the U.S. Securities and Exchange Commission.

Exam Probability: **Medium**

57. *Answer choices:*

(see index for correct answer)

- a. Comprehensive Performance Assessment
- b. Federal Accounting Standards Advisory Board
- c. Public Company Accounting Oversight Board
- d. Financial Accounting Foundation

Guidance: level 1

:: ::

A _____, or holiday, is a leave of absence from a regular occupation, or a specific trip or journey, usually for the purpose of recreation or tourism. People often take a _____ during specific holiday observances, or for specific festivals or celebrations. _____s are often spent with friends or family.

Exam Probability: **Low**

58. *Answer choices:*

(see index for correct answer)

- a. empathy
- b. cultural
- c. hierarchical perspective
- d. process perspective

Guidance: level 1

:: ::

An _____ is a comprehensive report on a company's activities throughout the preceding year. _____ s are intended to give shareholders and other interested people information about the company's activities and financial performance. They may be considered as grey literature. Most jurisdictions require companies to prepare and disclose _____ s, and many require the _____ to be filed at the company's registry. Companies listed on a stock exchange are also required to report at more frequent intervals.

Exam Probability: **High**

59. *Answer choices:*

(see index for correct answer)

- a. open system

- b. similarity-attraction theory
- c. hierarchical perspective
- d. Annual report

Guidance: level 1

Human resource management

Human resource (HR) management is the strategic approach to the effective management of organization workers so that they help the business gain a competitive advantage. It is designed to maximize employee performance in service of an employer's strategic objectives. HR is primarily concerned with the management of people within organizations, focusing on policies and on systems. HR departments are responsible for overseeing employee-benefits design, employee recruitment, training and development, performance appraisal, and rewarding (e.g., managing pay and benefit systems). HR also concerns itself with organizational change and industrial relations, that is, the balancing of organizational practices with requirements arising from collective bargaining and from governmental laws.

:: Labour relations ::

_____ is a field of study that can have different meanings depending on the context in which it is used. In an international context, it is a subfield of labor history that studies the human relations with regard to work – in its broadest sense – and how this connects to questions of social inequality. It explicitly encompasses unregulated, historical, and non-Western forms of labor. Here, _____ define "for or with whom one works and under what rules. These rules determine the type of work, type and amount of remuneration, working hours, degrees of physical and psychological strain, as well as the degree of freedom and autonomy associated with the work."

Exam Probability: **Medium**

1. *Answer choices:*

(see index for correct answer)

- a. Labor relations
- b. Two-tier system
- c. Eurocadres
- d. Union shop

Guidance: level 1

:: ::

An _____ is a period of work experience offered by an organization for a limited period of time. Once confined to medical graduates, the term is now used for a wide range of placements in businesses, non-profit organizations and government agencies. They are typically undertaken by students and graduates looking to gain relevant skills and experience in a particular field. Employers benefit from these placements because they often recruit employees from their best interns, who have known capabilities, thus saving time and money in the long run. _____s are usually arranged by third-party organizations which recruit interns on behalf of industry groups. Rules vary from country to country about when interns should be regarded as employees. The system can be open to exploitation by unscrupulous employers.

Exam Probability: **Low**

2. *Answer choices:*

(see index for correct answer)

- a. information systems assessment
- b. Internship
- c. empathy
- d. interpersonal communication

Guidance: level 1

:: Belief ::

_____ is the ability to acquire knowledge without proof, evidence, or conscious reasoning, or without understanding how the knowledge was acquired. Different writers give the word " _____ " a great variety of different meanings, ranging from direct access to unconscious knowledge, unconscious cognition, inner sensing, inner insight to unconscious pattern-recognition and the ability to understand something instinctively, without the need for conscious reasoning.

Exam Probability: **Medium**

3. *Answer choices:*

(see index for correct answer)

- a. Transubstantiation
- b. Anthropocentrism
- c. Intuition
- d. Availability cascade

Guidance: level 1

:: Human resource management ::

_____ is a continual process used to align the needs and priorities of the organization with those of its workforce to ensure it can meet its legislative, regulatory, service and production requirements and organizational objectives. _____ enables evidence based workforce development strategies.

Exam Probability: **Medium**

4. *Answer choices:*

(see index for correct answer)

- a. Employee silence
- b. Incentive program
- c. Service record
- d. Workforce planning

Guidance: level 1

:: Labour relations ::

A _____, also known as a post-entry closed shop, is a form of a union security clause. Under this, the employer agrees to either only hire labor union members or to require that any new employees who are not already union members become members within a certain amount of time. Use of the _____ varies widely from nation to nation, depending on the level of protection given trade unions in general.

Exam Probability: **Medium**

5. *Answer choices:*

(see index for correct answer)

- a. Eurocadres
- b. Association of German Chambers of Industry and Commerce

- c. Broad left
- d. Union shop

Guidance: level 1

:: Training ::

A _____ is commonly known as an individual taking part in a _____ program or a graduate program within a company after having graduated from university or college.

Exam Probability: **Medium**

6. *Answer choices:*

(see index for correct answer)

- a. Question Writer
- b. Trainee
- c. Large Group Capacitation
- d. National sports team

Guidance: level 1

:: Recruitment ::

_____ is a specialized recruitment service which organizations pay to seek out and recruit highly qualified candidates for senior-level and executive jobs. Headhunters may also seek out and recruit other highly specialized and/or skilled positions in organizations for which there is strong competition in the job market for the top talent, such as senior data analysts or computer programmers. The method usually involves commissioning a third-party organization, typically an _____ firm, but possibly a standalone consultant or consulting firm, to research the availability of suitable qualified candidates working for competitors or related businesses or organizations. Having identified a shortlist of qualified candidates who match the client's requirements, the _____ firm may act as an intermediary to contact the individual and see if they might be interested in moving to a new employer. The _____ firm may also carry out initial screening of the candidate, negotiations on remuneration and benefits, and preparing the employment contract. In some markets there has been a move towards using _____ for lower positions driven by the fact that there are less candidates for some positions even on lower levels than executive.

Exam Probability: **Low**

7. *Answer choices:*

(see index for correct answer)

- a. E-recruitment
- b. Work-at-home scheme
- c. South West African Native Labour Association
- d. Integrity Inventory

Guidance: level 1

:: Project management ::

_____ is a name for various theories of human motivation built on Douglas McGregor's Theory X and Theory Y. Theories X, Y and various versions of Z have been used in human resource management, organizational behavior, organizational communication and organizational development.

Exam Probability: **Low**

8. *Answer choices:*

(see index for correct answer)

- a. Technology roadmap
- b. Theory Z
- c. Product flow diagram
- d. Master of Science in Project Management

Guidance: level 1

:: Survey methodology ::

An _____ is a conversation where questions are asked and answers are given. In common parlance, the word "_____" refers to a one-on-one conversation between an _____ er and an _____ ee. The _____ er asks questions to which the _____ ee responds, usually so information may be transferred from _____ ee to _____ er. Sometimes, information can be transferred in both directions. It is a communication, unlike a speech, which produces a one-way flow of information.

Exam Probability: **Low**

9. *Answer choices:*

(see index for correct answer)

- a. Coverage error
- b. World Association for Public Opinion Research
- c. Interview
- d. National Health Interview Survey

Guidance: level 1

:: Management ::

A _____ is when two or more people come together to discuss one or more topics, often in a formal or business setting, but _____ s also occur in a variety of other environments. Many various types of _____ s exist.

Exam Probability: **Medium**

10. *Answer choices:*

(see index for correct answer)

- a. Fredmund Malik
- b. Identity formation
- c. Meeting system
- d. Earned value management

Guidance: level 1

:: Business terms ::

Centralisation or _____ is the process by which the activities of an organization, particularly those regarding planning and decision-making, framing strategy and policies become concentrated within a particular geographical location group. This moves the important decision-making and planning powers within the center of the organisation.

Exam Probability: **Low**

11. *Answer choices:*
(see index for correct answer)

- a. organizational capital
- b. customer base
- c. noncommercial
- d. Centralization

Guidance: level 1

:: ::

An _____ is a person temporarily or permanently residing in a country other than their native country. In common usage, the term often refers to professionals, skilled workers, or artists taking positions outside their home country, either independently or sent abroad by their employers, who can be companies, universities, governments, or non-governmental organisations. Effectively migrant workers, they usually earn more than they would at home, and less than local employees. However, the term ` _____ ` is also used for retirees and others who have chosen to live outside their native country. Historically, it has also referred to exiles.

Exam Probability: **Medium**

12. *Answer choices:*

(see index for correct answer)

- a. interpersonal communication
- b. functional perspective
- c. co-culture
- d. Expatriate

Guidance: level 1

:: Management ::

In organizational studies, _____ is the efficient and effective development of an organization's resources when they are needed. Such resources may include financial resources, inventory, human skills, production resources, or information technology and natural resources.

Exam Probability: **Medium**

13. *Answer choices:*

(see index for correct answer)

- a. Flat organization
- b. Records manager
- c. Resource management
- d. Supplier relationship management

Guidance: level 1

:: Cognitive biases ::

The _____ is a type of immediate judgement discrepancy, or cognitive bias, where a person making an initial assessment of another person, place, or thing will assume ambiguous information based upon concrete information. A simplified example of the _____ is when an individual noticing that the person in the photograph is attractive, well groomed, and properly attired, assumes, using a mental heuristic, that the person in the photograph is a good person based upon the rules of that individual's social concept. This constant error in judgment is reflective of the individual's preferences, prejudices, ideology, aspirations, and social perception. The _____ is an evaluation by an individual and can affect the perception of a decision, action, idea, business, person, group, entity, or other whenever concrete data is generalized or influences ambiguous information.

Exam Probability: **Medium**

14. Answer choices:

(see index for correct answer)

- a. Bandwagon effect
- b. Social comparison bias
- c. Ambiguity effect
- d. Ostrich effect

Guidance: level 1

:: Employee relations ::

> _____ ownership, or employee share ownership, is an ownership interest in a company held by the company's workforce. The ownership interest may be facilitated by the company as part of employees' remuneration or incentive compensation for work performed, or the company itself may be employee owned.

Exam Probability: **High**

15. Answer choices:

(see index for correct answer)

- a. Employee handbook
- b. Employee surveys
- c. Employee stock
- d. Employee engagement

Guidance: level 1

:: Bankruptcy ::

_____ is the concept of a person or group of people taking precedence over another person or group because the former is either older than the latter or has occupied a particular position longer than the latter. _____ is present between parents and children and may be present in other common relationships, such as among siblings of different ages or between workers and their managers.

Exam Probability: **Medium**

16. *Answer choices:*
(see index for correct answer)

- a. Strategic bankruptcy
- b. FitzPatrick 1932
- c. Assisted person
- d. Seniority

Guidance: level 1

:: Employment of foreign-born ::

_____ refers to the international labor pool of workers, including those employed by multinational companies and connected through a global system of networking and production, immigrant workers, transient migrant workers, telecommuting workers, those in export-oriented employment, contingent work or other precarious employment. As of 2012, the global labor pool consisted of approximately 3 billion workers, around 200 million unemployed.

Exam Probability: **High**

17. *Answer choices:*

(see index for correct answer)

- a. Reverse brain drain
- b. H-2B visa
- c. Foreign born
- d. L-1 visa

Guidance: level 1

:: Human resource management ::

_____ is a process for identifying and developing new leaders who can replace old leaders when they leave, retire or die. _____ increases the availability of experienced and capable employees that are prepared to assume these roles as they become available. Taken narrowly, "replacement planning" for key roles is the heart of _____ .

Exam Probability: **Medium**

18. *Answer choices:*

(see index for correct answer)

- a. Job performance
- b. Functional job analysis
- c. Succession planning
- d. T-shaped skills

Guidance: level 1

:: ::

In educational development, _____ provides a person, often a student, focus for selecting a career or subject to undertake in the future. Often educational institutions provide career counsellors to assist students with their educational development.

Exam Probability: **Low**

19. *Answer choices:*

(see index for correct answer)

- a. open system
- b. personal values
- c. functional perspective
- d. Career development

Guidance: level 1

:: Validity (statistics) ::

In psychometrics, _____ is the extent to which a score on a scale or test predicts scores on some criterion measure.

Exam Probability: **Low**

20. *Answer choices:*
(see index for correct answer)

- a. Statistical conclusion validity
- b. Predictive validity
- c. Face validity
- d. Discriminant validity

Guidance: level 1

:: United States employment discrimination case law ::

_____, 411 U.S. 792, is a US employment law case by the United States Supreme Court regarding the burdens and nature of proof in proving a Title VII case and the order in which plaintiffs and defendants present proof. It was the seminal case in the McDonnell Douglas burden-shifting framework.

Exam Probability: **High**

21. *Answer choices:*

(see index for correct answer)

- a. Kloeckner v. Solis
- b. Dothard v. Rawlinson
- c. Executive Order 11375
- d. New York City Transit Authority v. Beazer

Guidance: level 1

:: Management ::

_____ is a set of activities that ensure goals are met in an effective and efficient manner. _____ can focus on the performance of an organization, a department, an employee, or the processes in place to manage particular tasks. _____ standards are generally organized and disseminated by senior leadership at an organization, and by task owners.

Exam Probability: **High**

22. *Answer choices:*

(see index for correct answer)

- a. Business process interoperability
- b. Performance management

- c. Situational crisis communication theory
- d. Lead scoring

Guidance: level 1

:: Employment discrimination ::

A _____ is a metaphor used to represent an invisible barrier that keeps a given demographic from rising beyond a certain level in a hierarchy.

Exam Probability: **High**

23. *Answer choices:*

(see index for correct answer)

- a. Employment discrimination law in the European Union
- b. United Kingdom employment equality law
- c. New South Wales selection bias
- d. Glass ceiling

Guidance: level 1

:: ::

In organizational behavior and industrial/organizational psychology, proactivity or _____ behavior by individuals refers to anticipatory, change-oriented and self-initiated behavior in situations. _____ behavior involves acting in advance of a future situation, rather than just reacting. It means taking control and making things happen rather than just adjusting to a situation or waiting for something to happen. _____ employees generally do not need to be asked to act, nor do they require detailed instructions.

Exam Probability: **Medium**

24. *Answer choices:*

(see index for correct answer)

- a. Proactive
- b. personal values
- c. levels of analysis
- d. open system

Guidance: level 1

:: Human resource management ::

A _____ is a group of people with different functional expertise working toward a common goal. It may include people from finance, marketing, operations, and human resources departments. Typically, it includes employees from all levels of an organization. Members may also come from outside an organization.

Exam Probability: **High**

25. *Answer choices:*

(see index for correct answer)

- a. Employee value proposition
- b. Employment testing
- c. Cross-functional team
- d. Corporate Equality Index

Guidance: level 1

:: Business planning ::

_____ is an organization's process of defining its strategy, or direction, and making decisions on allocating its resources to pursue this strategy. It may also extend to control mechanisms for guiding the implementation of the strategy. _____ became prominent in corporations during the 1960s and remains an important aspect of strategic management. It is executed by strategic planners or strategists, who involve many parties and research sources in their analysis of the organization and its relationship to the environment in which it competes.

Exam Probability: **High**

26. *Answer choices:*

(see index for correct answer)

- a. Customer Demand Planning
- b. Gap analysis
- c. Business war games
- d. Community Futures

Guidance: level 1

:: Occupations ::

An _____ is a person who has a position of authority in a hierarchical organization. The term derives from the late Latin from officiarius, meaning "official".

Exam Probability: **Low**

27. *Answer choices:*
(see index for correct answer)

- a. Senior lecturer
- b. Shopkeeper
- c. Officer
- d. Business architect

Guidance: level 1

:: Employment ::

Onboarding, also known as _____, is management jargon first created in 1988 that refers to the mechanism through which new employees acquire the necessary knowledge, skills, and behaviors in order to become effective organizational members and insiders.

Exam Probability: **High**

28. *Answer choices:*

(see index for correct answer)

- a. Vanpool
- b. Employment Development Department
- c. Per diem
- d. Apprenticeship Ambassadors Network

Guidance: level 1

:: Training ::

_____ is the process of ensuring compliance with laws, regulations, rules, standards, or social norms. By enforcing laws and regulations, governments attempt to effectuate successful implementation of policies.

Exam Probability: **High**

29. *Answer choices:*

(see index for correct answer)

- a. Endurance training
- b. Makers Academy
- c. Confidence-based learning
- d. Enforcement

Guidance: level 1

:: United States employment discrimination case law ::

_____, 557 U.S. 557, is a US labor law case of the United States Supreme Court on unlawful discrimination through disparate impact under the Civil Rights Act of 1964.

Exam Probability: **Medium**

30. *Answer choices:*

(see index for correct answer)

- a. Ricci v. DeStefano
- b. Kloeckner v. Solis
- c. New York City Transit Authority v. Beazer
- d. Vance v. Ball State University

Guidance: level 1

:: ::

_____ involves the development of an action plan designed to motivate and guide a person or group toward a goal. _____ can be guided by goal-setting criteria such as SMART criteria. _____ is a major component of personal-development and management literature.

Exam Probability: **Low**

31. *Answer choices:*

(see index for correct answer)

- a. surface-level diversity
- b. Goal setting
- c. deep-level diversity
- d. hierarchical

Guidance: level 1

:: Validity (statistics) ::

In psychometrics, criterion or concrete validity is the extent to which a measure is related to an outcome. _____ is often divided into concurrent and predictive validity. Concurrent validity refers to a comparison between the measure in question and an outcome assessed at the same time. In Standards for Educational & Psychological Tests, it states, "concurrent validity reflects only the status quo at a particular time." Predictive validity, on the other hand, compares the measure in question with an outcome assessed at a later time. Although concurrent and predictive validity are similar, it is cautioned to keep the terms and findings separated. "Concurrent validity should not be used as a substitute for predictive validity without an appropriate supporting rationale."

Exam Probability: **High**

32. *Answer choices:*

(see index for correct answer)

- a. Content validity
- b. Predictive validity
- c. Concurrent validity
- d. Construct validity

Guidance: level 1

:: ::

_____, also known as drug abuse, is a patterned use of a drug in which the user consumes the substance in amounts or with methods which are harmful to themselves or others, and is a form of substance-related disorder. Widely differing definitions of drug abuse are used in public health, medical and criminal justice contexts. In some cases criminal or anti-social behaviour occurs when the person is under the influence of a drug, and long term personality changes in individuals may occur as well. In addition to possible physical, social, and psychological harm, use of some drugs may also lead to criminal penalties, although these vary widely depending on the local jurisdiction.

Exam Probability: **High**

33. *Answer choices:*

(see index for correct answer)

- a. empathy
- b. Substance abuse
- c. hierarchical
- d. process perspective

Guidance: level 1

:: Recruitment ::

A _____ or background investigation is the process of looking up and compiling criminal records, commercial records, and financial records of an individual or an organization. The frequency, purpose, and legitimacy of _____s varies between countries, industries, and individuals. A variety of methods are used to complete such a check, from comprehensive data base search to personal references.

Exam Probability: **High**

34. *Answer choices:*

(see index for correct answer)

- a. Blue Octopus Recruitment Ltd
- b. Employment counsellor
- c. Labour hire
- d. Background check

Guidance: level 1

:: Human resource management ::

_____ is the corporate management term for the act of reorganizing the legal, ownership, operational, or other structures of a company for the purpose of making it more profitable, or better organized for its present needs. Other reasons for _____ include a change of ownership or ownership structure, demerger, or a response to a crisis or major change in the business such as bankruptcy, repositioning, or buyout. _____ may also be described as corporate _____, debt _____ and financial _____.

35. *Answer choices:*

(see index for correct answer)

- a. Job enrichment
- b. Organization chart
- c. Employment testing
- d. Employeeship

Guidance: level 1

_____ is an important topic of Human Resource Management. It helps develop the career of the individual and the prosperous growth of the organization. On the job training is a form of training provided at the workplace. During the training, employees are familiarized with the working environment they will become part of. Employees also get a hands-on experience using machinery, equipment, tools, materials, etc. Part of is to face the challenges that occur during the performance of the job. An experienced employee or a manager are executing the role of the mentor who through written, or verbal instructions and demonstrations are passing on his/her knowledge and company-specific skills to the new employee. Executing the training on at the job location, rather than the classroom, creates a stress-free environment for the employees. _____ is the most popular method of training not only in the United States but in most of the developed countries, such as the United Kingdom, China, Russia, etc. Its effectiveness is based on the use of existing workplace tools, machines, documents and equipment, and the knowledge of specialists who are working in this field. _____ is easy to arrange and manage and it simplifies the process of adapting to the new workplace. OJT is highly used for practical tasks. It is inexpensive, and it doesn't require special equipment that is normally used for a specific job. Upon satisfaction of completion of the training, the employer is expected to retain participants as regular employees.

Exam Probability: **Medium**

36. *Answer choices:*

(see index for correct answer)

- a. On-the-job training
- b. information systems assessment
- c. corporate values
- d. Character

Guidance: level 1

:: Sociological terminology ::

In moral and political philosophy, the _____ is a theory or model that originated during the Age of Enlightenment and usually concerns the legitimacy of the authority of the state over the individual. _____ arguments typically posit that individuals have consented, either explicitly or tacitly, to surrender some of their freedoms and submit to the authority in exchange for protection of their remaining rights or maintenance of the social order. The relation between natural and legal rights is often a topic of _____ theory. The term takes its name from The _____, a 1762 book by Jean-Jacques Rousseau that discussed this concept. Although the antecedents of _____ theory are found in antiquity, in Greek and Stoic philosophy and Roman and Canon Law, the heyday of the _____ was the mid-17th to early 19th centuries, when it emerged as the leading doctrine of political legitimacy.

Exam Probability: **Low**

37. *Answer choices:*

(see index for correct answer)

- a. Social contract
- b. iron cage
- c. Typification
- d. latent function

Guidance: level 1

:: Employee relations ::

_____ is a fundamental concept in the effort to understand and describe, both qualitatively and quantitatively, the nature of the relationship between an organization and its employees. An "engaged employee" is defined as one who is fully absorbed by and enthusiastic about their work and so takes positive action to further the organization's reputation and interests. An engaged employee has a positive attitude towards the organization and its values. In contrast, a disengaged employee may range from someone doing the bare minimum at work, up to an employee who is actively damaging the company's work output and reputation.

Exam Probability: **Low**

38. *Answer choices:*

(see index for correct answer)

- a. Employee motivation
- b. Industry Federation of the State of Rio de Janeiro
- c. Employee engagement
- d. Employee handbook

Guidance: level 1

A _____ is an occupation founded upon specialized educational training, the purpose of which is to supply disinterested objective counsel and service to others, for a direct and definite compensation, wholly apart from expectation of other business gain. The term is a truncation of the term "liberal _____", which is, in turn, an Anglicization of the French term "_____ libérale". Originally borrowed by English users in the 19th century, it has been re-borrowed by international users from the late 20th, though the class overtones of the term do not seem to survive retranslation: "liberal _____ s" are, according to the European Union's Directive on Recognition of _____ al Qualifications "those practiced on the basis of relevant _____ al qualifications in a personal, responsible and _____ ally independent capacity by those providing intellectual and conceptual services in the interest of the client and the public".

Exam Probability: **Medium**

39. *Answer choices:*

(see index for correct answer)

- a. Character
- b. Profession
- c. personal values
- d. similarity-attraction theory

Guidance: level 1

:: Employment compensation ::

_____ is a notional derivative of a Health Reimbursement Arrangement, a type of US employer-funded health benefit plan that reimburses employees for out-of-pocket medical expenses and, in limited cases, to pay for health insurance plan premiums.

Exam Probability: **High**

40. *Answer choices:*

(see index for correct answer)

- a. Explanation of benefits
- b. Law Enforcement Availability Pay
- c. Stock appreciation right
- d. ADP, LLC

Guidance: level 1

:: Human resource management ::

An _____ is a software application that enables the electronic handling of recruitment needs. An ATS can be implemented or accessed online on an enterprise or small business level, depending on the needs of the company and there is also free and open source ATS software available. An ATS is very similar to customer relationship management systems, but are designed for recruitment tracking purposes. In many cases they filter applications automatically based on given criteria such as keywords, skills, former employers, years of experience and schools attended. This has caused many to adapt resume optimization techniques similar to those used in search engine optimization when creating and formatting their résumé.

Exam Probability: **Low**

41. *Answer choices:*

(see index for correct answer)

- a. E-HRM
- b. Progress, plans, problems
- c. Occupational Information Network
- d. Applicant tracking system

Guidance: level 1

:: Meetings ::

A _____ is a formal meeting of the representatives of different countries, constituent states, organizations, trade unions, political parties or other groups. The term, originally denoting a parley during battle in the Late Middle Ages, is derived from the Latin _____ us.

Exam Probability: **Low**

42. *Answer choices:*

(see index for correct answer)

- a. Congress
- b. Committee
- c. Prayer meeting

- d. CodeCamp

Guidance: level 1

:: ::

An _____ is a process where candidates are examined to determine their suitability for specific types of employment, especially management or military command. The candidates' personality and aptitudes are determined by techniques including interviews, group exercises, presentations, examinations and psychometric testing.

Exam Probability: **Low**

43. *Answer choices:*

(see index for correct answer)

- a. information systems assessment
- b. imperative
- c. Assessment center
- d. cultural

Guidance: level 1

:: Recruitment ::

A _____, also referred commonly as a career fair or career expo, is an event in which employers, recruiters, and schools give information to potential employees. Job seekers attend these while trying to make a good impression to potential coworkers by speaking face-to-face with one another, filling out résumés, and asking questions in attempt to get a good feel on the work needed. Likewise, online _____ s are held, giving job seekers another way to get in contact with probable employers using the internet.

Exam Probability: **High**

44. *Answer choices:*

(see index for correct answer)

- a. Homeworker
- b. Global Career Development Facilitator
- c. contract of employment
- d. Job fair

Guidance: level 1

:: Human resource management ::

_____ , also known as management by results, was first popularized by Peter Drucker in his 1954 book The Practice of Management. _____ is the process of defining specific objectives within an organization that management can convey to organization members, then deciding on how to achieve each objective in sequence. This process allows managers to take work that needs to be done one step at a time to allow for a calm, yet productive work environment. This process also helps organization members to see their accomplishments as they achieve each objective, which reinforces a positive work environment and a sense of achievement. An important part of MBO is the measurement and comparison of an employee's actual performance with the standards set. Ideally, when employees themselves have been involved with the goal-setting and choosing the course of action to be followed by them, they are more likely to fulfill their responsibilities. According to George S. Odiorne, the system of _____ can be described as a process whereby the superior and subordinate jointly identify common goals, define each individual's major areas of responsibility in terms of the results expected of him or her, and use these measures as guides for operating the unit and assessing the contribution of each of its members.

Exam Probability: **High**

45. *Answer choices:*

(see index for correct answer)

- a. Job design
- b. Selection ratio
- c. Management by objectives
- d. Income bracket

Guidance: level 1

:: Trade unions in the United States ::

The _____ is a labor union in the United States and Canada. Formed in 1903 by the merger of The Team Drivers International Union and The Teamsters National Union, the union now represents a diverse membership of blue-collar and professional workers in both the public and private sectors. The union had approximately 1.3 million members in 2013. Formerly known as the _____, Chauffeurs, Warehousemen and Helpers of America, the IBT is a member of the Change to Win Federation and Canadian Labour Congress.

Exam Probability: **Low**

46. *Answer choices:*

(see index for correct answer)

- a. Amalgamated Lithographers of America
- b. Art Directors Guild
- c. International Brotherhood of Teamsters
- d. Association of Professional Flight Attendants

Guidance: level 1

:: United States federal labor legislation ::

The _____ of 1967 is a US labor law that forbids employment discrimination against anyone at least 40 years of age in the United States. In 1967, the bill was signed into law by President Lyndon B. Johnson. The ADEA prevents age discrimination and provides equal employment opportunity under conditions that were not explicitly covered in Title VII of the Civil Rights Act of 1964. It also applies to the standards for pensions and benefits provided by employers, and requires that information concerning the needs of older workers be provided to the general public.

Exam Probability: **High**

47. *Answer choices:*

(see index for correct answer)

- a. National Whistleblowers Center
- b. Age Discrimination in Employment Act
- c. Anti-Pinkerton Act
- d. Landrum-Griffin Act

Guidance: level 1

:: Minimum wage ::

A _____ is the lowest remuneration that employers can legally pay their workers—the price floor below which workers may not sell their labor. Most countries had introduced _____ legislation by the end of the 20th century.

Exam Probability: **Medium**

48. *Answer choices:*

(see index for correct answer)

- a. Guaranteed minimum income
- b. Minimum Wage Fairness Act
- c. Minimum wage in the United States
- d. Minimum wage

Guidance: level 1

:: Power (social and political) ::

In a notable study of power conducted by social psychologists John R. P. French and Bertram Raven in 1959, power is divided into five separate and distinct forms. In 1965 Raven revised this model to include a sixth form by separating the informational power base as distinct from the _____ base.

Exam Probability: **Medium**

49. *Answer choices:*

(see index for correct answer)

- a. Expert power
- b. Hard power
- c. Referent power

Guidance: level 1

:: Behavior ::

_____ refers to behavior-change procedures that were employed during the 1970s and early 1980s. Based on methodological behaviorism, overt behavior was modified with presumed consequences, including artificial positive and negative reinforcement contingencies to increase desirable behavior, or administering positive and negative punishment and/or extinction to reduce problematic behavior. For the treatment of phobias, habituation and punishment were the basic principles used in flooding, a subcategory of desensitization.

Exam Probability: **Low**

50. *Answer choices:*
(see index for correct answer)

- a. Behavior modification
- b. theory of planned behavior

Guidance: level 1

:: ::

_____ is the combination of structured planning and the active management choice of one's own professional career. _____ was first defined in a social work doctoral thesis by Mary Valentich as the implementation of a career strategy through application of career tactics in relation to chosen career orientation. Career orientation referred to the overall design or pattern of one's career, shaped by particular goals and interests and identifiable by particular positions that embody these goals and interests. Career strategy pertains to the individual's general approach to the realization of career goals, and to the specificity of the goals themselves. Two general strategy approaches are adaptive and planned. Career tactics are actions to maintain oneself in a satisfactory employment situation. Tactics may be more or less assertive, with assertiveness in the work situation referring to actions taken to advance one's career interests or to exercise one's legitimate rights while respecting the rights of others.

Exam Probability: **High**

51. *Answer choices:*

(see index for correct answer)

- a. hierarchical
- b. Career management
- c. Character
- d. surface-level diversity

Guidance: level 1

In business strategy, _____ is establishing a competitive advantage by having the lowest cost of operation in the industry. _____ is often driven by company efficiency, size, scale, scope and cumulative experience. A _____ strategy aims to exploit scale of production, well-defined scope and other economies, producing highly standardized products, using advanced technology. In recent years, more and more companies have chosen a strategic mix to achieve market leadership. These patterns consist of simultaneous _____, superior customer service and product leadership. Walmart has succeeded across the world due to its _____ strategy. The company has cut down on exesses at every point of production and thus are able to provide the consumers with quality products at low prices.

Exam Probability: **High**

52. *Answer choices:*

(see index for correct answer)

- a. Cost leadership
- b. Sarbanes-Oxley act of 2002
- c. interpersonal communication
- d. process perspective

Guidance: level 1

:: Socialism ::

In sociology, _____ is the process of internalizing the norms and ideologies of society. _____ encompasses both learning and teaching and is thus "the means by which social and cultural continuity are attained".

Exam Probability: **High**

53. *Answer choices:*

(see index for correct answer)

- a. Socialist accumulation
- b. Frankfurt Declaration
- c. Red flag
- d. Socialization

Guidance: level 1

:: Telecommuting ::

_____, also called telework, teleworking, working from home, mobile work, remote work, and flexible workplace, is a work arrangement in which employees do not commute or travel to a central place of work, such as an office building, warehouse, or store. Teleworkers in the 21st century often use mobile telecommunications technology such as Wi-Fi-equipped laptop or tablet computers and smartphones to work from coffee shops; others may use a desktop computer and a landline phone at their home. According to a Reuters poll, approximately "one in five workers around the globe, particularly employees in the Middle East, Latin America and Asia, telecommute frequently and nearly 10 percent work from home every day." In the 2000s, annual leave or vacation in some organizations was seen as absence from the workplace rather than ceasing work, and some office employees used telework to continue to check work e-mails while on vacation.

Exam Probability: **High**

54. Answer choices:

(see index for correct answer)

- a. Homesourcing
- b. Telecommuting
- c. VenueGen
- d. OmNovia Technologies

Guidance: level 1

:: Business law ::

A pre-entry _____ is a form of union security agreement under which the employer agrees to hire union members only, and employees must remain members of the union at all times in order to remain employed. This is different from a post-entry _____, which is an agreement requiring all employees to join the union if they are not already members. In a union shop, the union must accept as a member any person hired by the employer.

Exam Probability: **Medium**

55. Answer choices:

(see index for correct answer)

- a. Double ticketing
- b. Negotiable instrument
- c. Facilitating payment
- d. Lien

Guidance: level 1

:: Trade unions ::

A _____ is an association of workers forming a legal unit or legal personhood, usually called a "bargaining unit", which acts as bargaining agent and legal representative for a unit of employees in all matters of law or right arising from or in the administration of a collective agreement. Labour unions typically fund the formal organisation, head office, and legal team functions of the labour union through regular fees or union dues. The delegate staff of the labour union representation in the workforce are made up of workplace volunteers who are appointed by members in democratic elections.

Exam Probability: **Medium**

56. *Answer choices:*

(see index for correct answer)

- a. Trade union
- b. Agency shop
- c. Givebacks
- d. Paper local

Guidance: level 1

:: Employment compensation ::

A _____ is a type of employee benefit plan offered in the United States pursuant to Section 125 of the Internal Revenue Code. Its name comes from the earliest such plans that allowed employees to choose between different types of benefits, similar to the ability of a customer to choose among available items in a cafeteria. Qualified _____ s are excluded from gross income. To qualify, a _____ must allow employees to choose from two or more benefits consisting of cash or qualified benefit plans. The Internal Revenue Code explicitly excludes deferred compensation plans from qualifying as a _____ subject to a gross income exemption. Section 125 also provides two exceptions.

Exam Probability: **High**

57. *Answer choices:*

(see index for correct answer)

- a. Compensation of employees
- b. Cafeteria plan
- c. Workers Compensation Act 1987
- d. Maximum wage

Guidance: level 1

:: Employment compensation ::

A _____ , also known as a flexible spending arrangement, is one of a number of tax-advantaged financial accounts, resulting in payroll tax savings. Before the Patient Protection and Affordable Care Act, one significant disadvantage to using an FSA was that funds not used by the end of the plan year were forfeited to the employer, known as the "use it or lose it" rule. Under the terms of the Affordable Care Act, a plan may permit an employee to carry over up to $500 into the following year without losing the funds.

Exam Probability: **Low**

58. *Answer choices:*

(see index for correct answer)

- a. Annual enrollment
- b. ADP, LLC
- c. Flexible spending account
- d. Law Enforcement Availability Pay

Guidance: level 1

:: Survey methodology ::

A _____ is the procedure of systematically acquiring and recording information about the members of a given population. The term is used mostly in connection with national population and housing _____ es; other common _____ es include agriculture, business, and traffic _____ es. The United Nations defines the essential features of population and housing _____ es as "individual enumeration, universality within a defined territory, simultaneity and defined periodicity", and recommends that population _____ es be taken at least every 10 years. United Nations recommendations also cover _____ topics to be collected, official definitions, classifications and other useful information to co-ordinate international practice.

Exam Probability: **Medium**

59. *Answer choices:*

(see index for correct answer)

- a. Scale analysis
- b. Census
- c. National Health Interview Survey
- d. Sampling

Guidance: level 1

Information systems

Information systems (IS) are formal, sociotechnical, organizational systems designed to collect, process, store, and distribute information. In a sociotechnical perspective Information Systems are composed by four components: technology, process, people and organizational structure.

:: Business process ::

A _____ or business method is a collection of related, structured activities or tasks by people or equipment which in a specific sequence produce a service or product for a particular customer or customers. _____ es occur at all organizational levels and may or may not be visible to the customers. A _____ may often be visualized as a flowchart of a sequence of activities with interleaving decision points or as a process matrix of a sequence of activities with relevance rules based on data in the process. The benefits of using _____ es include improved customer satisfaction and improved agility for reacting to rapid market change. Process-oriented organizations break down the barriers of structural departments and try to avoid functional silos.

Exam Probability: **Low**

1. *Answer choices:*

(see index for correct answer)

- a. Process capital
- b. Change order
- c. Business process
- d. Knowledge process outsourcing

Guidance: level 1

:: Data ::

_____ is a branch of mathematics working with data collection, organization, analysis, interpretation and presentation. In applying _____ to, for example, a scientific, industrial, or social problem, it is conventional to begin with a statistical population or a statistical model process to be studied. Populations can be diverse topics such as "all people living in a country" or "every atom composing a crystal". _____ deals with every aspect of data, including the planning of data collection in terms of the design of surveys and experiments.See glossary of probability and _____ .

Exam Probability: **Medium**

2. *Answer choices:*

(see index for correct answer)

- a. Dummy data
- b. Empress Embedded Database
- c. Data citation
- d. Statistics

Guidance: level 1

:: Data security ::

_____ are safeguards or countermeasures to avoid, detect, counteract, or minimize security risks to physical property, information, computer systems, or other assets.

Exam Probability: **High**

3. *Answer choices:*

(see index for correct answer)

- a. Biometric passport
- b. Security level management
- c. Airbackup
- d. Budapest Declaration on Machine Readable Travel Documents

Guidance: level 1

:: Business process ::

_____ is a discipline in operations management in which people use various methods to discover, model, analyze, measure, improve, optimize, and automate business processes. BPM focuses on improving corporate performance by managing business processes. Any combination of methods used to manage a company's business processes is BPM. Processes can be structured and repeatable or unstructured and variable. Though not required, enabling technologies are often used with BPM.

Exam Probability: **Medium**

4. *Answer choices:*

(see index for correct answer)

- a. Value process management

- b. Open door policy
- c. Business process management
- d. Tenant screening

Guidance: level 1

:: Cloud storage ::

_____ was an online backup service for both Windows and macOS users. Linux support was made available in Q3, 2014. In 2007 _____ was acquired by EMC, and in 2013 _____ was included in the EMC Backup Recovery Systems division's product list.On September 7, 2016, Dell Inc. acquired EMC Corporation to form Dell Technologies, restructuring the original Dell Inc. as a subsidiary of Dell Technologies.. On March 19, 2018 Carbonite acquired _____ from Dell for $148.5 million in cash and in 2019 shut down the service, incorporating _____ 's clients into its own online backup service programs.

Exam Probability: **High**

5. *Answer choices:*

(see index for correct answer)

- a. Zmanda Cloud Backup
- b. SlideRocket
- c. Mozy
- d. Scality

Guidance: level 1

:: Service-oriented (business computing) ::

_____ is a software licensing and delivery model in which software is licensed on a subscription basis and is centrally hosted. It is sometimes referred to as "on-demand software", and was formerly referred to as "software plus services" by Microsoft. SaaS is typically accessed by users using a thin client, e.g. via a web browser. SaaS has become a common delivery model for many business applications, including office software, messaging software, payroll processing software, DBMS software, management software, CAD software, development software, gamification, virtualization, accounting, collaboration, customer relationship management , Management Information Systems , enterprise resource planning , invoicing, human resource management , talent acquisition, learning management systems, content management , Geographic Information Systems , and service desk management. SaaS has been incorporated into the strategy of nearly all leading enterprise software companies.

Exam Probability: **Medium**

6. *Answer choices:*

(see index for correct answer)

- a. Service layer
- b. Service refactoring
- c. TOA Technologies
- d. SEMCI

Guidance: level 1

:: ::

In linguistics, a _____ is the smallest element that can be uttered in isolation with objective or practical meaning.

Exam Probability: **Medium**

7. *Answer choices:*

(see index for correct answer)

- a. empathy
- b. Word
- c. cultural
- d. functional perspective

Guidance: level 1

:: Market research ::

_____ is the action of defining, gathering, analyzing, and distributing intelligence about products, customers, competitors, and any aspect of the environment needed to support executives and managers in strategic decision making for an organization.

Exam Probability: **High**

8. *Answer choices:*

(see index for correct answer)

- a. PreTesting Company
- b. Market research
- c. Media-Analyse
- d. Competitive intelligence

Guidance: level 1

:: Metadata ::

_____ s usage can be discovered by inspection of software applications or application data files through a process of manual or automated Application Discovery and Understanding. Once _____ s are discovered they can be registered in a metadata registry.

Exam Probability: **Low**

9. *Answer choices:*

(see index for correct answer)

- a. Naming and Design Rules
- b. N-Triples
- c. Stitch Pipeline
- d. Data element

Guidance: level 1

:: Data management ::

> _____, or OLAP, is an approach to answer multi-dimensional analytical queries swiftly in computing. OLAP is part of the broader category of business intelligence, which also encompasses relational databases, report writing and data mining. Typical applications of OLAP include business reporting for sales, marketing, management reporting, business process management, budgeting and forecasting, financial reporting and similar areas, with new applications emerging, such as agriculture. The term OLAP was created as a slight modification of the traditional database term online transaction processing.

Exam Probability: **Low**

10. *Answer choices:*

(see index for correct answer)

- a. Transaction data
- b. Archive site
- c. Government Performance Management
- d. Online analytical processing

Guidance: level 1

:: Payment systems ::

A _____ is any system used to settle financial transactions through the transfer of monetary value. This includes the institutions, instruments, people, rules, procedures, standards, and technologies that make it exchange possible. A common type of _____ is called an operational network that links bank accounts and provides for monetary exchange using bank deposits. Some _____ s also include credit mechanisms, which are essentially a different aspect of payment.

Exam Probability: **High**

11. *Answer choices:*

(see index for correct answer)

- a. Teller
- b. Honesty bar
- c. Payment system
- d. Voluntary Collective Licensing

Guidance: level 1

:: Google services ::

A blog is a discussion or informational website published on the World Wide Web consisting of discrete, often informal diary-style text entries. Posts are typically displayed in reverse chronological order, so that the most recent post appears first, at the top of the web page. Until 2009, blogs were usually the work of a single individual, occasionally of a small group, and often covered a single subject or topic. In the 2010s, "multi-author blogs" emerged, featuring the writing of multiple authors and sometimes professionally edited. MABs from newspapers, other media outlets, universities, think tanks, advocacy groups, and similar institutions account for an increasing quantity of blog traffic. The rise of Twitter and other "microblogging" systems helps integrate MABs and single-author blogs into the news media. Blog can also be used as a verb, meaning to maintain or add content to a blog.

Exam Probability: **Medium**

12. *Answer choices:*

(see index for correct answer)

- a. Google Gadgets
- b. Google Sites
- c. Blogger
- d. Google Current

Guidance: level 1

:: ::

_____ Holdings, Inc. is an American company operating a worldwide online payments system that supports online money transfers and serves as an electronic alternative to traditional paper methods like checks and money orders. The company operates as a payment processor for online vendors, auction sites, and many other commercial users, for which it charges a fee in exchange for benefits such as one-click transactions and password memory. _____'s payment system, also called _____, is considered a type of payment rail.

Exam Probability: **Low**

13. *Answer choices:*

(see index for correct answer)

- a. hierarchical perspective
- b. PayPal
- c. interpersonal communication
- d. empathy

Guidance: level 1

:: Computer access control ::

_____ is the act of confirming the truth of an attribute of a single piece of data claimed true by an entity. In contrast with identification, which refers to the act of stating or otherwise indicating a claim purportedly attesting to a person or thing's identity, _____ is the process of actually confirming that identity. It might involve confirming the identity of a person by validating their identity documents, verifying the authenticity of a website with a digital certificate, determining the age of an artifact by carbon dating, or ensuring that a product is what its packaging and labeling claim to be. In other words, _____ often involves verifying the validity of at least one form of identification.

Exam Probability: **Medium**

14. *Answer choices:*

(see index for correct answer)

- a. Salute picture
- b. LOMAC
- c. Numina Application Framework
- d. Authentication

Guidance: level 1

:: Internet advertising ::

_____ , according to the United States federal law known as the Anti _____ Consumer Protection Act, is registering, trafficking in, or using an Internet domain name with bad faith intent to profit from the goodwill of a trademark belonging to someone else. The cybersquatter then offers to sell the domain to the person or company who owns a trademark contained within the name at an inflated price.

Exam Probability: **High**

15. *Answer choices:*

(see index for correct answer)

- a. Dove Real Beauty Sketches
- b. Adzerk
- c. Mediaocean
- d. Cybersquatting

Guidance: level 1

:: Security compliance ::

_____ refers to the inability to withstand the effects of a hostile environment. A window of _____ is a time frame within which defensive measures are diminished, compromised or lacking.

Exam Probability: **Medium**

16. *Answer choices:*

(see index for correct answer)

- a. Vulnerability
- b. Vulnerability management
- c. Information assurance vulnerability alert
- d. North American Electric Reliability Corporation

Guidance: level 1

:: ::

_____ is a set of documents provided on paper, or online, or on digital or analog media, such as audio tape or CDs. Examples are user guides, white papers, on-line help, quick-reference guides. It is becoming less common to see paper _____. _____ is distributed via websites, software products, and other on-line applications.

Exam Probability: **Medium**

17. *Answer choices:*

(see index for correct answer)

- a. open system
- b. empathy
- c. information systems assessment
- d. Documentation

Guidance: level 1

:: Management ::

In organizational studies, _____ is the efficient and effective development of an organization's resources when they are needed. Such resources may include financial resources, inventory, human skills, production resources, or information technology and natural resources.

Exam Probability: **Medium**

18. *Answer choices:*
(see index for correct answer)

- a. Productive efficiency
- b. Resource management
- c. Best practice
- d. Power to the edge

Guidance: level 1

:: Data management ::

_____ represents the business objects that contain the most valuable, agreed upon information shared across an organization. It can cover relatively static reference data, transactional, unstructured, analytical, hierarchical and metadata. It is the primary focus of the information technology discipline of _____ management.

Exam Probability: **Low**

19. *Answer choices:*

(see index for correct answer)

- a. Operational historian
- b. Master data
- c. Operational database
- d. Virtual facility

Guidance: level 1

:: Commercial item transport and distribution ::

In commerce, supply-chain management, the management of the flow of goods and services, involves the movement and storage of raw materials, of work-in-process inventory, and of finished goods from point of origin to point of consumption. Interconnected or interlinked networks, channels and node businesses combine in the provision of products and services required by end customers in a supply chain. Supply-chain management has been defined as the "design, planning, execution, control, and monitoring of supply-chain activities with the objective of creating net value, building a competitive infrastructure, leveraging worldwide logistics, synchronizing supply with demand and measuring performance globally." SCM practice draws heavily from the areas of industrial engineering, systems engineering, operations management, logistics, procurement, information technology, and marketing and strives for an integrated approach. Marketing channels play an important role in supply-chain management. Current research in supply-chain management is concerned with topics related to sustainability and risk management, among others. Some suggest that the "people dimension" of SCM, ethical issues, internal integration, transparency/visibility, and human capital/talent management are topics that have, so far, been underrepresented on the research agenda.

Exam Probability: **Low**

20. *Answer choices:*

(see index for correct answer)

- a. Plastic pallet
- b. Bonded warehouse
- c. Toll Domestic Forwarding
- d. Weigh station

Guidance: level 1

:: ::

_____ LLC is an American multinational technology company that specializes in Internet-related services and products, which include online advertising technologies, search engine, cloud computing, software, and hardware. It is considered one of the Big Four technology companies, alongside Amazon, Apple and Facebook.

Exam Probability: **Low**

21. *Answer choices:*

(see index for correct answer)

- a. Google
- b. interpersonal communication
- c. personal values
- d. Sarbanes-Oxley act of 2002

Guidance: level 1

:: Industrial automation ::

_____ is the technology by which a process or procedure is performed with minimal human assistance. _____ or automatic control is the use of various control systems for operating equipment such as machinery, processes in factories, boilers and heat treating ovens, switching on telephone networks, steering and stabilization of ships, aircraft and other applications and vehicles with minimal or reduced human intervention.

Exam Probability: **High**

22. *Answer choices:*

(see index for correct answer)

- a. EtherCAT
- b. Automation surprise
- c. Automation
- d. CODESYS

Guidance: level 1

:: Computer data ::

In computer science, _____ is the ability to access an arbitrary element of a sequence in equal time or any datum from a population of addressable elements roughly as easily and efficiently as any other, no matter how many elements may be in the set. It is typically contrasted to sequential access.

Exam Probability: **Medium**

23. *Answer choices:*

(see index for correct answer)

- a. Random access
- b. Header

- c. Persistent data
- d. Leading zero

Guidance: level 1

:: Information technology ::

_____ is the reorientation of product and service designs to focus on the end user as an individual consumer, in contrast with an earlier era of only organization-oriented offerings. Technologies whose first commercialization was at the inter-organization level thus have potential for later _____. The emergence of the individual consumer as the primary driver of product and service design is most commonly associated with the IT industry, as large business and government organizations dominated the early decades of computer usage and development. Thus the microcomputer revolution, in which electronic computing moved from exclusively enterprise and government use to include personal computing, is a cardinal example of _____. But many technology-based products, such as calculators and mobile phones, have also had their origins in business markets, and only over time did they become dominated by high-volume consumer usage, as these products commoditized and prices fell. An example of enterprise software that became consumer software is optical character recognition software, which originated with banks and postal systems but eventually became personal productivity software.

Exam Probability: **Low**

24. *Answer choices:*

(see index for correct answer)

- a. Mobile file management
- b. Information and communications technology

- c. ISO/IEC JTC 1/SC 23
- d. Consumerization

Guidance: level 1

:: Digital rights management ::

_____ tools or technological protection measures are a set of access control technologies for restricting the use of proprietary hardware and copyrighted works. DRM technologies try to control the use, modification, and distribution of copyrighted works , as well as systems within devices that enforce these policies.

Exam Probability: **Medium**

25. *Answer choices:*

(see index for correct answer)

- a. Digital rights management
- b. Secure Digital Music Initiative
- c. DIVX
- d. NTSC-C

Guidance: level 1

:: ::

_____ rate is the ratio of users who click on a specific link to the number of total users who view a page, email, or advertisement. It is commonly used to measure the success of an online advertising campaign for a particular website as well as the effectiveness of email campaigns.

Exam Probability: **Low**

26. *Answer choices:*

(see index for correct answer)

- a. personal values
- b. hierarchical
- c. deep-level diversity
- d. Click-through

Guidance: level 1

:: Service-oriented (business computing) ::

_____ is a style of software design where services are provided to the other components by application components, through a communication protocol over a network. The basic principles of _____ are independent of vendors, products and technologies. A service is a discrete unit of functionality that can be accessed remotely and acted upon and updated independently, such as retrieving a credit card statement online.

Exam Probability: **Medium**

27. *Answer choices:*

(see index for correct answer)

- a. DataNucleus
- b. Service-oriented architecture
- c. SAP Enterprise Architecture Framework
- d. SEMCI

Guidance: level 1

:: Information systems ::

_____ are formal, sociotechnical, organizational systems designed to collect, process, store, and distribute information. In a sociotechnical perspective, _____ are composed by four components: task, people, structure, and technology.

Exam Probability: **Medium**

28. *Answer choices:*

(see index for correct answer)

- a. Information systems
- b. Transport standards organisations
- c. Manufacturing execution system
- d. LabLynx, Inc.

Guidance: level 1

:: SQL ::

SQL is a domain-specific language used in programming and designed for managing data held in a relational database management system, or for stream processing in a relational data stream management system. It is particularly useful in handling structured data where there are relations between different entities/variables of the data. SQL offers two main advantages over older read/write APIs like ISAM or VSAM. First, it introduced the concept of accessing many records with one single command; and second, it eliminates the need to specify how to reach a record, e.g. with or without an index.

Exam Probability: **Low**

29. *Answer choices:*

(see index for correct answer)

- a. Windows Internal Database
- b. Correlated subquery
- c. Object-PL/SQL
- d. SQL/CLI

Guidance: level 1

:: World Wide Web ::

A _____ is a document that is suitable to act as a web resource on the World Wide Web. In order to graphically display a _____ , a web browser is needed. This is a type of software that can retrieve _____ s from the Internet. When accessed by a web browser it may be displayed as a _____ on a monitor or mobile device. Typical _____ s are hypertext documents which contain hyperlinks, often referred to as links, for browsing to other _____ s.

Exam Probability: **Medium**

30. *Answer choices:*

(see index for correct answer)

- a. Web page
- b. TatNet
- c. Link exchange
- d. Web Medica Acreditada

Guidance: level 1

:: Information technology ::

_____ is the use of computers to store, retrieve, transmit, and manipulate data, or information, often in the context of a business or other enterprise. IT is considered to be a subset of information and communications technology . An _____ system is generally an information system, a communications system or, more specifically speaking, a computer system – including all hardware, software and peripheral equipment – operated by a limited group of users.

Exam Probability: **Low**

31. *Answer choices:*

(see index for correct answer)

- a. Iomart Group plc
- b. Computer surveillance in the workplace
- c. Digital Researcher
- d. Information technology

Guidance: level 1

:: Payment systems ::

_____ is a mobile phone-based money transfer, financing and microfinancing service, launched in 2007 by Vodafone for Safaricom and Vodacom, the largest mobile network operators in Kenya and Tanzania. It has since expanded to Afghanistan, South Africa, India and in 2014 to Romania and in 2015 to Albania. _____ allows users to deposit, withdraw, transfer money and pay for goods and services easily with a mobile device.

Exam Probability: **High**

32. *Answer choices:*

(see index for correct answer)

- a. WorldPay
- b. M-Pesa

- c. Mobile purchasing
- d. Yang Cheng Tong

Guidance: level 1

:: Google services ::

_____ is a time-management and scheduling calendar service developed by Google. It became available in beta release April 13, 2006, and in general release in July 2009, on the web and as mobile apps for the Android and iOS platforms.

Exam Probability: **Medium**

33. *Answer choices:*

(see index for correct answer)

- a. Google Calendar
- b. Google Grants
- c. Google Map Maker
- d. Google Real-Time Search

Guidance: level 1

:: Information technology management ::

_____ is a collective term for all approaches to prepare, support and help individuals, teams, and organizations in making organizational change. The most common change drivers include: technological evolution, process reviews, crisis, and consumer habit changes; pressure from new business entrants, acquisitions, mergers, and organizational restructuring. It includes methods that redirect or redefine the use of resources, business process, budget allocations, or other modes of operation that significantly change a company or organization. Organizational _____ considers the full organization and what needs to change, while _____ may be used solely to refer to how people and teams are affected by such organizational transition. It deals with many different disciplines, from behavioral and social sciences to information technology and business solutions.

Exam Probability: **High**

34. *Answer choices:*

(see index for correct answer)

- a. Purchase order request
- b. IQuate
- c. Change management
- d. Document management system

Guidance: level 1

:: E-commerce ::

_____ is a method of e-commerce where shoppers' friends become involved in the shopping experience. _____ attempts to use technology to mimic the social interactions found in physical malls and stores. With the rise of mobile devices, _____ is now extending beyond the online world and into the offline world of shopping.

Exam Probability: **High**

35. *Answer choices:*

(see index for correct answer)

- a. Shopping directory
- b. Tor
- c. Social shopping
- d. USAePay

Guidance: level 1

:: Procurement practices ::

_____ or commercially available off-the-shelf products are packaged solutions which are then adapted to satisfy the needs of the purchasing organization, rather than the commissioning of custom-made, or bespoke, solutions. A related term, Mil-COTS, refers to COTS products for use by the U.S. military.

Exam Probability: **Low**

36. Answer choices:

(see index for correct answer)

- a. Commercial off-the-shelf
- b. Construction by configuration

Guidance: level 1

:: Computer memory ::

_____ is a type of non-volatile memory used in computers and other electronic devices. Data stored in ROM can only be modified slowly, with difficulty, or not at all, so it is mainly used to store firmware or application software in plug-in cartridges.

Exam Probability: **High**

37. Answer choices:

(see index for correct answer)

- a. Read-only memory
- b. Intel Memory Model
- c. Registered memory
- d. RAM parity

Guidance: level 1

:: Network theory ::

A _____ is a social structure made up of a set of social actors , sets of dyadic ties, and other social interactions between actors. The _____ perspective provides a set of methods for analyzing the structure of whole social entities as well as a variety of theories explaining the patterns observed in these structures. The study of these structures uses _____ analysis to identify local and global patterns, locate influential entities, and examine network dynamics.

Exam Probability: **Low**

38. *Answer choices:*

(see index for correct answer)

- a. Modularity
- b. Assortative mixing
- c. Betweenness centrality
- d. Social network

Guidance: level 1

:: Computer file formats ::

_____ is a communication protocol for peer-to-peer file sharing which is used to distribute data and electronic files over the Internet.

Exam Probability: **Low**

39. *Answer choices:*

(see index for correct answer)

- a. ISO/IEC JTC 1/SC 34
- b. PDB
- c. Secure Digital Container
- d. BitTorrent

Guidance: level 1

:: Computer access control protocols ::

An _____ is a type of computer communications protocol or cryptographic protocol specifically designed for transfer of authentication data between two entities. It allows the receiving entity to authenticate the connecting entity as well as authenticate itself to the connecting entity by declaring the type of information needed for authentication as well as syntax. It is the most important layer of protection needed for secure communication within computer networks.

Exam Probability: **Low**

40. *Answer choices:*

(see index for correct answer)

- a. RADIUS

- b. SMTP Authentication
- c. ID-MM7
- d. TACACS

Guidance: level 1

:: ::

A _____ , sometimes called a passcode, is a memorized secret used to confirm the identity of a user. Using the terminology of the NIST Digital Identity Guidelines, the secret is memorized by a party called the claimant while the party verifying the identity of the claimant is called the verifier. When the claimant successfully demonstrates knowledge of the _____ to the verifier through an established authentication protocol, the verifier is able to infer the claimant's identity.

Exam Probability: **Low**

41. *Answer choices:*
(see index for correct answer)

- a. Character
- b. Password
- c. Sarbanes-Oxley act of 2002
- d. functional perspective

Guidance: level 1

:: ::

A _____ is a telecommunications network that extends over a large geographical distance for the primary purpose of computer networking. _____ s are often established with leased telecommunication circuits.

Exam Probability: **Low**

42. *Answer choices:*

(see index for correct answer)

- a. Wide Area Network
- b. deep-level diversity
- c. personal values
- d. similarity-attraction theory

Guidance: level 1

:: Telecommunication theory ::

In reliability theory and reliability engineering, the term _____ has the following meanings.

Exam Probability: **Medium**

43. *Answer choices:*

(see index for correct answer)

- a. Intersymbol interference
- b. Anisochronous
- c. Availability
- d. Signal processing

Guidance: level 1

:: E-commerce ::

_____ , cybersecurity or information technology security is the protection of computer systems from theft or damage to their hardware, software or electronic data, as well as from disruption or misdirection of the services they provide.

Exam Probability: **Medium**

44. *Answer choices:*

(see index for correct answer)

- a. DigiCash
- b. Multichannel retailing
- c. Postback
- d. Computer security

Guidance: level 1

:: Credit cards ::

The _____ Company, also known as Amex, is an American multinational financial services corporation headquartered in Three World Financial Center in New York City. The company was founded in 1850 and is one of the 30 components of the Dow Jones Industrial Average. The company is best known for its charge card, credit card, and traveler's cheque businesses.

Exam Probability: **Low**

45. *Answer choices:*

(see index for correct answer)

- a. American Express
- b. Smiley v. Citibank
- c. Accolades Card
- d. Diners Club International

Guidance: level 1

:: ::

A _____ or data centre is a building, dedicated space within a building, or a group of buildings used to house computer systems and associated components, such as telecommunications and storage systems.

Exam Probability: **Low**

46. *Answer choices:*

(see index for correct answer)

- a. empathy
- b. Data center
- c. imperative
- d. cultural

Guidance: level 1

:: Global Positioning System ::

The _____, originally Navstar GPS, is a satellite-based radionavigation system owned by the United States government and operated by the United States Air Force. It is a global navigation satellite system that provides geolocation and time information to a GPS receiver anywhere on or near the Earth where there is an unobstructed line of sight to four or more GPS satellites. Obstacles such as mountains and buildings block the relatively weak GPS signals.

Exam Probability: **Medium**

47. *Answer choices:*

(see index for correct answer)

- a. StarFire

- b. Global Positioning System
- c. SiReNT
- d. European Geostationary Navigation Overlay Service

Guidance: level 1

:: Remote administration software ::

_____ is a protocol used on the Internet or local area network to provide a bidirectional interactive text-oriented communication facility using a virtual terminal connection. User data is interspersed in-band with _____ control information in an 8-bit byte oriented data connection over the Transmission Control Protocol.

Exam Probability: **High**

48. *Answer choices:*

(see index for correct answer)

- a. Telnet
- b. GoToAssist
- c. LiteManager
- d. Crossloop

Guidance: level 1

:: Information science ::

The United States National Forum on _____ defines _____ as "... the hyper ability to know when there is a need for information, to be able to identify, locate, evaluate, and effectively use that information for the issue or problem at hand." The American Library Association defines " _____ " as a set of abilities requiring individuals to "recognize when information is needed and have the ability to locate, evaluate, and use effectively the needed information. Other definitions incorporate aspects of "skepticism, judgement, free thinking, questioning, and understanding..." or incorporate competencies that an informed citizen of an information society ought to possess to participate intelligently and actively in that society.

Exam Probability: **High**

49. *Answer choices:*

(see index for correct answer)

- a. American Documentation Institute
- b. Information literacy
- c. Precision and recall
- d. The Royal School of Library and Information Science

Guidance: level 1

:: Data management ::

_____ involves combining data residing in different sources and providing users with a unified view of them. This process becomes significant in a variety of situations, which include both commercial and scientific domains. _____ appears with increasing frequency as the volume and the need to share existing data explodes. It has become the focus of extensive theoretical work, and numerous open problems remain unsolved. _____ encourages collaboration between internal as well as external users

Exam Probability: **High**

50. *Answer choices:*

(see index for correct answer)

- a. Processor data transfer
- b. DAMA
- c. Physical schema
- d. Junction table

Guidance: level 1

:: Commerce ::

_____, Inc. is an American media-services provider headquartered in Los Gatos, California, founded in 1997 by Reed Hastings and Marc Randolph in Scotts Valley, California. The company's primary business is its subscription-based streaming OTT service which offers online streaming of a library of films and television programs, including those produced in-house. As of April 2019, _____ had over 148 million paid subscriptions worldwide, including 60 million in the United States, and over 154 million subscriptions total including free trials. It is available almost worldwide except in mainland China as well as Syria, North Korea, and Crimea. The company also has offices in the Netherlands, Brazil, India, Japan, and South Korea. _____ is a member of the Motion Picture Association of America.

Exam Probability: **High**

51. *Answer choices:*

(see index for correct answer)

- a. Third-party source
- b. Linestanding
- c. Commerce
- d. Fast track

Guidance: level 1

:: Knowledge engineering ::

The _____ is an extension of the World Wide Web through standards by the World Wide Web Consortium . The standards promote common data formats and exchange protocols on the Web, most fundamentally the Resource Description Framework . According to the W3C, "The _____ provides a common framework that allows data to be shared and reused across application, enterprise, and community boundaries". The _____ is therefore regarded as an integrator across different content, information applications and systems.

Exam Probability: **Medium**

52. *Answer choices:*

(see index for correct answer)

- a. Semantic Web
- b. DTRules
- c. Knowledge engineering
- d. Semantic reasoner

Guidance: level 1

:: Information systems ::

In artificial intelligence, an _____ is a computer system that emulates the decision-making ability of a human expert. _____ s are designed to solve complex problems by reasoning through bodies of knowledge, represented mainly as if–then rules rather than through conventional procedural code. The first _____ s were created in the 1970s and then proliferated in the 1980s. _____ s were among the first truly successful forms of artificial intelligence software. However, some experts point out that _____ s were not part of true artificial intelligence since they lack the ability to learn autonomously from external data. An _____ is divided into two subsystems: the inference engine and the knowledge base. The knowledge base represents facts and rules. The inference engine applies the rules to the known facts to deduce new facts. Inference engines can also include explanation and debugging abilities.

Exam Probability: **High**

53. *Answer choices:*

(see index for correct answer)

- a. Censhare
- b. Expert system
- c. Joint Interface Control Officer
- d. Information Processes and Technology

Guidance: level 1

:: ::

_____ are electronic transfer of money from one bank account to another, either within a single financial institution or across multiple institutions, via computer-based systems, without the direct intervention of bank staff.

Exam Probability: **High**

54. *Answer choices:*

(see index for correct answer)

- a. imperative
- b. hierarchical
- c. levels of analysis
- d. Electronic funds transfer

Guidance: level 1

:: ::

The _____ of 1996 was enacted by the 104th United States Congress and signed by President Bill Clinton in 1996. It was created primarily to modernize the flow of healthcare information, stipulate how Personally Identifiable Information maintained by the healthcare and healthcare insurance industries should be protected from fraud and theft, and address limitations on healthcare insurance coverage.

Exam Probability: **High**

55. *Answer choices:*

(see index for correct answer)

- a. Sarbanes-Oxley act of 2002
- b. cultural
- c. functional perspective
- d. imperative

Guidance: level 1

:: ::

_____ is the function of specifying access rights/privileges to resources, which is related to information security and computer security in general and to access control in particular. More formally, "to authorize" is to define an access policy. For example, human resources staff are normally authorized to access employee records and this policy is usually formalized as access control rules in a computer system. During operation, the system uses the access control rules to decide whether access requests from consumers shall be approved or disapproved. Resources include individual files or an item's data, computer programs, computer devices and functionality provided by computer applications. Examples of consumers are computer users, computer Software and other Hardware on the computer.

Exam Probability: **High**

56. *Answer choices:*

(see index for correct answer)

- a. open system
- b. personal values
- c. Authorization
- d. empathy

Guidance: level 1

:: ::

Within the Internet, _____ s are formed by the rules and procedures of the _____ System. Any name registered in the DNS is a _____. _____ s are used in various networking contexts and for application-specific naming and addressing purposes. In general, a _____ represents an Internet Protocol resource, such as a personal computer used to access the Internet, a server computer hosting a web site, or the web site itself or any other service communicated via the Internet. In 2017, 330.6 million _____ s had been registered.

Exam Probability: **High**

57. *Answer choices:*

(see index for correct answer)

- a. Character
- b. functional perspective
- c. personal values
- d. Domain name

Guidance: level 1

:: Business process ::

Business process re-engineering is a business management strategy, originally pioneered in the early 1990s, focusing on the analysis and design of workflows and business processes within an organization. BPR aimed to help organizations fundamentally rethink how they do their work in order to improve customer service, cut operational costs, and become world-class competitors.

Exam Probability: **Medium**

58. *Answer choices:*

(see index for correct answer)

- a. Extended Enterprise Modeling Language
- b. Hi-tech export
- c. Business process reengineering
- d. Change order

Guidance: level 1

:: Network analyzers ::

A _____ , meaning "meat eater" , is an organism that derives its energy and nutrient requirements from a diet consisting mainly or exclusively of animal tissue, whether through predation or scavenging. Animals that depend solely on animal flesh for their nutrient requirements are called obligate _____ s while those that also consume non-animal food are called facultative _____ s. Omnivores also consume both animal and non-animal food, and, apart from the more general definition, there is no clearly defined ratio of plant to animal material that would distinguish a facultative _____ from an omnivore. A _____ at the top of the food chain, not preyed upon by other animals, is termed an apex predator.

Exam Probability: **Medium**

59. *Answer choices:*
(see index for correct answer)

- a. Zx Sniffer
- b. Weplab
- c. Network intelligence
- d. KisMAC

Guidance: level 1

Marketing

Marketing is the study and management of exchange relationships. Marketing is the business process of creating relationships with and satisfying customers. With its focus on the customer, marketing is one of the premier components of business management.

Marketing is defined by the American Marketing Association as "the activity, set of institutions, and processes for creating, communicating, delivering, and exchanging offerings that have value for customers, clients, partners, and society at large."

:: Marketing ::

_____ is the percentage of a market accounted for by a specific entity. In a survey of nearly 200 senior marketing managers, 67% responded that they found the revenue- "dollar _____" metric very useful, while 61% found "unit _____" very useful.

Exam Probability: **Low**

1. *Answer choices:*

(see index for correct answer)

- a. Decoy effect
- b. Market share
- c. Golden sample
- d. Pitching engine

Guidance: level 1

:: Manufacturing ::

A _____ is a building for storing goods. _____ s are used by manufacturers, importers, exporters, wholesalers, transport businesses, customs, etc. They are usually large plain buildings in industrial parks on the outskirts of cities, towns or villages.

Exam Probability: **High**

2. *Answer choices:*

(see index for correct answer)

- a. Factory Physics
- b. Axiomatic design
- c. Warehouse
- d. Air bearing

Guidance: level 1

:: ::

> An _____ is a contingent motivator. Traditional _____ s are extrinsic motivators which reward actions to yield a desired outcome. The effectiveness of traditional _____ s has changed as the needs of Western society have evolved. While the traditional _____ model is effective when there is a defined procedure and goal for a task, Western society started to require a higher volume of critical thinkers, so the traditional model became less effective. Institutions are now following a trend in implementing strategies that rely on intrinsic motivations rather than the extrinsic motivations that the traditional _____ s foster.

Exam Probability: **High**

3. *Answer choices:*

(see index for correct answer)

- a. interpersonal communication
- b. imperative
- c. Incentive

- d. Character

Guidance: level 1

:: ::

A _____ is a person who trades in commodities produced by other people. Historically, a _____ is anyone who is involved in business or trade. _____ s have operated for as long as industry, commerce, and trade have existed. During the 16th-century, in Europe, two different terms for _____ s emerged: One term, meerseniers, described local traders such as bakers, grocers, etc.; while a new term, koopman (Dutch: koopman, described _____ s who operated on a global stage, importing and exporting goods over vast distances, and offering added-value services such as credit and finance.

Exam Probability: **Medium**

4. *Answer choices:*
(see index for correct answer)

- a. functional perspective
- b. surface-level diversity
- c. process perspective
- d. interpersonal communication

Guidance: level 1

:: Marketing ::

_____ is a market strategy in which a firm decides to ignore market segment differences and appeal the whole market with one offer or one strategy, which supports the idea of broadcasting a message that will reach the largest number of people possible. Traditionally _____ has focused on radio, television and newspapers as the media used to reach this broad audience. By reaching the largest audience possible, exposure to the product is maximized, and in theory this would directly correlate with a larger number of sales or buys into the product.

Exam Probability: **Low**

5. *Answer choices:*

(see index for correct answer)

- a. Mystery shopping
- b. Digital billboard
- c. Customer interaction tracker
- d. Mass marketing

Guidance: level 1

:: ::

In production, research, retail, and accounting, a _____ is the value of money that has been used up to produce something or deliver a service, and hence is not available for use anymore. In business, the _____ may be one of acquisition, in which case the amount of money expended to acquire it is counted as _____ . In this case, money is the input that is gone in order to acquire the thing. This acquisition _____ may be the sum of the _____ of production as incurred by the original producer, and further _____ s of transaction as incurred by the acquirer over and above the price paid to the producer. Usually, the price also includes a mark-up for profit over the _____ of production.

Exam Probability: **High**

6. *Answer choices:*

(see index for correct answer)

- a. similarity-attraction theory
- b. cultural
- c. interpersonal communication
- d. Cost

Guidance: level 1

:: ::

Competition arises whenever at least two parties strive for a goal which cannot be shared: where one`s gain is the other`s loss .

Exam Probability: **Medium**

7. *Answer choices:*

(see index for correct answer)

- a. similarity-attraction theory
- b. hierarchical perspective
- c. functional perspective
- d. empathy

Guidance: level 1

:: Pricing ::

_____ is unwanted sound judged to be unpleasant, loud or disruptive to hearing. From a physics standpoint, _____ is indistinguishable from sound, as both are vibrations through a medium, such as air or water. The difference arises when the brain receives and perceives a sound.

Exam Probability: **Low**

8. *Answer choices:*

(see index for correct answer)

- a. Two-tiered pricing
- b. Noise
- c. Big ticket item

- d. Nonlinear pricing

Guidance: level 1

:: ::

The _____ is an agreement signed by Canada, Mexico, and the United States, creating a trilateral trade bloc in North America. The agreement came into force on January 1, 1994, and superseded the 1988 Canada–United States Free Trade Agreement between the United States and Canada. The NAFTA trade bloc is one of the largest trade blocs in the world by gross domestic product.

Exam Probability: **Medium**

9. *Answer choices:*
(see index for correct answer)

- a. levels of analysis
- b. North American Free Trade Agreement
- c. co-culture
- d. similarity-attraction theory

Guidance: level 1

:: Commerce ::

A _____ is a company or individual that purchases goods or services with the intention of selling them rather than consuming or using them. This is usually done for profit. One example can be found in the industry of telecommunications, where companies buy excess amounts of transmission capacity or call time from other carriers and resell it to smaller carriers.

Exam Probability: **Low**

10. *Answer choices:*

(see index for correct answer)

- a. Factory
- b. Staple right
- c. Oxygen bar
- d. Reseller

Guidance: level 1

:: Consumer behaviour ::

_____ refers to the ability of a company or product to retain its customers over some specified period. High _____ means customers of the product or business tend to return to, continue to buy or in some other way not defect to another product or business, or to non-use entirely. Selling organizations generally attempt to reduce customer defections. _____ starts with the first contact an organization has with a customer and continues throughout the entire lifetime of a relationship and successful retention efforts take this entire lifecycle into account. A company's ability to attract and retain new customers is related not only to its product or services, but also to the way it services its existing customers, the value the customers actually generate as a result of utilizing the solutions, and the reputation it creates within and across the marketplace.

Exam Probability: **Medium**

11. *Answer choices:*

(see index for correct answer)

- a. Social norms approach
- b. Psychological continuum model
- c. Customer analytics
- d. Consumer socialization

Guidance: level 1

:: Marketing ::

_____s are structured marketing strategies designed by merchants to encourage customers to continue to shop at or use the services of businesses associated with each program. These programs exist covering most types of commerce, each one having varying features and rewards-schemes.

Exam Probability: **Medium**

12. *Answer choices:*

(see index for correct answer)

- a. Carrying cost
- b. Loyalty program
- c. Lingerie party
- d. Contact centre

Guidance: level 1

:: ::

A _____ is an organization, usually a group of people or a company, authorized to act as a single entity and recognized as such in law. Early incorporated entities were established by charter. Most jurisdictions now allow the creation of new _____s through registration.

Exam Probability: **Low**

13. *Answer choices:*

(see index for correct answer)

- a. information systems assessment
- b. deep-level diversity
- c. Corporation
- d. empathy

Guidance: level 1

:: Internet privacy ::

An _____ is a private network accessible only to an organization's staff. Often, a wide range of information and services are available on an organization's internal _____ that are unavailable to the public, unlike the Internet. A company-wide _____ can constitute an important focal point of internal communication and collaboration, and provide a single starting point to access internal and external resources. In its simplest form, an _____ is established with the technologies for local area networks and wide area networks . Many modern _____ s have search engines, user profiles, blogs, mobile apps with notifications, and events planning within their infrastructure.

Exam Probability: **High**

14. *Answer choices:*
(see index for correct answer)

- a. Real-name system
- b. Intranet portal

- c. DoNotTrackMe
- d. Bitmessage

Guidance: level 1

:: Marketing ::

_____ is a marketing practice of individuals or organizations. It allows them to sell products or services to other companies or organizations that resell them, use them in their products or services or use them to support their works.

Exam Probability: **Low**

15. *Answer choices:*

(see index for correct answer)

- a. Branded asset management
- b. Gambling advertising
- c. Business marketing
- d. Private label

Guidance: level 1

:: Data interchange standards ::

_____ is the concept of businesses electronically communicating information that was traditionally communicated on paper, such as purchase orders and invoices. Technical standards for EDI exist to facilitate parties transacting such instruments without having to make special arrangements.

Exam Probability: **High**

16. *Answer choices:*

(see index for correct answer)

- a. Domain Application Protocol
- b. Electronic data interchange
- c. Data Interchange Standards Association
- d. Uniform Communication Standard

Guidance: level 1

:: Retailing ::

A _____ is a self-service shop offering a wide variety of food, beverages and household products, organized into sections and shelves. It is larger and has a wider selection than earlier grocery stores, but is smaller and more limited in the range of merchandise than a hypermarket or big-box market.

Exam Probability: **Low**

17. *Answer choices:*

(see index for correct answer)

- a. Supermarket
- b. Strip mall
- c. Hobby shop
- d. Buy Here Pay Here

Guidance: level 1

:: Marketing ::

> _____ is a growth strategy that identifies and develops new market segments for current products. A _____ strategy targets non-buying customers in currently targeted segments. It also targets new customers in new segments.

Exam Probability: **Low**

18. *Answer choices:*

(see index for correct answer)

- a. Marketing brochure
- b. societal marketing
- c. Market development
- d. Marketing mix

Guidance: level 1

:: Cognitive dissonance ::

In the field of psychology, _____ is the mental discomfort experienced by a person who holds two or more contradictory beliefs, ideas, or values. This discomfort is triggered by a situation in which a person's belief clashes with new evidence perceived by the person. When confronted with facts that contradict beliefs, ideals, and values, people will try to find a way to resolve the contradiction to reduce their discomfort.

Exam Probability: **Medium**

19. *Answer choices:*

(see index for correct answer)

- a. Emotional conflict
- b. Cognitive dissonance
- c. The Fox and the Grapes
- d. Self-refuting idea

Guidance: level 1

:: Industry ::

_____ describes various measures of the efficiency of production. Often, a _____ measure is expressed as the ratio of an aggregate output to a single input or an aggregate input used in a production process, i.e. output per unit of input. Most common example is the labour _____ measure, e.g., such as GDP per worker. There are many different definitions of _____ and the choice among them depends on the purpose of the _____ measurement and/or data availability. The key source of difference between various _____ measures is also usually related to how the outputs and the inputs are aggregated into scalars to obtain such a ratio-type measure of _____.

Exam Probability: **Low**

20. *Answer choices:*

(see index for correct answer)

- a. Group technology
- b. Recommended exposure limit
- c. Cartoning machine
- d. Exposure action value

Guidance: level 1

:: Project management ::

A _____ is a source or supply from which a benefit is produced and it has some utility. _____ s can broadly be classified upon their availability—they are classified into renewable and non-renewable _____ s.Examples of non renewable _____ s are coal ,crude oil natural gas nuclear energy etc. Examples of renewable _____ s are air,water,wind,solar energy etc. They can also be classified as actual and potential on the basis of level of development and use, on the basis of origin they can be classified as biotic and abiotic, and on the basis of their distribution, as ubiquitous and localized . An item becomes a _____ with time and developing technology. Typically, _____ s are materials, energy, services, staff, knowledge, or other assets that are transformed to produce benefit and in the process may be consumed or made unavailable. Benefits of _____ utilization may include increased wealth, proper functioning of a system, or enhanced well-being. From a human perspective a natural _____ is anything obtained from the environment to satisfy human needs and wants. From a broader biological or ecological perspective a _____ satisfies the needs of a living organism .

Exam Probability: **Medium**

21. *Answer choices:*

(see index for correct answer)

- a. Schedule chicken
- b. Project anatomy
- c. Rapid Results
- d. Project management 2.0

Guidance: level 1

In _____ relations and communication science, _____ s are groups of individual people, and the _____ is the totality of such groupings. This is a different concept to the sociological concept of the Öffentlichkeit or _____ sphere. The concept of a _____ has also been defined in political science, psychology, marketing, and advertising. In _____ relations and communication science, it is one of the more ambiguous concepts in the field. Although it has definitions in the theory of the field that have been formulated from the early 20th century onwards, it has suffered in more recent years from being blurred, as a result of conflation of the idea of a _____ with the notions of audience, market segment, community, constituency, and stakeholder.

Exam Probability: **Medium**

22. *Answer choices:*

(see index for correct answer)

- a. functional perspective
- b. personal values
- c. Public
- d. open system

Guidance: level 1

:: Basic financial concepts ::

_____ is a sustained increase in the general price level of goods and services in an economy over a period of time. When the general price level rises, each unit of currency buys fewer goods and services; consequently, _____ reflects a reduction in the purchasing power per unit of money a loss of real value in the medium of exchange and unit of account within the economy. The measure of _____ is the _____ rate, the annualized percentage change in a general price index, usually the consumer price index, over time. The opposite of _____ is deflation.

Exam Probability: **High**

23. *Answer choices:*

(see index for correct answer)

- a. Future-oriented
- b. Financial transaction
- c. balloon payment
- d. Inflation

Guidance: level 1

:: ::

In international relations, _____ is – from the perspective of governments – a voluntary transfer of resources from one country to another.

Exam Probability: **High**

24. Answer choices:

(see index for correct answer)

- a. Sarbanes-Oxley act of 2002
- b. process perspective
- c. Aid
- d. cultural

Guidance: level 1

:: Market research ::

An _____ or lighthouse customer is an early customer of a given company, product, or technology. The term originates from Everett M. Rogers' Diffusion of Innovations.

Exam Probability: **Medium**

25. Answer choices:

(see index for correct answer)

- a. Qualtrics
- b. Media Technology Monitor
- c. Early adopter
- d. Market research and opinion polling in China

Guidance: level 1

:: ::

_____ is a concept of English common law and is a necessity for simple contracts but not for special contracts. The concept has been adopted by other common law jurisdictions, including the US.

Exam Probability: **Low**

26. *Answer choices:*

(see index for correct answer)

- a. open system
- b. deep-level diversity
- c. levels of analysis
- d. Consideration

Guidance: level 1

:: Management ::

In economics and marketing, _____ is the process of distinguishing a product or service from others, to make it more attractive to a particular target market. This involves differentiating it from competitors' products as well as a firm's own products. The concept was proposed by Edward Chamberlin in his 1933 The Theory of Monopolistic Competition.

Exam Probability: **Low**

27. *Answer choices:*

(see index for correct answer)

- a. Modes of leadership
- b. Product differentiation
- c. Job rotation
- d. Enterprise planning system

Guidance: level 1

:: ::

_____ is change in the heritable characteristics of biological populations over successive generations. These characteristics are the expressions of genes that are passed on from parent to offspring during reproduction. Different characteristics tend to exist within any given population as a result of mutation, genetic recombination and other sources of genetic variation. _____ occurs when _____ ary processes such as natural selection and genetic drift act on this variation, resulting in certain characteristics becoming more common or rare within a population. It is this process of _____ that has given rise to biodiversity at every level of biological organisation, including the levels of species, individual organisms and molecules.

Exam Probability: **Medium**

28. *Answer choices:*

(see index for correct answer)

- a. deep-level diversity
- b. information systems assessment
- c. co-culture
- d. Evolution

Guidance: level 1

:: Social psychology ::

_____ s is a qualitative methodology used to describe consumers on psychological attributes. _____ s have been applied to the study of personality, values, opinions, attitudes, interests, and lifestyles. While _____ s are often equated with lifestyle research, it has been argued that _____ s should apply to the study of cognitive attributes such as attitudes, interests, opinions, and beliefs while lifestyle should apply to the study of overt behavior. Because this area of research focuses on activities, interests, and opinions, _____ factors are sometimes abbreviated to `AIO variables`.

Exam Probability: **Low**

29. *Answer choices:*

(see index for correct answer)

- a. Psychographic
- b. externalization
- c. Mutual engagement

- d. social loafing

Guidance: level 1

:: Product management ::

` _____ ` is a phrase used in the marketing industry which describes the value of having a well-known brand name, based on the idea that the owner of a well-known brand name can generate more revenue simply from brand recognition; that is from products with that brand name than from products with a less well known name, as consumers believe that a product with a well-known name is better than products with less well-known names.

Exam Probability: **Low**

30. *Answer choices:*
(see index for correct answer)

- a. Requirement prioritization
- b. Service life
- c. Rapid prototyping
- d. Discontinuation

Guidance: level 1

:: Advertising techniques ::

In promotion and of advertising, a _____ or show consists of a person's written or spoken statement extolling the virtue of a product. The term "_____" most commonly applies to the sales-pitches attributed to ordinary citizens, whereas the word "endorsement" usually applies to pitches by celebrities. _____s can be part of communal marketing. Sometimes, the cartoon character can be a _____ in a commercial.

Exam Probability: **Medium**

31. *Answer choices:*
(see index for correct answer)

- a. Two Cunts in a Kitchen
- b. Unipole sign
- c. Testimonial
- d. Hard sell

Guidance: level 1

:: ::

A _____ is a discussion or informational website published on the World Wide Web consisting of discrete, often informal diary-style text entries. Posts are typically displayed in reverse chronological order, so that the most recent post appears first, at the top of the web page. Until 2009, _____ s were usually the work of a single individual, occasionally of a small group, and often covered a single subject or topic. In the 2010s, "multi-author _____ s" emerged, featuring the writing of multiple authors and sometimes professionally edited. MABs from newspapers, other media outlets, universities, think tanks, advocacy groups, and similar institutions account for an increasing quantity of _____ traffic. The rise of Twitter and other "micro _____ ging" systems helps integrate MABs and single-author _____ s into the news media. _____ can also be used as a verb, meaning to maintain or add content to a _____ .

Exam Probability: **Medium**

32. *Answer choices:*

(see index for correct answer)

- a. Character
- b. co-culture
- c. Blog
- d. levels of analysis

Guidance: level 1

:: Advertising ::

A _____ is a document used by creative professionals and agencies to develop creative deliverables: visual design, copy, advertising, web sites, etc. The document is usually developed by the requestor and approved by the creative team of designers, writers, and project managers. In some cases, the project's _____ may need creative director approval before work will commence.

Exam Probability: **Medium**

33. *Answer choices:*

(see index for correct answer)

- a. Brand Development Index
- b. Under the Anheuser Bush
- c. Social advertising
- d. Reply marketing

Guidance: level 1

:: ::

_____ s are formal, sociotechnical, organizational systems designed to collect, process, store, and distribute information. In a sociotechnical perspective, _____ s are composed by four components: task, people, structure, and technology.

Exam Probability: **High**

34. Answer choices:

(see index for correct answer)

- a. Information system
- b. open system
- c. corporate values
- d. functional perspective

Guidance: level 1

:: ::

The _____ is a U.S. business-focused, English-language international daily newspaper based in New York City. The Journal, along with its Asian and European editions, is published six days a week by Dow Jones & Company, a division of News Corp. The newspaper is published in the broadsheet format and online. The Journal has been printed continuously since its inception on July 8, 1889, by Charles Dow, Edward Jones, and Charles Bergstresser.

Exam Probability: **Low**

35. Answer choices:

(see index for correct answer)

- a. Character
- b. Wall Street Journal
- c. Sarbanes-Oxley act of 2002
- d. corporate values

Guidance: level 1

:: National accounts ::

_____ is a monetary measure of the market value of all the final goods and services produced in a period of time, often annually. GDP per capita does not, however, reflect differences in the cost of living and the inflation rates of the countries; therefore using a basis of GDP per capita at purchasing power parity is arguably more useful when comparing differences in living standards between nations.

Exam Probability: **Low**

36. *Answer choices:*

(see index for correct answer)

- a. National Income
- b. Fixed capital
- c. capital formation

Guidance: level 1

:: Promotion and marketing communications ::

_____ is one of the elements of the promotional mix. . _____ uses both media and non-media marketing communications for a pre-determined, limited time to increase consumer demand, stimulate market demand or improve product availability. Examples include contests, coupons, freebies, loss leaders, point of purchase displays, premiums, prizes, product samples, and rebates.

Exam Probability: **Low**

37. *Answer choices:*

(see index for correct answer)

- a. FLIP Publicity
- b. Aeroplan
- c. Sales promotion
- d. Promotional representative

Guidance: level 1

:: Marketing ::

_____, sometimes called trigger-based or event-driven marketing, is a marketing strategy that uses two-way communication channels to allow consumers to connect with a company directly. Although this exchange can take place in person, in the last decade it has increasingly taken place almost exclusively online through email, social media, and blogs.

Exam Probability: **Low**

38. *Answer choices:*

(see index for correct answer)

- a. Outsourcing relationship management
- b. Niche market
- c. Interactive marketing
- d. Penetration pricing

Guidance: level 1

:: ::

_____ is the act of conveying meanings from one entity or group to another through the use of mutually understood signs, symbols, and semiotic rules.

Exam Probability: **Medium**

39. *Answer choices:*

(see index for correct answer)

- a. open system
- b. Communication
- c. hierarchical perspective
- d. corporate values

Guidance: level 1

:: Materials ::

A _____, also known as a feedstock, unprocessed material, or primary commodity, is a basic material that is used to produce goods, finished products, energy, or intermediate materials which are feedstock for future finished products. As feedstock, the term connotes these materials are bottleneck assets and are highly important with regard to producing other products. An example of this is crude oil, which is a _____ and a feedstock used in the production of industrial chemicals, fuels, plastics, and pharmaceutical goods; lumber is a _____ used to produce a variety of products including all types of furniture. The term "_____" denotes materials in minimally processed or unprocessed in states; e.g., raw latex, crude oil, cotton, coal, raw biomass, iron ore, air, logs, or water i.e. "...any product of agriculture, forestry, fishing and any other mineral that is in its natural form or which has undergone the transformation required to prepare it for internationally marketing in substantial volumes."

Exam Probability: **Medium**

40. *Answer choices:*
(see index for correct answer)

- a. Raw material
- b. Ultralight material
- c. Glass microsphere
- d. Cellulose fiber

Guidance: level 1

:: ::

A _____ service is an online platform which people use to build social networks or social relationship with other people who share similar personal or career interests, activities, backgrounds or real-life connections.

Exam Probability: **Low**

41. *Answer choices:*

(see index for correct answer)

- a. functional perspective
- b. personal values
- c. surface-level diversity
- d. Social networking

Guidance: level 1

:: ::

A _____ or sample _____ is a single measure of some attribute of a sample. It is calculated by applying a function to the values of the items of the sample, which are known together as a set of data.

Exam Probability: **High**

42. Answer choices:

(see index for correct answer)

- a. open system
- b. personal values
- c. empathy
- d. Statistic

Guidance: level 1

:: ::

> Retail is the process of selling consumer goods or services to customers through multiple channels of distribution to earn a profit. Retailers satisfy demand identified through a supply chain. The term "retailer" is typically applied where a service provider fills the small orders of a large number of individuals, who are end-users, rather than large orders of a small number of wholesale, corporate or government clientele. Shopping generally refers to the act of buying products. Sometimes this is done to obtain final goods, including necessities such as food and clothing; sometimes it takes place as a recreational activity. Recreational shopping often involves window shopping and browsing: it does not always result in a purchase.

Exam Probability: **Medium**

43. Answer choices:

(see index for correct answer)

- a. similarity-attraction theory

- b. hierarchical
- c. co-culture
- d. Retailing

Guidance: level 1

:: Health promotion ::

_____ , as defined by the World _____ Organization , is "a state of complete physical, mental and social well-being and not merely the absence of disease or infirmity." This definition has been subject to controversy, as it may have limited value for implementation. _____ may be defined as the ability to adapt and manage physical, mental and social challenges throughout life.

Exam Probability: **Medium**

44. *Answer choices:*

(see index for correct answer)

- a. Unwarranted variation
- b. American Frontiers: A Public Lands Journey
- c. High-deductible health plan
- d. NHS Health Scotland

Guidance: level 1

:: Brand management ::

_____ is defined as positive feelings towards a brand and dedication to purchase the same product or service repeatedly now and in the future from the same brand, regardless of a competitor's actions or changes in the environment. It can also be demonstrated with other behaviors such as positive word-of-mouth advocacy. _____ is where an individual buys products from the same manufacturer repeatedly rather than from other suppliers. Businesses whose financial and ethical values, for example ESG responsibilities, rest in large part on their _____ are said to use the loyalty business model.

Exam Probability: **Medium**

45. *Answer choices:*

(see index for correct answer)

- a. Saban Capital Group
- b. Boomerang Media
- c. Operator logo
- d. Brand loyalty

Guidance: level 1

:: Debt ::

_____ is the trust which allows one party to provide money or resources to another party wherein the second party does not reimburse the first party immediately, but promises either to repay or return those resources at a later date. In other words, _____ is a method of making reciprocity formal, legally enforceable, and extensible to a large group of unrelated people.

Exam Probability: **Low**

46. *Answer choices:*

(see index for correct answer)

- a. Credit
- b. Compulsive buying disorder
- c. Financial assistance
- d. Internal debt

Guidance: level 1

:: Management accounting ::

In economics, _____ s, indirect costs or overheads are business expenses that are not dependent on the level of goods or services produced by the business. They tend to be time-related, such as interest or rents being paid per month, and are often referred to as overhead costs. This is in contrast to variable costs, which are volume-related and unknown at the beginning of the accounting year. For a simple example, such as a bakery, the monthly rent for the baking facilities, and the monthly payments for the security system and basic phone line are _____ s, as they do not change according to how much bread the bakery produces and sells. On the other hand, the wage costs of the bakery are variable, as the bakery will have to hire more workers if the production of bread increases. Economists reckon _____ as a entry barrier for new entrepreneurs.

Exam Probability: **High**

47. *Answer choices:*

(see index for correct answer)

- a. Double counting
- b. Fixed cost
- c. Net present value
- d. Resource consumption accounting

Guidance: level 1

:: ::

Market segmentation is the activity of dividing a broad consumer or business market, normally consisting of existing and potential customers, into sub-groups of consumers based on some type of shared characteristics. In dividing or segmenting markets, researchers typically look for common characteristics such as shared needs, common interests, similar lifestyles or even similar demographic profiles. The overall aim of segmentation is to identify high yield segments – that is, those segments that are likely to be the most profitable or that have growth potential – so that these can be selected for special attention .

Exam Probability: **Medium**

48. *Answer choices:*

(see index for correct answer)

- a. information systems assessment
- b. similarity-attraction theory
- c. co-culture
- d. Market segments

Guidance: level 1

:: Generally Accepted Accounting Principles ::

Expenditure is an outflow of money to another person or group to pay for an item or service, or for a category of costs. For a tenant, rent is an _____. For students or parents, tuition is an _____. Buying food, clothing, furniture or an automobile is often referred to as an _____. An _____ is a cost that is "paid" or "remitted", usually in exchange for something of value. Something that seems to cost a great deal is "expensive". Something that seems to cost little is "inexpensive". "_____s of the table" are _____s of dining, refreshments, a feast, etc.

Exam Probability: **High**

49. *Answer choices:*

(see index for correct answer)

- a. Net income
- b. Access to finance
- c. Liability
- d. Expense

Guidance: level 1

:: Commercial item transport and distribution ::

In commerce, supply-chain management, the management of the flow of goods and services, involves the movement and storage of raw materials, of work-in-process inventory, and of finished goods from point of origin to point of consumption. Interconnected or interlinked networks, channels and node businesses combine in the provision of products and services required by end customers in a supply chain. Supply-chain management has been defined as the "design, planning, execution, control, and monitoring of supply-chain activities with the objective of creating net value, building a competitive infrastructure, leveraging worldwide logistics, synchronizing supply with demand and measuring performance globally."SCM practice draws heavily from the areas of industrial engineering, systems engineering, operations management, logistics, procurement, information technology, and marketing and strives for an integrated approach. Marketing channels play an important role in supply-chain management. Current research in supply-chain management is concerned with topics related to sustainability and risk management, among others. Some suggest that the "people dimension" of SCM, ethical issues, internal integration, transparency/visibility, and human capital/talent management are topics that have, so far, been underrepresented on the research agenda.

Exam Probability: **Low**

50. *Answer choices:*

(see index for correct answer)

- a. Supply chain management
- b. Shipping container
- c. Blue Water Trucking
- d. Transshipment problem

Guidance: level 1

:: Advertising ::

A _____ is a large outdoor advertising structure, typically found in high-traffic areas such as alongside busy roads. _____ s present large advertisements to passing pedestrians and drivers. Typically showing witty slogans and distinctive visuals, _____ s are highly visible in the top designated market areas.

Exam Probability: **High**

51. *Answer choices:*

(see index for correct answer)

- a. Visual pollution
- b. Cretic
- c. Billboard
- d. Cidade Limpa

Guidance: level 1

:: Progressive Era in the United States ::

The Clayton Antitrust Act of 1914, was a part of United States antitrust law with the goal of adding further substance to the U.S. antitrust law regime; the _____ sought to prevent anticompetitive practices in their incipiency. That regime started with the Sherman Antitrust Act of 1890, the first Federal law outlawing practices considered harmful to consumers. The _____ specified particular prohibited conduct, the three-level enforcement scheme, the exemptions, and the remedial measures.

Exam Probability: **High**

52. *Answer choices:*

(see index for correct answer)

- a. Clayton Antitrust Act
- b. Mann Act
- c. Clayton Act

Guidance: level 1

:: ::

An _____ is the production of goods or related services within an economy. The major source of revenue of a group or company is the indicator of its relevant _____ . When a large group has multiple sources of revenue generation, it is considered to be working in different industries. Manufacturing _____ became a key sector of production and labour in European and North American countries during the Industrial Revolution, upsetting previous mercantile and feudal economies. This came through many successive rapid advances in technology, such as the production of steel and coal.

Exam Probability: **Medium**

53. *Answer choices:*

(see index for correct answer)

- a. hierarchical
- b. corporate values
- c. personal values
- d. Character

Guidance: level 1

:: Evaluation methods ::

In natural and social sciences, and sometimes in other fields, _____ is the systematic empirical investigation of observable phenomena via statistical, mathematical, or computational techniques. The objective of _____ is to develop and employ mathematical models, theories, and hypotheses pertaining to phenomena. The process of measurement is central to _____ because it provides the fundamental connection between empirical observation and mathematical expression of quantitative relationships.

Exam Probability: **Medium**

54. *Answer choices:*

(see index for correct answer)

- a. Rubric
- b. Poll average
- c. Quantitative research
- d. Analog observation

Guidance: level 1

:: International trade ::

In finance, an _____ is the rate at which one currency will be exchanged for another. It is also regarded as the value of one country's currency in relation to another currency. For example, an interbank _____ of 114 Japanese yen to the United States dollar means that ¥114 will be exchanged for each US$1 or that US$1 will be exchanged for each ¥114. In this case it is said that the price of a dollar in relation to yen is ¥114, or equivalently that the price of a yen in relation to dollars is $1/114.

Exam Probability: **High**

55. *Answer choices:*

(see index for correct answer)

- a. Trade mandate
- b. Indo-Roman relations
- c. Booze cruise
- d. Orderly marketing arrangement

Guidance: level 1

:: Credit cards ::

The _____ Company, also known as Amex, is an American multinational financial services corporation headquartered in Three World Financial Center in New York City. The company was founded in 1850 and is one of the 30 components of the Dow Jones Industrial Average. The company is best known for its charge card, credit card, and traveler's cheque businesses.

Exam Probability: **Low**

56. *Answer choices:*

(see index for correct answer)

- a. Alpha Card Services
- b. American Express

- c. HSBC
- d. Payments as a service

Guidance: level 1

:: Television commercials ::

_____ is a characteristic that distinguishes physical entities that have biological processes, such as signaling and self-sustaining processes, from those that do not, either because such functions have ceased , or because they never had such functions and are classified as inanimate. Various forms of _____ exist, such as plants, animals, fungi, protists, archaea, and bacteria. The criteria can at times be ambiguous and may or may not define viruses, viroids, or potential synthetic _____ as "living". Biology is the science concerned with the study of _____ .

Exam Probability: **Medium**

57. *Answer choices:*
(see index for correct answer)

- a. Cheer Up!
- b. Time Sculpture
- c. Batman OnStar commercials
- d. Life

Guidance: level 1

:: Types of marketing ::

_____ is "marketing on a worldwide scale reconciling or taking commercial advantage of global operational differences, similarities and opportunities in order to meet global objectives".

Exam Probability: **Medium**

58. *Answer choices:*

(see index for correct answer)

- a. Ethical marketing
- b. Project SCUM
- c. Customer advocacy
- d. Close Range Marketing

Guidance: level 1

:: Market research ::

_____, an acronym for Information through Disguised Experimentation is an annual market research fair conducted by the students of IIM-Lucknow. Students create games and use various other simulated environments to capture consumers' subconscious thoughts. This innovative method of market research removes the sensitization effect that might bias peoples answers to questions. This ensures that the most truthful answers are captured to research questions. The games are designed in such a way that the observers can elicit all the required information just by observing and noting down the behaviour and the responses of the participants.

Exam Probability: **High**

59. *Answer choices:*

(see index for correct answer)

- a. Landing page optimization
- b. INDEX
- c. Vehicle Dependability Study
- d. TNS NIPO

Guidance: level 1

Manufacturing

Manufacturing is the production of merchandise for use or sale using labor and machines, tools, chemical and biological processing, or formulation. The term may refer to a range of human activity, from handicraft to high tech, but is most commonly applied to industrial design , in which raw materials are transformed into finished goods on a large scale. Such finished goods may be sold to other manufacturers for the production of other, more complex products, such as aircraft, household appliances, furniture, sports equipment or automobiles, or sold to wholesalers, who in turn sell them to retailers, who then sell them to end users and consumers.

:: Project management ::

_____ is a process of setting goals, planning and/or controlling the organizing and leading the execution of any type of activity, such as.

Exam Probability: **Medium**

1. *Answer choices:*

(see index for correct answer)

- a. TELOS
- b. Management process
- c. Product flow diagram
- d. Design structure matrix

Guidance: level 1

:: Costs ::

In process improvement efforts, _____ or cost of quality is a means to quantify the total cost of quality-related efforts and deficiencies. It was first described by Armand V. Feigenbaum in a 1956 Harvard Business Review article.

Exam Probability: **Low**

2. *Answer choices:*

(see index for correct answer)

- a. Social cost
- b. Total cost
- c. Quality costs
- d. Road Logistics Costing in South Africa

Guidance: level 1

:: Management ::

_____ is the discipline of strategically planning for, and managing, all interactions with third party organizations that supply goods and/or services to an organization in order to maximize the value of those interactions. In practice, SRM entails creating closer, more collaborative relationships with key suppliers in order to uncover and realize new value and reduce risk of failure.

Exam Probability: **Medium**

3. *Answer choices:*

(see index for correct answer)

- a. Jarratt report
- b. Management cockpit
- c. Supplier relationship management
- d. Relational view

Guidance: level 1

:: Management ::

_____ is a formal technique useful where many possible courses of action are competing for attention. In essence, the problem-solver estimates the benefit delivered by each action, then selects a number of the most effective actions that deliver a total benefit reasonably close to the maximal possible one.

Exam Probability: **Medium**

4. *Answer choices:*
(see index for correct answer)

- a. Functional management
- b. Pareto analysis
- c. Strategic lenses
- d. Relevance paradox

Guidance: level 1

:: Help desk ::

Data center management is the collection of tasks performed by those responsible for managing ongoing operation of a data center This includes Business service management and planning for the future.

Exam Probability: **Low**

5. *Answer choices:*

(see index for correct answer)

- a. Liberum Help Desk
- b. Technical support
- c. SysAid Technologies
- d. Web Help Desk

Guidance: level 1

:: Information systems ::

_____ is the process of creating, sharing, using and managing the knowledge and information of an organisation. It refers to a multidisciplinary approach to achieving organisational objectives by making the best use of knowledge.

Exam Probability: **High**

6. *Answer choices:*

(see index for correct answer)

- a. System for Electronic Document Analysis and Retrieval
- b. Legal expert system
- c. Complex event processing
- d. Knowledge management

Guidance: level 1

:: Industrial design ::

In physics and mathematics, the _____ of a mathematical space is informally defined as the minimum number of coordinates needed to specify any point within it. Thus a line has a _____ of one because only one coordinate is needed to specify a point on it for example, the point at 5 on a number line. A surface such as a plane or the surface of a cylinder or sphere has a _____ of two because two coordinates are needed to specify a point on it for example, both a latitude and longitude are required to locate a point on the surface of a sphere. The inside of a cube, a cylinder or a sphere is three- _____ al because three coordinates are needed to locate a point within these spaces.

Exam Probability: **Low**

7. *Answer choices:*

(see index for correct answer)

- a. Air-augmented rocket
- b. User interface design
- c. Sustainable furniture design
- d. Dimension

Guidance: level 1

:: Production and manufacturing ::

_____ is a set of techniques and tools for process improvement. Though as a shortened form it may be found written as 6S, it should not be confused with the methodology known as 6S.

Exam Probability: **Medium**

8. *Answer choices:*

(see index for correct answer)

- a. Dynamic Manufacturing Network
- b. Subir Chowdhury
- c. Six Sigma
- d. Craft production

Guidance: level 1

:: Casting (manufacturing) ::

A _____ is a regularity in the world, man-made design, or abstract ideas. As such, the elements of a _____ repeat in a predictable manner. A geometric _____ is a kind of _____ formed of geometric shapes and typically repeated like a wallpaper design.

Exam Probability: **Low**

9. *Answer choices:*

(see index for correct answer)

- a. Semi-steel
- b. Continuous casting
- c. Pattern
- d. Hydrogen gas porosity

Guidance: level 1

:: Business process ::

_____ is the value to an enterprise which is derived from the techniques, procedures, and programs that implement and enhance the delivery of goods and services. _____ is one of the three components of structural capital, itself a component of intellectual capital. _____ can be seen as the value of processes to any entity, whether for profit or not-for profit, but is most commonly used in reference to for-profit entities.

Exam Probability: **Medium**

10. *Answer choices:*
(see index for correct answer)

- a. Business Motivation Model
- b. Process capital
- c. Feasibility study
- d. Intention mining

Guidance: level 1

:: Production economics ::

_____ is the creation of a whole that is greater than the simple sum of its parts. The term _____ comes from the Attic Greek word sea synergia from synergos, , meaning "working together".

Exam Probability: **Medium**

11. *Answer choices:*

(see index for correct answer)

- a. Factor price
- b. Constant elasticity of transformation
- c. Synergy
- d. Partial productivity

Guidance: level 1

:: Production and manufacturing ::

_____ is a theory of management that analyzes and synthesizes workflows. Its main objective is improving economic efficiency, especially labor productivity. It was one of the earliest attempts to apply science to the engineering of processes and to management. _____ is sometimes known as Taylorism after its founder, Frederick Winslow Taylor.

Exam Probability: **Medium**

12. *Answer choices:*

(see index for correct answer)

- a. Citect
- b. Scientific management
- c. Job shop
- d. Product data record

Guidance: level 1

:: Production economics ::

In economics and related disciplines, a _____ is a cost in making any economic trade when participating in a market.

Exam Probability: **Medium**

13. *Answer choices:*

(see index for correct answer)

- a. Economies of scale
- b. Capitalist mode of production
- c. Marginal cost
- d. Choice of techniques

Guidance: level 1

:: Project management ::

A _____ is a type of bar chart that illustrates a project schedule, named after its inventor, Henry Gantt , who designed such a chart around the years 1910–1915. Modern _____ s also show the dependency relationships between activities and current schedule status.

Exam Probability: **Low**

14. *Answer choices:*

(see index for correct answer)

- a. The Practice Standard for Scheduling
- b. Gantt chart
- c. Milestone
- d. Dependency

Guidance: level 1

:: Packaging materials ::

_____ is a thin material produced by pressing together moist fibres of cellulose pulp derived from wood, rags or grasses, and drying them into flexible sheets. It is a versatile material with many uses, including writing, printing, packaging, cleaning, decorating, and a number of industrial and construction processes. _____ s are essential in legal or non-legal documentation.

Exam Probability: **Low**

15. *Answer choices:*

(see index for correct answer)

- a. Corrugated plastic
- b. Kraft paper
- c. Saran
- d. Paper

Guidance: level 1

:: Data management ::

_____ is an object-oriented program and library developed by CERN. It was originally designed for particle physics data analysis and contains several features specific to this field, but it is also used in other applications such as astronomy and data mining. The latest release is 6.16.00, as of 2018-11-14.

Exam Probability: **Low**

16. Answer choices:

(see index for correct answer)

- a. Data custodian
- b. Customer data management
- c. National Information Governance Board for Health and Social Care
- d. ROOT

Guidance: level 1

:: Asset ::

In financial accounting, an _____ is any resource owned by the business. Anything tangible or intangible that can be owned or controlled to produce value and that is held by a company to produce positive economic value is an _____. Simply stated, _____ s represent value of ownership that can be converted into cash. The balance sheet of a firm records the monetary value of the _____ s owned by that firm. It covers money and other valuables belonging to an individual or to a business.

Exam Probability: **High**

17. Answer choices:

(see index for correct answer)

- a. Fixed asset
- b. Current asset

Guidance: level 1

:: Management ::

_____ is a process by which entities review the quality of all factors involved in production. ISO 9000 defines _____ as "A part of quality management focused on fulfilling quality requirements".

Exam Probability: **Low**

18. *Answer choices:*

(see index for correct answer)

- a. Managerial economics
- b. Control
- c. Quality control
- d. Virtual customer environment

Guidance: level 1

:: Industrial processes ::

_____ is a technique involving the condensation of vapors and the return of this condensate to the system from which it originated. It is used in industrial and laboratory distillations. It is also used in chemistry to supply energy to reactions over a long period of time.

Exam Probability: **High**

19. *Answer choices:*

(see index for correct answer)

- a. Girdler sulfide process
- b. Reflux
- c. Air separation
- d. Kroll process

Guidance: level 1

:: Procurement ::

Purchasing is the formal process of buying goods and services. The _____ can vary from one organization to another, but there are some common key elements.

Exam Probability: **Low**

20. *Answer choices:*

(see index for correct answer)

- a. Purchasing process
- b. Request price quotation
- c. Commodity management
- d. Request for quotation

Guidance: level 1

:: Project management ::

Rolling-wave planning is the process of project planning in waves as the project proceeds and later details become clearer; similar to the techniques used in agile software development approaches like Scrum..

Exam Probability: **Low**

21. *Answer choices:*

(see index for correct answer)

- a. Rolling Wave planning
- b. Financial plan
- c. Project initiation document
- d. Time horizon

Guidance: level 1

:: Natural materials ::

_____ is a finely-grained natural rock or soil material that combines one or more _____ minerals with possible traces of quartz, metal oxides and organic matter. Geologic _____ deposits are mostly composed of phyllosilicate minerals containing variable amounts of water trapped in the mineral structure. _____ s are plastic due to particle size and geometry as well as water content, and become hard, brittle and non–plastic upon drying or firing. Depending on the soil's content in which it is found, _____ can appear in various colours from white to dull grey or brown to deep orange-red.

Exam Probability: **Medium**

22. *Answer choices:*

(see index for correct answer)

- a. Cob
- b. Dry stone
- c. Natural material
- d. Clay

Guidance: level 1

:: Project management ::

A _____ is a source or supply from which a benefit is produced and it has some utility. _____ s can broadly be classified upon their availability—they are classified into renewable and non-renewable _____ s. Examples of non renewable _____ s are coal, crude oil natural gas nuclear energy etc. Examples of renewable _____ s are air, water, wind, solar energy etc. They can also be classified as actual and potential on the basis of level of development and use, on the basis of origin they can be classified as biotic and abiotic, and on the basis of their distribution, as ubiquitous and localized. An item becomes a _____ with time and developing technology. Typically, _____ s are materials, energy, services, staff, knowledge, or other assets that are transformed to produce benefit and in the process may be consumed or made unavailable. Benefits of _____ utilization may include increased wealth, proper functioning of a system, or enhanced well-being. From a human perspective a natural _____ is anything obtained from the environment to satisfy human needs and wants. From a broader biological or ecological perspective a _____ satisfies the needs of a living organism.

Exam Probability: **Low**

23. *Answer choices:*

(see Index for correct answer)

- a. Resource
- b. Australian Institute of Project Management
- c. Case competition
- d. Project management office

Guidance: level 1

:: Unit operations ::

_____ is a discipline of thermal engineering that concerns the generation, use, conversion, and exchange of thermal energy between physical systems. _____ is classified into various mechanisms, such as thermal conduction, thermal convection, thermal radiation, and transfer of energy by phase changes. Engineers also consider the transfer of mass of differing chemical species, either cold or hot, to achieve _____. While these mechanisms have distinct characteristics, they often occur simultaneously in the same system.

Exam Probability: **Medium**

24. *Answer choices:*

(see index for correct answer)

- a. Unit operation
- b. Heat transfer
- c. Clearing factor
- d. Homogenization

Guidance: level 1

:: Costs ::

In microeconomic theory, the _____, or alternative cost, of making a particular choice is the value of the most valuable choice out of those that were not taken. In other words, opportunity that will require sacrifices.

Exam Probability: **High**

25. *Answer choices:*

(see index for correct answer)

- a. Opportunity cost
- b. Psychic cost
- c. Quality costs
- d. Customer Cost

Guidance: level 1

:: Marketing techniques ::

A _____ is an award to be given to a person, a group of people like a sports team, or organization to recognise and reward actions or achievements. Official _____ s often involve monetary rewards as well as the fame that comes with them. Some _____ s are also associated with extravagant awarding ceremonies, such as the Academy Awards.

Exam Probability: **Medium**

26. *Answer choices:*

(see index for correct answer)

- a. Real-time marketing
- b. Wait marketing
- c. unique selling point
- d. Prize

Guidance: level 1

:: Materials science ::

An _____ is a polymer with viscoelasticity and very weak intermolecular forces, and generally low Young's modulus and high failure strain compared with other materials. The term, a portmanteau of elastic polymer, is often used interchangeably with rubber, although the latter is preferred when referring to vulcanisates. Each of the monomers which link to form the polymer is usually a compound of several elements among carbon, hydrogen, oxygen and silicon. _____ s are amorphous polymers maintained above their glass transition temperature, so that considerable molecular reconformation, without breaking of covalent bonds, is feasible. At ambient temperatures, such rubbers are thus relatively soft and deformable. Their primary uses are for seals, adhesives and molded flexible parts. Application areas for different types of rubber are manifold and cover segments as diverse as tires, soles for shoes, and damping and insulating elements. The importance of these rubbers can be judged from the fact that global revenues are forecast to rise to US$56 billion in 2020.

Exam Probability: **Low**

27. *Answer choices:*

(see index for correct answer)

- a. Mohs scale of mineral hardness
- b. Quietstone
- c. Bauschinger effect
- d. Elastomer

Guidance: level 1

:: Management ::

In inventory management, _____ is the order quantity that minimizes the total holding costs and ordering costs. It is one of the oldest classical production scheduling models. The model was developed by Ford W. Harris in 1913, but R. H. Wilson, a consultant who applied it extensively, and K. Andler are given credit for their in-depth analysis.

Exam Probability: **Low**

28. *Answer choices:*

(see index for correct answer)

- a. Empowerment
- b. Downstream
- c. Energy management software
- d. Focused improvement

Guidance: level 1

:: Metal forming ::

_____ is a type of motion that combines rotation and translation of that object with respect to a surface, such that, if ideal conditions exist, the two are in contact with each other without sliding.

Exam Probability: **Low**

29. *Answer choices:*

(see index for correct answer)

- a. Rolling
- b. Tube drawing
- c. Planishing
- d. Goldbeating

Guidance: level 1

:: Commercial item transport and distribution ::

_____ in logistics and supply chain management is an organization's use of third-party businesses to outsource elements of its distribution, warehousing, and fulfillment services.

Exam Probability: **Medium**

30. *Answer choices:*

(see index for correct answer)

- a. Mid-stream operation
- b. Tank chassis
- c. Air cargo
- d. Voice-directed warehousing

Guidance: level 1

:: Project management ::

_____ is a marketing activity that does an aggregate plan for the production process, in advance of 6 to 18 months, to give an idea to management as to what quantity of materials and other resources are to be procured and when, so that the total cost of operations of the organization is kept to the minimum over that period.

Exam Probability: **Low**

31. *Answer choices:*

(see index for correct answer)

- a. PRINCE2
- b. Project blog
- c. Soft Costs
- d. Task

Guidance: level 1

:: Quality awards ::

The _____ recognizes U.S. organizations in the business, health care, education, and nonprofit sectors for performance excellence. The Baldrige Award is the only formal recognition of the performance excellence of both public and private U.S. organizations given by the President of the United States. It is administered by the Baldrige Performance Excellence Program, which is based at and managed by the National Institute of Standards and Technology, an agency of the U.S. Department of Commerce.

Exam Probability: **High**

32. *Answer choices:*

(see index for correct answer)

- a. Philippine Quality Award
- b. European Quality Award
- c. Canada Awards for Excellence
- d. Malcolm Baldrige National Quality Award

Guidance: level 1

:: ::

A _____ is a covering that is applied to the surface of an object, usually referred to as the substrate. The purpose of applying the _____ may be decorative, functional, or both. The _____ itself may be an all-over _____, completely covering the substrate, or it may only cover parts of the substrate. An example of all of these types of _____ is a product label on many drinks bottles- one side has an all-over functional _____ and the other side has one or more decorative _____s in an appropriate pattern to form the words and images.

Exam Probability: **Low**

33. *Answer choices:*

(see index for correct answer)

- a. imperative
- b. Coating
- c. deep-level diversity
- d. information systems assessment

Guidance: level 1

:: Management ::

Business _____ is a discipline in operations management in which people use various methods to discover, model, analyze, measure, improve, optimize, and automate business processes. BPM focuses on improving corporate performance by managing business processes. Any combination of methods used to manage a company's business processes is BPM. Processes can be structured and repeatable or unstructured and variable. Though not required, enabling technologies are often used with BPM.

Exam Probability: **Medium**

34. *Answer choices:*
(see index for correct answer)

- a. Process management
- b. Cross ownership
- c. Identity formation
- d. Personal offshoring

Guidance: level 1

:: Insulators ::

A _____ is a piece of soft cloth large enough either to cover or to enfold a great portion of the user's body, usually when sleeping or otherwise at rest, thereby trapping radiant bodily heat that otherwise would be lost through convection, and so keeping the body warm.

Exam Probability: **High**

35. *Answer choices:*

(see index for correct answer)

- a. Draught excluder
- b. Pipe insulation
- c. Blanket
- d. Fill power

Guidance: level 1

:: Information technology management ::

_____ is a collective term for all approaches to prepare, support and help individuals, teams, and organizations in making organizational change. The most common change drivers include: technological evolution, process reviews, crisis, and consumer habit changes; pressure from new business entrants, acquisitions, mergers, and organizational restructuring. It includes methods that redirect or redefine the use of resources, business process, budget allocations, or other modes of operation that significantly change a company or organization. Organizational _____ considers the full organization and what needs to change, while _____ may be used solely to refer to how people and teams are affected by such organizational transition. It deals with many different disciplines, from behavioral and social sciences to information technology and business solutions.

Exam Probability: **Low**

36. *Answer choices:*

(see index for correct answer)

- a. Wire data
- b. OpenACS
- c. Change management
- d. Storage virtualization

Guidance: level 1

:: Direct marketing ::

> _____ Inc. is an American privately owned multi-level marketing company. According to Direct Selling News, _____ was the sixth largest network marketing company in the world in 2018, with a wholesale volume of US$3.25 billion. _____ is based in Addison, Texas, outside Dallas. The company was founded by _____ Ash in 1963. Richard Rogers, _____'s son, is the chairman, and David Holl is president and was named CEO in 2006.

Exam Probability: **Low**

37. *Answer choices:*
(see index for correct answer)

- a. Peter Lemongello
- b. Mary Kay
- c. Stream Energy
- d. Drayton Bird

Guidance: level 1

:: Project management ::

_____ is a work methodology emphasizing the parallelisation of tasks, which is sometimes called simultaneous engineering or integrated product development using an integrated product team approach. It refers to an approach used in product development in which functions of design engineering, manufacturing engineering, and other functions are integrated to reduce the time required to bring a new product to market.

Exam Probability: **High**

38. *Answer choices:*

(see index for correct answer)

- a. Costab
- b. Theory Z
- c. Social project management
- d. Concurrent engineering

Guidance: level 1

:: Marketing ::

_____ or stock is the goods and materials that a business holds for the ultimate goal of resale.

Exam Probability: **Medium**

39. *Answer choices:*

(see index for correct answer)

- a. Customer lifetime value
- b. Marketing spending
- c. Customer reference program
- d. Inventory

Guidance: level 1

:: Lean manufacturing ::

_____ is a Japanese term that means "mistake-proofing" or "inadvertent error prevention". A _____ is any mechanism in any process that helps an equipment operator avoid mistakes . Its purpose is to eliminate product defects by preventing, correcting, or drawing attention to human errors as they occur. The concept was formalised, and the term adopted, by Shigeo Shingo as part of the Toyota Production System. It was originally described as baka-yoke, but as this means "fool-proofing" the name was changed to the milder _____ .

Exam Probability: **Medium**

40. *Answer choices:*

(see index for correct answer)

- a. Lean laboratory
- b. Lean product development

- c. Kanban board
- d. Poka-yoke

Guidance: level 1

:: Computer memory companies ::

> _____ Corporation is a Japanese multinational conglomerate headquartered in Tokyo, Japan. Its diversified products and services include information technology and communications equipment and systems, electronic components and materials, power systems, industrial and social infrastructure systems, consumer electronics, household appliances, medical equipment, office equipment, as well as lighting and logistics.

Exam Probability: **Medium**

41. *Answer choices:*
(see index for correct answer)

- a. Anobit
- b. Virage Logic
- c. Grandis
- d. G.Skill

Guidance: level 1

:: Goods ::

In most contexts, the concept of _____ denotes the conduct that should be preferred when posed with a choice between possible actions. _____ is generally considered to be the opposite of evil, and is of interest in the study of morality, ethics, religion and philosophy. The specific meaning and etymology of the term and its associated translations among ancient and contemporary languages show substantial variation in its inflection and meaning depending on circumstances of place, history, religious, or philosophical context.

Exam Probability: **Low**

42. *Answer choices:*

(see index for correct answer)

- a. Search good
- b. Superior good
- c. Club good
- d. Global commons

Guidance: level 1

:: Production and manufacturing ::

_____ was a management-led program to eliminate defects in industrial production that enjoyed brief popularity in American industry from 1964 to the early 1970s. Quality expert Philip Crosby later incorporated it into his "Absolutes of Quality Management" and it enjoyed a renaissance in the American automobile industry—as a performance goal more than as a program—in the 1990s. Although applicable to any type of enterprise, it has been primarily adopted within supply chains wherever large volumes of components are being purchased .

Exam Probability: **Low**

43. *Answer choices:*

(see index for correct answer)

- a. Pegging report
- b. Original design manufacturer
- c. Direct numerical control
- d. LPA512

Guidance: level 1

:: Metrics ::

_____ is a computer model developed by the University of Idaho, that uses Landsat satellite data to compute and map evapotranspiration. _____ calculates ET as a residual of the surface energy balance, where ET is estimated by keeping account of total net short wave and long wave radiation at the vegetation or soil surface, the amount of heat conducted into soil, and the amount of heat convected into the air above the surface. The difference in these three terms represents the amount of energy absorbed during the conversion of liquid water to vapor, which is ET. _____ expresses near-surface temperature gradients used in heat convection as indexed functions of radio _____ surface temperature, thereby eliminating the need for absolutely accurate surface temperature and the need for air-temperature measurements.

Exam Probability: **Medium**

44. *Answer choices:*

(see index for correct answer)

- a. Parts-per notation
- b. Neighbourhood unit
- c. Cleanroom suitability
- d. METRIC

Guidance: level 1

:: Product development ::

In business and engineering, _____ covers the complete process of bringing a new product to market. A central aspect of NPD is product design, along with various business considerations. _____ is described broadly as the transformation of a market opportunity into a product available for sale. The product can be tangible or intangible , though sometimes services and other processes are distinguished from "products." NPD requires an understanding of customer needs and wants, the competitive environment, and the nature of the market.Cost, time and quality are the main variables that drive customer needs. Aiming at these three variables, innovative companies develop continuous practices and strategies to better satisfy customer requirements and to increase their own market share by a regular development of new products. There are many uncertainties and challenges which companies must face throughout the process. The use of best practices and the elimination of barriers to communication are the main concerns for the management of the NPD .

Exam Probability: **Low**

45. *Answer choices:*

(see index for correct answer)

- a. DFMA
- b. New product development
- c. Material selection
- d. Line extension

Guidance: level 1

:: Product management ::

_____ s, also known as Shewhart charts or process-behavior charts, are a statistical process control tool used to determine if a manufacturing or business process is in a state of control.

Exam Probability: **High**

46. *Answer choices:*

(see index for correct answer)

- a. Visual brand language
- b. Trademark look
- c. Obsolescence
- d. Trademark distinctiveness

Guidance: level 1

:: Industrial organization ::

In economics, specifically general equilibrium theory, a perfect market is defined by several idealizing conditions, collectively called _____ . In theoretical models where conditions of _____ hold, it has been theoretically demonstrated that a market will reach an equilibrium in which the quantity supplied for every product or service, including labor, equals the quantity demanded at the current price. This equilibrium would be a Pareto optimum.

Exam Probability: **Medium**

47. Answer choices:

(see index for correct answer)

- a. Williamson trade-off model
- b. Industrial organization
- c. Tapered integration
- d. Perfect competition

Guidance: level 1

:: ::

In production, research, retail, and accounting, a _____ is the value of money that has been used up to produce something or deliver a service, and hence is not available for use anymore. In business, the _____ may be one of acquisition, in which case the amount of money expended to acquire it is counted as _____ . In this case, money is the input that is gone in order to acquire the thing. This acquisition _____ may be the sum of the _____ of production as incurred by the original producer, and further _____ s of transaction as incurred by the acquirer over and above the price paid to the producer. Usually, the price also includes a mark-up for profit over the _____ of production.

Exam Probability: **Low**

48. Answer choices:

(see index for correct answer)

- a. hierarchical

- b. levels of analysis
- c. cultural
- d. Cost

Guidance: level 1

:: Metalworking ::

A _____ is a round object with various uses. It is used in _____ games, where the play of the game follows the state of the _____ as it is hit, kicked or thrown by players. _____ s can also be used for simpler activities, such as catch or juggling. _____ s made from hard-wearing materials are used in engineering applications to provide very low friction bearings, known as _____ bearings. Black-powder weapons use stone and metal _____ s as projectiles.

Exam Probability: **Low**

49. *Answer choices:*

(see index for correct answer)

- a. Hot pressing
- b. Ball
- c. Cupola furnace
- d. Flame cleaning

Guidance: level 1

:: Production and manufacturing ::

_____ is the production under license of technology developed elsewhere. It is an especially prominent commercial practice in developing nations, which often approach _____ as a starting point for indigenous industrial development.

Exam Probability: **Medium**

50. *Answer choices:*
(see index for correct answer)

- a. Engineering validation test
- b. Process control
- c. Licensed production
- d. Production part approval process

Guidance: level 1

:: Outsourcing ::

_____ is an institutional procurement process that continuously improves and re-evaluates the purchasing activities of a company. In the services industry, _____ refers to a service solution, sometimes called a strategic partnership, which is specifically customized to meet the client's individual needs. In a production environment, it is often considered one component of supply chain management. Modern supply chain management professionals have placed emphasis on defining the distinct differences between _____ and procurement. Procurement operations support tactical day-to-day transactions such as issuing Purchase Orders to suppliers, whereas _____ represents to strategic planning, supplier development, contract negotiation, supply chain infrastructure, and outsourcing models.

Exam Probability: **High**

51. *Answer choices:*

(see index for correct answer)

- a. Engineering process outsourcing
- b. Strategic sourcing
- c. Minacs
- d. Media Process Outsourcing

Guidance: level 1

:: Procurement ::

A _____ is a standard business process whose purpose is to invite suppliers into a bidding process to bid on specific products or services. RfQ generally means the same thing as Call for bids and Invitation for bid.

Exam Probability: **Low**

52. *Answer choices:*

(see index for correct answer)

- a. Supplier diversity
- b. Full operational capability
- c. Request price quotation
- d. Request for quotation

Guidance: level 1

:: Retailing ::

_____ is the process of selling consumer goods or services to customers through multiple channels of distribution to earn a profit. _____ers satisfy demand identified through a supply chain. The term "_____er" is typically applied where a service provider fills the small orders of a large number of individuals, who are end-users, rather than large orders of a small number of wholesale, corporate or government clientele. Shopping generally refers to the act of buying products. Sometimes this is done to obtain final goods, including necessities such as food and clothing; sometimes it takes place as a recreational activity. Recreational shopping often involves window shopping and browsing: it does not always result in a purchase.

Exam Probability: **Low**

53. *Answer choices:*

(see index for correct answer)

- a. Till roll
- b. Retail
- c. Shop in a box
- d. Catalog merchant

Guidance: level 1

:: Chemical processes ::

_____ is the understanding and application of the fundamental principles and laws of nature that allow us to transform raw material and energy into products that are useful to society, at an industrial level. By taking advantage of the driving forces of nature such as pressure, temperature and concentration gradients, as well as the law of conservation of mass, process engineers can develop methods to synthesize and purify large quantities of desired chemical products. _____ focuses on the design, operation, control, optimization and intensification of chemical, physical, and biological processes. _____ encompasses a vast range of industries, such as agriculture, automotive, biotechnical, chemical, food, material development, mining, nuclear, petrochemical, pharmaceutical, and software development. The application of systematic computer-based methods to _____ is "process systems engineering".

Exam Probability: **Low**

54. *Answer choices:*

(see index for correct answer)

- a. Densitation
- b. Catalytic combustion

- c. Process engineering
- d. Electropolishing

Guidance: level 1

:: Production and manufacturing ::

> _____ consists of organization-wide efforts to "install and make permanent climate where employees continuously improve their ability to provide on demand products and services that customers will find of particular value." "Total" emphasizes that departments in addition to production are obligated to improve their operations; "management" emphasizes that executives are obligated to actively manage quality through funding, training, staffing, and goal setting. While there is no widely agreed-upon approach, TQM efforts typically draw heavily on the previously developed tools and techniques of quality control. TQM enjoyed widespread attention during the late 1980s and early 1990s before being overshadowed by ISO 9000, Lean manufacturing, and Six Sigma.

Exam Probability: **High**

55. *Answer choices:*
(see index for correct answer)

- a. International MTM Directorate
- b. Total quality management
- c. Craft production
- d. Virtual manufacturing network

Guidance: level 1

:: Process management ::

A _____ is a diagram commonly used in chemical and process engineering to indicate the general flow of plant processes and equipment. The PFD displays the relationship between major equipment of a plant facility and does not show minor details such as piping details and designations. Another commonly used term for a PFD is a flowsheet.

Exam Probability: **Low**

56. *Answer choices:*

(see index for correct answer)

- a. business process re-engineering
- b. Process flow diagram
- c. Process modeling
- d. Process capability index

Guidance: level 1

:: Commerce ::

A _____ is an employee within a company, business or other organization who is responsible at some level for buying or approving the acquisition of goods and services needed by the company. Responsible for buying the best quality products, goods and services for their company at the most competitive prices, _____ s work in a wide range of sectors for many different organizations. The position responsibilities may be the same as that of a buyer or purchasing agent, or may include wider supervisory or managerial responsibilities. A _____ may oversee the acquisition of materials needed for production, general supplies for offices and facilities, equipment, or construction contracts. A _____ often supervises purchasing agents and buyers, but in small companies the _____ may also be the purchasing agent or buyer. The _____ position may also carry the title "Procurement Manager" or in the public sector, "Procurement Officer". He or she can come from both an Engineering or Economics background.

Exam Probability: **High**

57. *Answer choices:*

(see index for correct answer)

- a. Hauls
- b. Purchasing manager
- c. Third-party source
- d. Uttarapatha

Guidance: level 1

:: Alchemical processes ::

In chemistry, a _____ is a special type of homogeneous mixture composed of two or more substances. In such a mixture, a solute is a substance dissolved in another substance, known as a solvent. The mixing process of a _____ happens at a scale where the effects of chemical polarity are involved, resulting in interactions that are specific to solvation. The _____ assumes the phase of the solvent when the solvent is the larger fraction of the mixture, as is commonly the case. The concentration of a solute in a _____ is the mass of that solute expressed as a percentage of the mass of the whole _____ . The term aqueous _____ is when one of the solvents is water.

Exam Probability: **Medium**

58. *Answer choices:*

(see index for correct answer)

- a. Ceration
- b. Digestion
- c. Solution
- d. Fermentation

Guidance: level 1

:: Quality management ::

_____ ensures that an organization, product or service is consistent. It has four main components: quality planning, quality assurance, quality control and quality improvement. _____ is focused not only on product and service quality, but also on the means to achieve it. _____, therefore, uses quality assurance and control of processes as well as products to achieve more consistent quality. What a customer wants and is willing to pay for it determines quality. It is written or unwritten commitment to a known or unknown consumer in the market. Thus, quality can be defined as fitness for intended use or, in other words, how well the product performs its intended function

Exam Probability: **High**

59. *Answer choices:*

(see index for correct answer)

- a. Good Clinical Laboratory Practice
- b. Bureau Veritas
- c. Quality management
- d. ISO 9000

Guidance: level 1

Commerce

Commerce relates to "the exchange of goods and services, especially on a large scale." It includes legal, economic, political, social, cultural and technological systems that operate in any country or internationally.

_____ is the collection of techniques, skills, methods, and processes used in the production of goods or services or in the accomplishment of objectives, such as scientific investigation. _____ can be the knowledge of techniques, processes, and the like, or it can be embedded in machines to allow for operation without detailed knowledge of their workings. Systems applying _____ by taking an input, changing it according to the system's use, and then producing an outcome are referred to as _____ systems or technological systems.

Exam Probability: **Medium**

1. *Answer choices:*

(see index for correct answer)

- a. surface-level diversity
- b. corporate values
- c. Technology
- d. interpersonal communication

Guidance: level 1

:: ::

Walter Elias Disney was an American entrepreneur, animator, voice actor and film producer. A pioneer of the American animation industry, he introduced several developments in the production of cartoons. As a film producer, Disney holds the record for most Academy Awards earned by an individual, having won 22 Oscars from 59 nominations. He was presented with two Golden Globe Special Achievement Awards and an Emmy Award, among other honors. Several of his films are included in the National Film Registry by the Library of Congress.

Exam Probability: **Low**

2. *Answer choices:*

(see index for correct answer)

- a. information systems assessment
- b. Walt Disney
- c. Character
- d. similarity-attraction theory

Guidance: level 1

:: Workplace ::

_____ is asystematic determination of a subject's merit, worth and significance, using criteria governed by a set of standards. It can assist an organization, program, design, project or any other intervention or initiative to assess any aim, realisable concept/proposal, or any alternative, to help in decision-making; or to ascertain the degree of achievement or value in regard to the aim and objectives and results of any such action that has been completed. The primary purpose of _____ , in addition to gaining insight into prior or existing initiatives, is to enable reflection and assist in the identification of future change.

Exam Probability: **Medium**

3. *Answer choices:*

(see index for correct answer)

- a. Workplace conflict
- b. Occupational stress
- c. Queen bee syndrome
- d. Workplace health surveillance

Guidance: level 1

:: International trade ::

An _____ is a good brought into a jurisdiction, especially across a national border, from an external source. The party bringing in the good is called an _____ er. An _____ in the receiving country is an export from the sending country. _____ ation and exportation are the defining financial transactions of international trade.

Exam Probability: **High**

4. *Answer choices:*

(see index for correct answer)

- a. Cross-border cooperation
- b. Trade and Investment Framework Agreement
- c. Reciprocity
- d. Import

Guidance: level 1

:: Industrial automation ::

_____ is the technology by which a process or procedure is performed with minimal human assistance. _____ or automatic control is the use of various control systems for operating equipment such as machinery, processes in factories, boilers and heat treating ovens, switching on telephone networks, steering and stabilization of ships, aircraft and other applications and vehicles with minimal or reduced human intervention.

Exam Probability: **Medium**

5. *Answer choices:*

(see index for correct answer)

- a. DirectLOGIC
- b. Advanced Plant Management System

- c. CODESYS
- d. Automation

Guidance: level 1

:: ::

The _____ is a U.S. business-focused, English-language international daily newspaper based in New York City. The Journal, along with its Asian and European editions, is published six days a week by Dow Jones & Company, a division of News Corp. The newspaper is published in the broadsheet format and online. The Journal has been printed continuously since its inception on July 8, 1889, by Charles Dow, Edward Jones, and Charles Bergstresser.

Exam Probability: **High**

6. *Answer choices:*

(see index for correct answer)

- a. interpersonal communication
- b. Wall Street Journal
- c. similarity-attraction theory
- d. surface-level diversity

Guidance: level 1

:: Insolvency ::

_____ is a legal process through which people or other entities who cannot repay debts to creditors may seek relief from some or all of their debts. In most jurisdictions, _____ is imposed by a court order, often initiated by the debtor.

Exam Probability: **Low**

7. *Answer choices:*

(see index for correct answer)

- a. Insolvency law of Russia
- b. George Samuel Ford
- c. Bankruptcy
- d. Preferential creditor

Guidance: level 1

:: Warrants issued in Hong Kong Stock Exchange ::

_____ is a chemical element with symbol Ag and atomic number 47. A soft, white, lustrous transition metal, it exhibits the highest electrical conductivity, thermal conductivity, and reflectivity of any metal. The metal is found in the Earth's crust in the pure, free elemental form, as an alloy with gold and other metals, and in minerals such as argentite and chlorargyrite. Most _____ is produced as a byproduct of copper, gold, lead, and zinc refining.

Exam Probability: **Medium**

8. *Answer choices:*

(see index for correct answer)

- a. Taiwan Capitalization Weighted Stock Index
- b. BOC Hong Kong
- c. Silver
- d. Ping An Insurance

Guidance: level 1

:: Credit cards ::

A _____ is a payment card issued to users to enable the cardholder to pay a merchant for goods and services based on the cardholder's promise to the card issuer to pay them for the amounts plus the other agreed charges. The card issuer creates a revolving account and grants a line of credit to the cardholder, from which the cardholder can borrow money for payment to a merchant or as a cash advance.

Exam Probability: **Low**

9. *Answer choices:*

(see index for correct answer)

- a. Credit card
- b. CardLab
- c. Universal Air Travel Plan
- d. Payments as a service

Guidance: level 1

:: E-commerce ::

A _____ is a hosted service offering that acts as an intermediary between business partners sharing standards based or proprietary data via shared business processes. The offered service is referred to as " _____ services".

Exam Probability: **Medium**

10. *Answer choices:*

(see index for correct answer)

- a. Authorize.Net
- b. Segundamano
- c. Paid content
- d. Value-added network

Guidance: level 1

:: Investment ::

In finance, the benefit from an _____ is called a return. The return may consist of a gain realised from the sale of property or an _____, unrealised capital appreciation, or _____ income such as dividends, interest, rental income etc., or a combination of capital gain and income. The return may also include currency gains or losses due to changes in foreign currency exchange rates.

Exam Probability: **Medium**

11. *Answer choices:*

(see index for correct answer)

- a. Asia Frontier Capital Ltd.
- b. Insurance bond
- c. Laddering
- d. Investment

Guidance: level 1

:: Export and import control ::

"_____" means the Government Service which is responsible for the administration of _____ law and the collection of duties and taxes and which also has the responsibility for the application of other laws and regulations relating to the importation, exportation, movement or storage of goods.

Exam Probability: **Low**

12. *Answer choices:*

(see index for correct answer)

- a. Export parity price
- b. Customs
- c. Plant Protection and Quarantine
- d. ATA Carnet

Guidance: level 1

:: Meetings ::

A _____ is a body of one or more persons that is subordinate to a deliberative assembly. Usually, the assembly sends matters into a _____ as a way to explore them more fully than would be possible if the assembly itself were considering them. _____ s may have different functions and their type of work differ depending on the type of the organization and its needs.

Exam Probability: **Medium**

13. *Answer choices:*

(see index for correct answer)

- a. Minutes
- b. Annual Georgia European Union Summit
- c. Moment of silence
- d. Committee

Guidance: level 1

:: Confidence tricks ::

> _____ is the fraudulent attempt to obtain sensitive information such as usernames, passwords and credit card details by disguising oneself as a trustworthy entity in an electronic communication. Typically carried out by email spoofing or instant messaging, it often directs users to enter personal information at a fake website which matches the look and feel of the legitimate site.

Exam Probability: **High**

14. *Answer choices:*

(see index for correct answer)

- a. Salting
- b. The switch
- c. Phishing
- d. Private investment capital subscription

Guidance: level 1

:: Costs ::

In economics, _____ is the total economic cost of production and is made up of variable cost, which varies according to the quantity of a good produced and includes inputs such as labour and raw materials, plus fixed cost, which is independent of the quantity of a good produced and includes inputs that cannot be varied in the short term: fixed costs such as buildings and machinery, including sunk costs if any. Since cost is measured per unit of time, it is a flow variable.

Exam Probability: **High**

15. *Answer choices:*

(see index for correct answer)

- a. Total cost
- b. Economic cost
- c. Road Logistics Costing in South Africa
- d. Cost competitiveness of fuel sources

Guidance: level 1

:: ::

_____ is a type of government support for the citizens of that society. _____ may be provided to people of any income level, as with social security, but it is usually intended to ensure that the poor can meet their basic human needs such as food and shelter. _____ attempts to provide poor people with a minimal level of well-being, usually either a free- or a subsidized-supply of certain goods and social services, such as healthcare, education, and vocational training.

Exam Probability: **Medium**

16. *Answer choices:*

(see index for correct answer)

- a. similarity-attraction theory
- b. Welfare
- c. information systems assessment
- d. co-culture

Guidance: level 1

:: Project management ::

In political science, an _____ is a means by which a petition signed by a certain minimum number of registered voters can force a government to choose to either enact a law or hold a public vote in parliament in what is called indirect _____ , or under direct _____ , the proposition is immediately put to a plebiscite or referendum, in what is called a Popular initiated Referendum or citizen-initiated referendum).

Exam Probability: **Medium**

17. *Answer choices:*

(see index for correct answer)

- a. Basis of estimate
- b. Graphical path method

- c. Initiative
- d. PM Declaration of Interdependence

Guidance: level 1

:: Management ::

> In business, a _____ is the attribute that allows an organization to outperform its competitors. A _____ may include access to natural resources, such as high-grade ores or a low-cost power source, highly skilled labor, geographic location, high entry barriers, and access to new technology.

Exam Probability: **Low**

18. *Answer choices:*

(see index for correct answer)

- a. Product breakdown structure
- b. Logistics support analysis
- c. Wireless informatics
- d. Competitive advantage

Guidance: level 1

:: ::

Competition arises whenever at least two parties strive for a goal which cannot be shared: where one's gain is the other's loss.

Exam Probability: **High**

19. *Answer choices:*

(see index for correct answer)

- a. information systems assessment
- b. interpersonal communication
- c. Competitor
- d. Character

Guidance: level 1

:: ::

_____ is the amount of time someone works beyond normal working hours. The term is also used for the pay received for this time. Normal hours may be determined in several ways.

Exam Probability: **High**

20. *Answer choices:*

(see index for correct answer)

- a. levels of analysis
- b. process perspective
- c. Overtime
- d. functional perspective

Guidance: level 1

:: ::

_____ refers to the overall process of attracting, shortlisting, selecting and appointing suitable candidates for jobs within an organization. _____ can also refer to processes involved in choosing individuals for unpaid roles. Managers, human resource generalists and _____ specialists may be tasked with carrying out _____, but in some cases public-sector employment agencies, commercial _____ agencies, or specialist search consultancies are used to undertake parts of the process. Internet-based technologies which support all aspects of _____ have become widespread.

Exam Probability: **Low**

21. *Answer choices:*

(see index for correct answer)

- a. process perspective
- b. Character
- c. hierarchical
- d. interpersonal communication

Guidance: level 1

:: ::

In financial markets, a share is a unit used as mutual funds, limited partnerships, and real estate investment trusts. The owner of _____ in the corporation/company is a shareholder of the corporation. A share is an indivisible unit of capital, expressing the ownership relationship between the company and the shareholder. The denominated value of a share is its face value, and the total of the face value of issued _____ represent the capital of a company, which may not reflect the market value of those _____ .

Exam Probability: **Low**

22. *Answer choices:*
(see index for correct answer)

- a. surface-level diversity
- b. hierarchical perspective
- c. process perspective
- d. Shares

Guidance: level 1

:: ::

Business Model Canvas is a strategic management and lean startup template for developing new or documenting existing business models. It is a visual chart with elements describing a firm's or product's value proposition, infrastructure, customers, and finances. It assists firms in aligning their activities by illustrating potential trade-offs.

Exam Probability: **Medium**

23. *Answer choices:*

(see index for correct answer)

- a. Cost structure
- b. personal values
- c. hierarchical
- d. process perspective

Guidance: level 1

:: E-commerce ::

IBM _____ also known as WCS is a software platform framework for e-commerce, including marketing, sales, customer and order processing functionality in a tailorable, integrated package. It is a single, unified platform which offers the ability to do business directly with consumers, with businesses, indirectly through channel partners, or all of these simultaneously. _____ is a customizable, scalable and high availability solution built on the Java - Java EE platform using open standards, such as XML, and Web services.

Exam Probability: **Medium**

24. *Answer choices:*

(see index for correct answer)

- a. Optimize Capital Markets
- b. WebSphere Commerce
- c. Eagle Cash
- d. Andy Dunn

Guidance: level 1

:: Payment systems ::

_____ s are part of a payment system issued by financial institutions, such as a bank, to a customer that enables its owner to access the funds in the customer's designated bank accounts, or through a credit account and make payments by electronic funds transfer and access automated teller machines. Such cards are known by a variety of names including bank cards, ATM cards, MAC , client cards, key cards or cash cards.

Exam Probability: **Medium**

25. *Answer choices:*

(see index for correct answer)

- a. ACI Worldwide
- b. Visa Buxx

- c. TSYS
- d. Payment card

Guidance: level 1

:: Human resource management ::

> An organizational chart is a diagram that shows the structure of an organization and the relationships and relative ranks of its parts and positions/jobs. The term is also used for similar diagrams, for example ones showing the different elements of a field of knowledge or a group of languages.

Exam Probability: **Medium**

26. *Answer choices:*
(see index for correct answer)

- a. Organization chart
- b. Experticity
- c. Mentorship
- d. Continuing professional development

Guidance: level 1

:: Debt ::

_____ is the trust which allows one party to provide money or resources to another party wherein the second party does not reimburse the first party immediately, but promises either to repay or return those resources at a later date. In other words, _____ is a method of making reciprocity formal, legally enforceable, and extensible to a large group of unrelated people.

Exam Probability: **High**

27. *Answer choices:*

(see index for correct answer)

- a. Interest
- b. Credit
- c. Medical debt
- d. Money disorders

Guidance: level 1

:: Evaluation ::

_____ is a way of preventing mistakes and defects in manufactured products and avoiding problems when delivering products or services to customers; which ISO 9000 defines as "part of quality management focused on providing confidence that quality requirements will be fulfilled". This defect prevention in _____ differs subtly from defect detection and rejection in quality control and has been referred to as a shift left since it focuses on quality earlier in the process.

Exam Probability: **Medium**

28. *Answer choices:*

(see index for correct answer)

- a. Immanent evaluation
- b. Cryptographic Module Testing Laboratory
- c. Quality assurance
- d. Server Efficiency Rating Tool

Guidance: level 1

:: ::

_____ , also referred to as orthostasis, is a human position in which the body is held in an upright position and supported only by the feet.

Exam Probability: **Low**

29. *Answer choices:*

(see index for correct answer)

- a. surface-level diversity
- b. cultural
- c. hierarchical perspective
- d. similarity-attraction theory

Guidance: level 1

:: Marketing by medium ::

_____ , also called online marketing or Internet advertising or web advertising, is a form of marketing and advertising which uses the Internet to deliver promotional marketing messages to consumers. Many consumers find _____ disruptive and have increasingly turned to ad blocking for a variety of reasons. When software is used to do the purchasing, it is known as programmatic advertising.

Exam Probability: **Low**

30. *Answer choices:*
(see index for correct answer)

- a. Digital marketing
- b. Social intelligence architect
- c. New media marketing
- d. Growth hacking

Guidance: level 1

:: ::

Competition law is a law that promotes or seeks to maintain market competition by regulating anti-competitive conduct by companies. Competition law is implemented through public and private enforcement. Competition law is known as "_____ law" in the United States for historical reasons, and as "anti-monopoly law" in China and Russia. In previous years it has been known as trade practices law in the United Kingdom and Australia. In the European Union, it is referred to as both _____ and competition law.

Exam Probability: **High**

31. *Answer choices:*

(see index for correct answer)

- a. Antitrust
- b. levels of analysis
- c. open system
- d. hierarchical

Guidance: level 1

:: Management ::

_____ is the process of thinking about the activities required to achieve a desired goal. It is the first and foremost activity to achieve desired results. It involves the creation and maintenance of a plan, such as psychological aspects that require conceptual skills. There are even a couple of tests to measure someone's capability of _____ well. As such, _____ is a fundamental property of intelligent behavior. An important further meaning, often just called "_____" is the legal context of permitted building developments.

Exam Probability: **High**

32. *Answer choices:*

(see index for correct answer)

- a. Planning
- b. Management fad
- c. Topple rate
- d. Automated decision support

Guidance: level 1

:: Cryptography ::

In cryptography, _____ is the process of encoding a message or information in such a way that only authorized parties can access it and those who are not authorized cannot. _____ does not itself prevent interference, but denies the intelligible content to a would-be interceptor. In an _____ scheme, the intended information or message, referred to as plaintext, is encrypted using an _____ algorithm – a cipher – generating ciphertext that can be read only if decrypted. For technical reasons, an _____ scheme usually uses a pseudo-random _____ key generated by an algorithm. It is in principle possible to decrypt the message without possessing the key, but, for a well-designed _____ scheme, considerable computational resources and skills are required. An authorized recipient can easily decrypt the message with the key provided by the originator to recipients but not to unauthorized users.

Exam Probability: **Medium**

33. *Answer choices:*

(see index for correct answer)

- a. backdoor
- b. Electronic Signature
- c. Anonymous matching
- d. plaintext

Guidance: level 1

:: Minimum wage ::

A _____ is the lowest remuneration that employers can legally pay their workers—the price floor below which workers may not sell their labor. Most countries had introduced _____ legislation by the end of the 20th century.

Exam Probability: **Medium**

34. *Answer choices:*

(see index for correct answer)

- a. Working poor
- b. National Anti-Sweating League
- c. Minimum wage in Taiwan
- d. Minimum Wage Fairness Act

Guidance: level 1

:: Decision theory ::

Within economics the concept of _____ is used to model worth or value, but its usage has evolved significantly over time. The term was introduced initially as a measure of pleasure or satisfaction within the theory of utilitarianism by moral philosophers such as Jeremy Bentham and John Stuart Mill. But the term has been adapted and reapplied within neoclassical economics, which dominates modern economic theory, as a _____ function that represents a consumer's preference ordering over a choice set. As such, it is devoid of its original interpretation as a measurement of the pleasure or satisfaction obtained by the consumer from that choice.

Exam Probability: **Low**

35. *Answer choices:*

(see index for correct answer)

- a. Nominal group technique
- b. Belief decision matrix
- c. Utility
- d. Decision-matrix method

Guidance: level 1

:: E-commerce ::

A _____ is a financial transaction involving a very small sum of money and usually one that occurs online. A number of _____ systems were proposed and developed in the mid-to-late 1990s, all of which were ultimately unsuccessful. A second generation of _____ systems emerged in the 2010s.

Exam Probability: **Low**

36. *Answer choices:*

(see index for correct answer)

- a. XIPWIRE
- b. Micropayment
- c. IDEAL

- d. AS 2805

Guidance: level 1

:: Generally Accepted Accounting Principles ::

In accounting, _____ is the income that a business have from its normal business activities, usually from the sale of goods and services to customers. _____ is also referred to as sales or turnover. Some companies receive _____ from interest, royalties, or other fees. _____ may refer to business income in general, or it may refer to the amount, in a monetary unit, earned during a period of time, as in "Last year, Company X had _____ of $42 million". Profits or net income generally imply total _____ minus total expenses in a given period. In accounting, in the balance statement it is a subsection of the Equity section and _____ increases equity, it is often referred to as the "top line" due to its position on the income statement at the very top. This is to be contrasted with the "bottom line" which denotes net income.

Exam Probability: **Medium**

37. *Answer choices:*

(see index for correct answer)

- a. Management accounting principles
- b. Deferred income
- c. Consolidation
- d. Revenue

Guidance: level 1

:: Business law ::

A _____ is a contractual arrangement calling for the lessee to pay the lessor for use of an asset. Property, buildings and vehicles are common assets that are _____ d. Industrial or business equipment is also _____ d.

Exam Probability: **Low**

38. *Answer choices:*

(see index for correct answer)

- a. Chattel mortgage
- b. Participation
- c. Facilitating payment
- d. Lease

Guidance: level 1

:: Income ::

_____ is a ratio between the net profit and cost of investment resulting from an investment of some resources. A high ROI means the investment's gains favorably to its cost. As a performance measure, ROI is used to evaluate the efficiency of an investment or to compare the efficiencies of several different investments. In purely economic terms, it is one way of relating profits to capital invested. _____ is a performance measure used by businesses to identify the efficiency of an investment or number of different investments.

Exam Probability: **Medium**

39. *Answer choices:*

(see index for correct answer)

- a. Meetup fee
- b. Family income
- c. Return on investment
- d. Passive income

Guidance: level 1

:: Management ::

A _____ is an idea of the future or desired result that a person or a group of people envisions, plans and commits to achieve. People endeavor to reach _____ s within a finite time by setting deadlines.

Exam Probability: **Low**

40. *Answer choices:*

(see index for correct answer)

- a. Goal
- b. Enterprise planning system
- c. Perth leadership outcome model
- d. Topple rate

Guidance: level 1

:: ::

A trade fair is an exhibition organized so that companies in a specific industry can showcase and demonstrate their latest products and services, meet with industry partners and customers, study activities of rivals, and examine recent market trends and opportunities. In contrast to consumer fairs, only some trade fairs are open to the public, while others can only be attended by company representatives and members of the press, therefore _____ s are classified as either "public" or "trade only". A few fairs are hybrids of the two; one example is the Frankfurt Book Fair, which is trade only for its first three days and open to the general public on its final two days. They are held on a continuing basis in virtually all markets and normally attract companies from around the globe. For example, in the U.S., there are currently over 10,000 _____ s held every year, and several online directories have been established to help organizers, attendees, and marketers identify appropriate events.

Exam Probability: **Medium**

41. *Answer choices:*

(see index for correct answer)

- a. corporate values
- b. interpersonal communication
- c. process perspective
- d. Trade show

Guidance: level 1

:: Stock market ::

The _____ of a corporation is all of the shares into which ownership of the corporation is divided. In American English, the shares are commonly known as "_____ s". A single share of the _____ represents fractional ownership of the corporation in proportion to the total number of shares. This typically entitles the _____ holder to that fraction of the company's earnings, proceeds from liquidation of assets, or voting power, often dividing these up in proportion to the amount of money each _____ holder has invested. Not all _____ is necessarily equal, as certain classes of _____ may be issued for example without voting rights, with enhanced voting rights, or with a certain priority to receive profits or liquidation proceeds before or after other classes of shareholders.

Exam Probability: **High**

42. *Answer choices:*

(see index for correct answer)

- a. Stock

- b. Reverse stock split
- c. General Standard
- d. Follow-on offering

Guidance: level 1

:: Marketing ::

A _____ is an overall experience of a customer that distinguishes an organization or product from its rivals in the eyes of the customer. _____ s are used in business, marketing, and advertising. Name _____ s are sometimes distinguished from generic or store _____ s.

Exam Probability: **Low**

43. *Answer choices:*

(see index for correct answer)

- a. Price point
- b. Nia effect
- c. Contact centre
- d. Brand

Guidance: level 1

:: Auctioneering ::

A _____ is one of several similar kinds of auctions. Most commonly, it means an auction in which the auctioneer begins with a high asking price, and lowers it until some participant accepts the price, or it reaches a predetermined reserve price. This has also been called a clock auction or open-outcry descending-price auction. This type of auction is good for auctioning goods quickly, since a sale never requires more than one bid. Strategically, it's similar to a first-price sealed-bid auction.

Exam Probability: **Medium**

44. *Answer choices:*

(see index for correct answer)

- a. Proxy bid
- b. Dutch auction
- c. Vehicle impoundment
- d. World Livestock Auctioneer Championship

Guidance: level 1

:: Dot-com bubble ::

_____, Inc., is a web search engine and web portal established in 1994, spun out of Carnegie Mellon University. _____ also encompasses a network of email, webhosting, social networking, and entertainment websites. The company is based in Waltham, Massachusetts, and is currently a subsidiary of Kakao.

Exam Probability: **High**

45. *Answer choices:*

(see index for correct answer)

- a. Inktomi
- b. Dot-com company
- c. Fucked Company
- d. Lycos

Guidance: level 1

:: Public relations ::

_____ is the public visibility or awareness for any product, service or company. It may also refer to the movement of information from its source to the general public, often but not always via the media. The subjects of _____ include people, goods and services, organizations, and works of art or entertainment.

Exam Probability: **Low**

46. *Answer choices:*

(see index for correct answer)

- a. Publicity
- b. Zakazukha

- c. Hearts and minds
- d. Litigation public relations

Guidance: level 1

:: ::

The _____ of 1990 is a civil rights law that prohibits discrimination based on disability. It affords similar protections against discrimination to Americans with disabilities as the Civil Rights Act of 1964, which made discrimination based on race, religion, sex, national origin, and other characteristics illegal. In addition, unlike the Civil Rights Act, the ADA also requires covered employers to provide reasonable accommodations to employees with disabilities, and imposes accessibility requirements on public accommodations.

Exam Probability: **Low**

47. *Answer choices:*

(see index for correct answer)

- a. open system
- b. levels of analysis
- c. surface-level diversity
- d. Americans with Disabilities Act

Guidance: level 1

:: Supply chain management ::

A _____ is a type of auction in which the traditional roles of buyer and seller are reversed. Thus, there is one buyer and many potential sellers. In an ordinary auction, buyers compete to obtain goods or services by offering increasingly higher prices. In contrast, in a _____ , the sellers compete to obtain business from the buyer and prices will typically decrease as the sellers underbid each other.

Exam Probability: **High**

48. *Answer choices:*

(see index for correct answer)

- a. DIFOT
- b. Reverse auction
- c. National Centre for Cold-chain Development
- d. Dell Theory of Conflict Prevention

Guidance: level 1

:: ::

_____ , or auditory perception, is the ability to perceive sounds by detecting vibrations, changes in the pressure of the surrounding medium through time, through an organ such as the ear. The academic field concerned with _____ is auditory science.

Exam Probability: **High**

49. *Answer choices:*

(see index for correct answer)

- a. hierarchical
- b. interpersonal communication
- c. Character
- d. deep-level diversity

Guidance: level 1

:: Customs duties ::

> A _____ is a tax on imports or exports between sovereign states. It is a form of regulation of foreign trade and a policy that taxes foreign products to encourage or safeguard domestic industry. _____ s are the simplest and oldest instrument of trade policy. Traditionally, states have used them as a source of income. Now, they are among the most widely used instruments of protection, along with import and export quotas.

Exam Probability: **Low**

50. *Answer choices:*

(see index for correct answer)

- a. Russian Customs Tariff
- b. Duty-free shop

- c. Immigration tariff
- d. Court of Exchequer

Guidance: level 1

:: ::

A _____ or _____ s is a type of footwear and not a specific type of shoe. Most _____ s mainly cover the foot and the ankle, while some also cover some part of the lower calf. Some _____ s extend up the leg, sometimes as far as the knee or even the hip. Most _____ s have a heel that is clearly distinguishable from the rest of the sole, even if the two are made of one piece. Traditionally made of leather or rubber, modern _____ s are made from a variety of materials. _____ s are worn both for their functionality protecting the foot and leg from water, extreme cold, mud or hazards or providing additional ankle support for strenuous activities with added traction requirements , or may have hobnails on their undersides to protect against wear and to get better grip; and for reasons of style and fashion.

Exam Probability: **High**

51. *Answer choices:*

(see index for correct answer)

- a. co-culture
- b. information systems assessment
- c. Boot
- d. corporate values

Guidance: level 1

:: Market research ::

_____ is an organized effort to gather information about target markets or customers. It is a very important component of business strategy. The term is commonly interchanged with marketing research; however, expert practitioners may wish to draw a distinction, in that marketing research is concerned specifically about marketing processes, while _____ is concerned specifically with markets.

Exam Probability: **High**

52. *Answer choices:*

(see index for correct answer)

- a. Incite
- b. Market research
- c. Customer experience analytics
- d. Marketing Fair

Guidance: level 1

:: ::

_____ is the exchange of capital, goods, and services across international borders or territories.

Exam Probability: **Low**

53. *Answer choices:*

(see index for correct answer)

- a. International trade
- b. surface-level diversity
- c. Character
- d. imperative

Guidance: level 1

:: Free market ::

In economics, a _____ is a system in which the prices for goods and services are determined by the open market and by consumers. In a _____, the laws and forces of supply and demand are free from any intervention by a government or other authority and from all forms of economic privilege, monopolies and artificial scarcities. Proponents of the concept of _____ contrast it with a regulated market in which a government intervenes in supply and demand through various methods, such as tariffs, used to restrict trade and to protect the local economy. In an idealized free-market economy, prices for goods and services are set freely by the forces of supply and demand and are allowed to reach their point of equilibrium without intervention by government policy.

Exam Probability: **Medium**

54. *Answer choices:*

(see index for correct answer)

- a. Free market
- b. Piece rate

Guidance: level 1

:: Payments ::

A _____ or government incentive is a form of financial aid or support extended to an economic sector generally with the aim of promoting economic and social policy. Although commonly extended from government, the term _____ can relate to any type of support – for example from NGOs or as implicit subsidies. Subsidies come in various forms including: direct and indirect .

Exam Probability: **Low**

55. *Answer choices:*

(see index for correct answer)

- a. Incentive payments
- b. Market transition payments
- c. Subsidy
- d. Deficiency payments

Guidance: level 1

:: ::

Advertising is a marketing communication that employs an openly sponsored, non-personal message to promote or sell a product, service or idea. Sponsors of advertising are typically businesses wishing to promote their products or services. Advertising is differentiated from public relations in that an advertiser pays for and has control over the message. It differs from personal selling in that the message is non-personal, i.e., not directed to a particular individual. Advertising is communicated through various mass media, including traditional media such as newspapers, magazines, television, radio, outdoor advertising or direct mail; and new media such as search results, blogs, social media, websites or text messages. The actual presentation of the message in a medium is referred to as an _____, or "ad" or advert for short.

Exam Probability: **Low**

56. *Answer choices:*

(see index for correct answer)

- a. Advertisement
- b. hierarchical perspective
- c. functional perspective
- d. Character

Guidance: level 1

:: Land value taxation ::

> _____, sometimes referred to as dry _____, is the solid surface of Earth that is not permanently covered by water. The vast majority of human activity throughout history has occurred in _____ areas that support agriculture, habitat, and various natural resources. Some life forms have developed from predecessor species that lived in bodies of water.

Exam Probability: **High**

57. *Answer choices:*

(see index for correct answer)

- a. Land
- b. Physiocracy
- c. Harry Gunnison Brown
- d. Prosper Australia

Guidance: level 1

:: ::

An _____ is the production of goods or related services within an economy. The major source of revenue of a group or company is the indicator of its relevant _____ . When a large group has multiple sources of revenue generation, it is considered to be working in different industries. Manufacturing _____ became a key sector of production and labour in European and North American countries during the Industrial Revolution, upsetting previous mercantile and feudal economies. This came through many successive rapid advances in technology, such as the production of steel and coal.

Exam Probability: **Low**

58. *Answer choices:*

(see index for correct answer)

- a. Sarbanes-Oxley act of 2002
- b. Industry
- c. open system
- d. information systems assessment

Guidance: level 1

:: ::

In the broadest sense, _____ is any practice which contributes to the sale of products to a retail consumer. At a retail in-store level, _____ refers to the variety of products available for sale and the display of those products in such a way that it stimulates interest and entices customers to make a purchase.

Exam Probability: **Low**

59. *Answer choices:*

(see index for correct answer)

- a. hierarchical perspective
- b. process perspective
- c. open system
- d. Merchandising

Guidance: level 1

Business ethics

Business ethics (also known as corporate ethics) is a form of applied ethics or professional ethics, that examines ethical principles and moral or ethical problems that can arise in a business environment. It applies to all aspects of business conduct and is relevant to the conduct of individuals and entire organizations. These ethics originate from individuals, organizational statements or from the legal system. These norms, values, ethical, and unethical practices are what is used to guide business. They help those businesses maintain a better connection with their stakeholders.

_____ , O.S.A. was a German professor of theology, composer, priest, monk, and a seminal figure in the Protestant Reformation.

Exam Probability: **Medium**

1. *Answer choices:*

(see index for correct answer)

- a. process perspective
- b. Martin Luther
- c. functional perspective
- d. cultural

Guidance: level 1

:: Anti-competitive behaviour ::

_____ is a secret cooperation or deceitful agreement in order to deceive others, although not necessarily illegal, as a conspiracy. A secret agreement between two or more parties to limit open competition by deceiving, misleading, or defrauding others of their legal rights, or to obtain an objective forbidden by law typically by defrauding or gaining an unfair market advantage is an example of _____ . It is an agreement among firms or individuals to divide a market, set prices, limit production or limit opportunities. It can involve "unions, wage fixing, kickbacks, or misrepresenting the independence of the relationship between the colluding parties". In legal terms, all acts effected by _____ are considered void.

Exam Probability: **High**

2. *Answer choices:*

(see index for correct answer)

- a. Collusion
- b. Anti-siphoning laws in Australia
- c. Competition regulator
- d. Barriers to entry

Guidance: level 1

:: Occupational safety and health ::

_____ is a chemical element with symbol Pb and atomic number 82. It is a heavy metal that is denser than most common materials. _____ is soft and malleable, and also has a relatively low melting point. When freshly cut, _____ is silvery with a hint of blue; it tarnishes to a dull gray color when exposed to air. _____ has the highest atomic number of any stable element and three of its isotopes are endpoints of major nuclear decay chains of heavier elements.

Exam Probability: **Medium**

3. *Answer choices:*

(see index for correct answer)

- a. Work method statement

- b. Lead
- c. Samuel Stockhausen
- d. Hot work

Guidance: level 1

:: Separation of investment and commercial banking ::

The _____ refers to § 619 of the Dodd–Frank Wall Street Reform and Consumer Protection Act. The rule was originally proposed by American economist and former United States Federal Reserve Chairman Paul Volcker to restrict United States banks from making certain kinds of speculative investments that do not benefit their customers. Volcker argued that such speculative activity played a key role in the financial crisis of 2007–2008. The rule is often referred to as a ban on proprietary trading by commercial banks, whereby deposits are used to trade on the bank's own accounts, although a number of exceptions to this ban were included in the Dodd-Frank law.

Exam Probability: **Medium**

4. *Answer choices:*
(see index for correct answer)

- a. investment bank
- b. Volcker Rule
- c. Bank Holding Company Act
- d. Merchant bank

Guidance: level 1

:: Progressive Era in the United States ::

The Clayton Antitrust Act of 1914, was a part of United States antitrust law with the goal of adding further substance to the U.S. antitrust law regime; the _____ sought to prevent anticompetitive practices in their incipiency. That regime started with the Sherman Antitrust Act of 1890, the first Federal law outlawing practices considered harmful to consumers. The _____ specified particular prohibited conduct, the three-level enforcement scheme, the exemptions, and the remedial measures.

Exam Probability: **Low**

5. *Answer choices:*

(see index for correct answer)

- a. Clayton Antitrust Act
- b. pragmatism
- c. Mann Act

Guidance: level 1

:: ::

The _____ is an American stock exchange located at 11 Wall Street, Lower Manhattan, New York City, New York. It is by far the world's largest stock exchange by market capitalization of its listed companies at US$30.1 trillion as of February 2018. The average daily trading value was approximately US$169 billion in 2013. The NYSE trading floor is located at 11 Wall Street and is composed of 21 rooms used for the facilitation of trading. A fifth trading room, located at 30 Broad Street, was closed in February 2007. The main building and the 11 Wall Street building were designated National Historic Landmarks in 1978.

Exam Probability: **High**

6. *Answer choices:*

(see index for correct answer)

- a. open system
- b. hierarchical
- c. imperative
- d. hierarchical perspective

Guidance: level 1

:: ::

The American Recovery and Reinvestment Act of 2009, nicknamed the _____, was a stimulus package enacted by the 111th U.S. Congress and signed into law by President Barack Obama in February 2009. Developed in response to the Great Recession, the ARRA's primary objective was to save existing jobs and create new ones as soon as possible. Other objectives were to provide temporary relief programs for those most affected by the recession and invest in infrastructure, education, health, and renewable energy.

Exam Probability: **Medium**

7. *Answer choices:*

(see index for correct answer)

- a. surface-level diversity
- b. hierarchical
- c. open system
- d. Recovery Act

Guidance: level 1

:: Minimum wage ::

A _____ is the lowest remuneration that employers can legally pay their workers—the price floor below which workers may not sell their labor. Most countries had introduced _____ legislation by the end of the 20th century.

Exam Probability: **Low**

8. *Answer choices:*

(see index for correct answer)

- a. Minimum Wage Fairness Act
- b. Minimum wage
- c. Working poor
- d. Minimum wage in Taiwan

Guidance: level 1

:: Electronic waste ::

_____ or e-waste describes discarded electrical or electronic devices. Used electronics which are destined for refurbishment, reuse, resale, salvage, recycling through material recovery, or disposal are also considered e-waste. Informal processing of e-waste in developing countries can lead to adverse human health effects and environmental pollution.

Exam Probability: **High**

9. *Answer choices:*

(see index for correct answer)

- a. Solving the E-waste Problem
- b. World Reuse, Repair and Recycling Association
- c. Electronic waste
- d. E-Stewards

Guidance: level 1

:: Natural gas ::

_____ is a naturally occurring hydrocarbon gas mixture consisting primarily of methane, but commonly including varying amounts of other higher alkanes, and sometimes a small percentage of carbon dioxide, nitrogen, hydrogen sulfide, or helium. It is formed when layers of decomposing plant and animal matter are exposed to intense heat and pressure under the surface of the Earth over millions of years. The energy that the plants originally obtained from the sun is stored in the form of chemical bonds in the gas.

Exam Probability: **Low**

10. *Answer choices:*

(see index for correct answer)

- a. Natural gas
- b. Renewable natural gas
- c. Wet gas
- d. Production fluid

Guidance: level 1

:: ::

The _____ Group is a global financial investment management and insurance company headquartered in Des Moines, Iowa.

Exam Probability: **High**

11. *Answer choices:*

(see index for correct answer)

- a. functional perspective
- b. imperative
- c. open system
- d. Character

Guidance: level 1

:: Ethical banking ::

A _____ or community development finance institution - abbreviated in both cases to CDFI - is a financial institution that provides credit and financial services to underserved markets and populations, primarily in the USA but also in the UK. A CDFI may be a community development bank, a community development credit union , a community development loan fund , a community development venture capital fund , a microenterprise development loan fund, or a community development corporation.

Exam Probability: **Low**

12. *Answer choices:*

(see index for correct answer)

- a. Community development financial institution
- b. GLS Bank
- c. Citizens Bank of Canada
- d. Wilhelm Ernst Barkhoff

Guidance: level 1

:: Business law ::

A _____ is an arrangement where parties, known as partners, agree to cooperate to advance their mutual interests. The partners in a _____ may be individuals, businesses, interest-based organizations, schools, governments or combinations. Organizations may partner to increase the likelihood of each achieving their mission and to amplify their reach. A _____ may result in issuing and holding equity or may be only governed by a contract.

Exam Probability: **Low**

13. *Answer choices:*

(see index for correct answer)

- a. Enhanced use lease
- b. Starting a Business Index
- c. Partnership
- d. Copyright transfer agreement

Guidance: level 1

:: Auditing ::

_____ , as defined by accounting and auditing, is a process for assuring of an organization's objectives in operational effectiveness and efficiency, reliable financial reporting, and compliance with laws, regulations and policies. A broad concept, _____ involves everything that controls risks to an organization.

Exam Probability: **High**

14. *Answer choices:*

(see index for correct answer)

- a. Internal audit
- b. Lease audit
- c. Mainframe audit
- d. Verified Audit Circulation

Guidance: level 1

:: Industry ::

_____ is the manner in which a given entity has decided to address issues of energy development including energy production, distribution and consumption. The attributes of _____ may include legislation, international treaties, incentives to investment, guidelines for energy conservation, taxation and other public policy techniques. Energy is a core component of modern economies. A functioning economy requires not only labor and capital but also energy, for manufacturing processes, transportation, communication, agriculture, and more.

Exam Probability: **Low**

15. *Answer choices:*

(see index for correct answer)

- a. Energy policy
- b. Reindustrialization
- c. Industrial archaeology
- d. Boilery

Guidance: level 1

:: United States federal labor legislation ::

The _____ of 1988 is a United States federal law that generally prevents employers from using polygraph tests, either for pre-employment screening or during the course of employment, with certain exemptions.

Exam Probability: **Low**

16. *Answer choices:*

(see index for correct answer)

- a. Adamson Act
- b. Landrum-Griffin Act
- c. Employee Polygraph Protection Act
- d. Employment Act of 1946

Guidance: level 1

:: ::

_____ is the introduction of contaminants into the natural environment that cause adverse change. _____ can take the form of chemical substances or energy, such as noise, heat or light. Pollutants, the components of _____ , can be either foreign substances/energies or naturally occurring contaminants. _____ is often classed as point source or nonpoint source _____ .In 2015, _____ killed 9 million people in the world.

Exam Probability: **Low**

17. *Answer choices:*

(see index for correct answer)

- a. surface-level diversity
- b. Pollution
- c. open system
- d. similarity-attraction theory

Guidance: level 1

:: ::

The _____ , the Calvinist work ethic or the Puritan work ethic is a work ethic concept in theology, sociology, economics and history that emphasizes that hard work, discipline and frugality are a result of a person's subscription to the values espoused by the Protestant faith, particularly Calvinism. The phrase was initially coined in 1904–1905 by Max Weber in his book The Protestant Ethic and the Spirit of Capitalism.

Exam Probability: **High**

18. *Answer choices:*

(see index for correct answer)

- a. interpersonal communication
- b. deep-level diversity
- c. levels of analysis
- d. Protestant work ethic

Guidance: level 1

:: ::

A _____ is a proceeding by a party or parties against another in the civil court of law. The archaic term "suit in law" is found in only a small number of laws still in effect today. The term "_____" is used in reference to a civil action brought in a court of law in which a plaintiff, a party who claims to have incurred loss as a result of a defendant's actions, demands a legal or equitable remedy. The defendant is required to respond to the plaintiff's complaint. If the plaintiff is successful, judgment is in the plaintiff's favor, and a variety of court orders may be issued to enforce a right, award damages, or impose a temporary or permanent injunction to prevent an act or compel an act. A declaratory judgment may be issued to prevent future legal disputes.

Exam Probability: **Low**

19. *Answer choices:*

(see index for correct answer)

- a. hierarchical
- b. imperative
- c. Character
- d. Lawsuit

Guidance: level 1

:: ::

The _____ of 1977 is a United States federal law known primarily for two of its main provisions: one that addresses accounting transparency requirements under the Securities Exchange Act of 1934 and another concerning bribery of foreign officials. The Act was amended in 1988 and in 1998, and has been subject to continued congressional concerns, namely whether its enforcement discourages U.S. companies from investing abroad.

Exam Probability: **Medium**

20. *Answer choices:*

(see index for correct answer)

- a. Sarbanes-Oxley act of 2002
- b. deep-level diversity
- c. hierarchical
- d. Foreign Corrupt Practices Act

Guidance: level 1

:: Hazard analysis ::

Broadly speaking, a _____ is the combined effort of 1. identifying and analyzing potential events that may negatively impact individuals, assets, and/or the environment ; and 2. making judgments "on the tolerability of the risk on the basis of a risk analysis" while considering influencing factors . Put in simpler terms, a _____ analyzes what can go wrong, how likely it is to happen, what the potential consequences are, and how tolerable the identified risk is. As part of this process, the resulting determination of risk may be expressed in a quantitative or qualitative fashion. The _____ is an inherent part of an overall risk management strategy, which attempts to, after a _____ , "introduce control measures to eliminate or reduce" any potential risk-related consequences.

Exam Probability: **High**

21. *Answer choices:*

(see index for correct answer)

- a. Hazard identification
- b. Hazardous Materials Identification System
- c. Risk assessment

Guidance: level 1

:: International trade ::

_____ involves the transfer of goods or services from one person or entity to another, often in exchange for money. A system or network that allows _____ is called a market.

Exam Probability: **Medium**

22. *Answer choices:*

(see index for correct answer)

- a. Gravity model of trade
- b. Trade mandate
- c. International commodity agreement
- d. Trade

Guidance: level 1

:: Utilitarianism ::

_____ is a school of thought that argues that the pursuit of pleasure and intrinsic goods are the primary or most important goals of human life. A hedonist strives to maximize net pleasure . However upon finally gaining said pleasure, happiness may remain stationary.

Exam Probability: **Low**

23. *Answer choices:*

(see index for correct answer)

- a. The Theory of Good and Evil
- b. Preference utilitarianism
- c. Rule utilitarianism

- d. Informed judge

Guidance: level 1

:: Renewable energy ::

A _____ is a fuel that is produced through contemporary biological processes, such as agriculture and anaerobic digestion, rather than a fuel produced by geological processes such as those involved in the formation of fossil fuels, such as coal and petroleum, from prehistoric biological matter. If the source biomatter can regrow quickly, the resulting fuel is said to be a form of renewable energy.

Exam Probability: **Medium**

24. *Answer choices:*
(see index for correct answer)

- a. Copper indium gallium selenide
- b. Tidal power
- c. Market transformation
- d. Biofuel

Guidance: level 1

:: Supply chain management terms ::

In business and finance, _____ is a system of organizations, people, activities, information, and resources involved in moving a product or service from supplier to customer. _____ activities involve the transformation of natural resources, raw materials, and components into a finished product that is delivered to the end customer. In sophisticated _____ systems, used products may re-enter the _____ at any point where residual value is recyclable. _____ s link value chains.

Exam Probability: **Medium**

25. *Answer choices:*

(see index for correct answer)

- a. inventory management
- b. Supply Chain
- c. Most valuable customers
- d. Work in process

Guidance: level 1

:: ::

A _____ is an organization, usually a group of people or a company, authorized to act as a single entity and recognized as such in law. Early incorporated entities were established by charter. Most jurisdictions now allow the creation of new _____ s through registration.

Exam Probability: **Medium**

26. Answer choices:

(see index for correct answer)

- a. surface-level diversity
- b. Corporation
- c. corporate values
- d. interpersonal communication

Guidance: level 1

:: Public relations terminology ::

_____ , also called "green sheen", is a form of spin in which green PR or green marketing is deceptively used to promote the perception that an organization's products, aims or policies are environmentally friendly. Evidence that an organization is _____ often comes from pointing out the spending differences: when significantly more money or time has been spent advertising being "green" , than is actually spent on environmentally sound practices. _____ efforts can range from changing the name or label of a product to evoke the natural environment on a product that contains harmful chemicals to multimillion-dollar marketing campaigns portraying highly polluting energy companies as eco-friendly. Publicized accusations of _____ have contributed to the term's increasing use.

Exam Probability: **Medium**

27. Answer choices:

(see index for correct answer)

- a. Green PR
- b. Greenwashing
- c. Crisis communication
- d. PR Gallery

Guidance: level 1

:: Business ethics ::

_____ is a type of harassment technique that relates to a sexual nature and the unwelcome or inappropriate promise of rewards in exchange for sexual favors. _____ includes a range of actions from mild transgressions to sexual abuse or assault. Harassment can occur in many different social settings such as the workplace, the home, school, churches, etc. Harassers or victims may be of any gender.

Exam Probability: **Medium**

28. *Answer choices:*
(see index for correct answer)

- a. Anatomy of Greed
- b. Interfaith Center on Corporate Responsibility
- c. Business and Professional Ethics Journal
- d. Third-party technique

Guidance: level 1

:: Market-based policy instruments ::

Cause marketing is defined as a type of corporate social responsibility, in which a company's promotional campaign has the dual purpose of increasing profitability while bettering society.

Exam Probability: **High**

29. *Answer choices:*

(see index for correct answer)

- a. Tree credits
- b. The Other Invisible Hand
- c. Regional Clean Air Incentives Market
- d. Cause-related marketing

Guidance: level 1

:: Financial markets ::

The _____ is a United States federal government organization, established by Title I of the Dodd–Frank Wall Street Reform and Consumer Protection Act, which was signed into law by President Barack Obama on July 21, 2010. The Office of Financial Research is intended to provide support to the council.

Exam Probability: **Medium**

30. *Answer choices:*

(see index for correct answer)

- a. Financial Stability Oversight Council
- b. Market basket
- c. Internal financing
- d. Index cohesive force

Guidance: level 1

:: ::

_____ is the practice of deliberately managing the spread of information between an individual or an organization and the public. _____ may include an organization or individual gaining exposure to their audiences using topics of public interest and news items that do not require direct payment. This differentiates it from advertising as a form of marketing communications. _____ is the idea of creating coverage for clients for free, rather than marketing or advertising. But now, advertising is also a part of greater PR Activities. An example of good _____ would be generating an article featuring a client, rather than paying for the client to be advertised next to the article. The aim of _____ is to inform the public, prospective customers, investors, partners, employees, and other stakeholders and ultimately persuade them to maintain a positive or favorable view about the organization, its leadership, products, or political decisions. _____ professionals typically work for PR and marketing firms, businesses and companies, government, and public officials as PIOs and nongovernmental organizations, and nonprofit organizations. Jobs central to _____ include account coordinator, account executive, account supervisor, and media relations manager.

Exam Probability: **Low**

31. *Answer choices:*

(see index for correct answer)

- a. process perspective
- b. imperative
- c. Public relations
- d. empathy

Guidance: level 1

:: ::

The Catholic Church, also known as the Roman Catholic Church, is the largest Christian church, with approximately 1.3 billion baptised Catholics worldwide as of 2017. As the world's oldest continuously functioning international institution, it has played a prominent role in the history and development of Western civilisation. The church is headed by the Bishop of Rome, known as the pope. Its central administration, the Holy See, is in the Vatican City, an enclave within the city of Rome in Italy.

Exam Probability: **High**

32. *Answer choices:*

(see index for correct answer)

- a. Character

- b. hierarchical perspective
- c. deep-level diversity
- d. Catholicism

Guidance: level 1

:: Business ethics ::

> The _____ are the names of two corporate codes of conduct, developed by the African-American preacher Rev. Leon Sullivan, promoting corporate social responsibility.

Exam Probability: **High**

33. *Answer choices:*
(see index for correct answer)

- a. Hostile work environment
- b. Voluntary compliance
- c. Sullivan principles
- d. Corporate Knights

Guidance: level 1

:: ::

_____ is a private Dominican liberal arts college in Madison, Wisconsin. The college occupies a 55 acres campus overlooking the shores of Lake Wingra.

Exam Probability: **Low**

34. *Answer choices:*

(see index for correct answer)

- a. surface-level diversity
- b. levels of analysis
- c. process perspective
- d. Edgewood College

Guidance: level 1

:: Management ::

_____ or executive pay is composed of the financial compensation and other non-financial awards received by an executive from their firm for their service to the organization. It is typically a mixture of salary, bonuses, shares of or call options on the company stock, benefits, and perquisites, ideally configured to take into account government regulations, tax law, the desires of the organization and the executive, and rewards for performance.

Exam Probability: **High**

35. *Answer choices:*

(see index for correct answer)

- a. Community of practice
- b. Executive compensation
- c. Swarm Development Group
- d. Interim management

Guidance: level 1

:: ::

A _____ is a problem offering two possibilities, neither of which is unambiguously acceptable or preferable. The possibilities are termed the horns of the _____ , a clichéd usage, but distinguishing the _____ from other kinds of predicament as a matter of usage.

Exam Probability: **Low**

36. *Answer choices:*

(see index for correct answer)

- a. cultural
- b. functional perspective
- c. similarity-attraction theory
- d. imperative

Guidance: level 1

:: Marketing ::

_____ is the marketing of products that are presumed to be environmentally safe. It incorporates a broad range of activities, including product modification, changes to the production process, sustainable packaging, as well as modifying advertising. Yet defining _____ is not a simple task where several meanings intersect and contradict each other; an example of this will be the existence of varying social, environmental and retail definitions attached to this term. Other similar terms used are environmental marketing and ecological marketing.

Exam Probability: **High**

37. *Answer choices:*
(see index for correct answer)

- a. Personalized marketing
- b. Green marketing
- c. Price war
- d. Negotiation

Guidance: level 1

:: Confidence tricks ::

A _____ is a form of fraud that lures investors and pays profits to earlier investors with funds from more recent investors. The scheme leads victims to believe that profits are coming from product sales or other means, and they remain unaware that other investors are the source of funds. A _____ can maintain the illusion of a sustainable business as long as new investors contribute new funds, and as long as most of the investors do not demand full repayment and still believe in the non-existent assets they are purported to own.

Exam Probability: **High**

38. *Answer choices:*

(see index for correct answer)

- a. Vanity gallery
- b. Private investment capital subscription
- c. Ponzi scheme
- d. Thai tailor scam

Guidance: level 1

The _____ of 1906 was the first of a series of significant consumer protection laws which was enacted by Congress in the 20th century and led to the creation of the Food and Drug Administration. Its main purpose was to ban foreign and interstate traffic in adulterated or mislabeled food and drug products, and it directed the U.S. Bureau of Chemistry to inspect products and refer offenders to prosecutors. It required that active ingredients be placed on the label of a drug's packaging and that drugs could not fall below purity levels established by the United States Pharmacopeia or the National Formulary. The Jungle by Upton Sinclair with its graphic and revolting descriptions of unsanitary conditions and unscrupulous practices rampant in the meatpacking industry, was an inspirational piece that kept the public's attention on the important issue of unhygienic meat processing plants that later led to food inspection legislation. Sinclair quipped, "I aimed at the public's heart and by accident I hit it in the stomach," as outraged readers demanded and got the pure food law.

Exam Probability: **Low**

39. *Answer choices:*

(see index for correct answer)

- a. Pure Food and Drug Act
- b. process perspective
- c. interpersonal communication
- d. information systems assessment

Guidance: level 1

:: Euthenics ::

_____ is an ethical framework and suggests that an entity, be it an organization or individual, has an obligation to act for the benefit of society at large. _____ is a duty every individual has to perform so as to maintain a balance between the economy and the ecosystems. A trade-off may exist between economic development, in the material sense, and the welfare of the society and environment, though this has been challenged by many reports over the past decade. _____ means sustaining the equilibrium between the two. It pertains not only to business organizations but also to everyone whose any action impacts the environment. This responsibility can be passive, by avoiding engaging in socially harmful acts, or active, by performing activities that directly advance social goals. _____ must be intergenerational since the actions of one generation have consequences on those following.

Exam Probability: **Medium**

40. *Answer choices:*

(see index for correct answer)

- a. Home economics
- b. Euthenics
- c. Family and consumer science
- d. Social responsibility

Guidance: level 1

:: Coal ::

_____ is a combustible black or brownish-black sedimentary rock, formed as rock strata called _____ seams. _____ is mostly carbon with variable amounts of other elements; chiefly hydrogen, sulfur, oxygen, and nitrogen. _____ is formed if dead plant matter decays into peat and over millions of years the heat and pressure of deep burial converts the peat into _____. Vast deposits of _____ originates in former wetlands—called _____ forests—that covered much of the Earth's tropical land areas during the late Carboniferous and Permian times.

Exam Probability: **High**

41. *Answer choices:*

(see index for correct answer)

- a. Coal
- b. Coal water
- c. Leonardite
- d. Liptinite

Guidance: level 1

:: Environmental economics ::

_____ is the process of people maintaining change in a balanced environment, in which the exploitation of resources, the direction of investments, the orientation of technological development and institutional change are all in harmony and enhance both current and future potential to meet human needs and aspirations. For many in the field, _____ is defined through the following interconnected domains or pillars: environment, economic and social, which according to Fritjof Capra is based on the principles of Systems Thinking. Sub-domains of sustainable development have been considered also: cultural, technological and political. While sustainable development may be the organizing principle for _____ for some, for others, the two terms are paradoxical. Sustainable development is the development that meets the needs of the present without compromising the ability of future generations to meet their own needs. Brundtland Report for the World Commission on Environment and Development introduced the term of sustainable development.

Exam Probability: **High**

42. *Answer choices:*

(see index for correct answer)

- a. Sustainability
- b. Green growth
- c. Forests Now Declaration
- d. Environmental economics

Guidance: level 1

_____ is "property consisting of land and the buildings on it, along with its natural resources such as crops, minerals or water; immovable property of this nature; an interest vested in this an item of real property, buildings or housing in general. Also: the business of _____ ; the profession of buying, selling, or renting land, buildings, or housing." It is a legal term used in jurisdictions whose legal system is derived from English common law, such as India, England, Wales, Northern Ireland, United States, Canada, Pakistan, Australia, and New Zealand.

Exam Probability: **Low**

43. *Answer choices:*

(see index for correct answer)

- a. Character
- b. functional perspective
- c. co-culture
- d. Real estate

Guidance: level 1

:: ::

A _____ is the ability to carry out a task with determined results often within a given amount of time, energy, or both. _____s can often be divided into domain-general and domain-specific _____s. For example, in the domain of work, some general _____s would include time management, teamwork and leadership, self-motivation and others, whereas domain-specific _____s would be used only for a certain job. _____ usually requires certain environmental stimuli and situations to assess the level of _____ being shown and used.

Exam Probability: **High**

44. *Answer choices:*

(see index for correct answer)

- a. Skill
- b. similarity-attraction theory
- c. information systems assessment
- d. interpersonal communication

Guidance: level 1

:: ::

MCI, Inc. was an American telecommunication corporation, currently a subsidiary of Verizon Communications, with its main office in Ashburn, Virginia. The corporation was formed originally as a result of the merger of _____ and MCI Communications corporations, and used the name MCI _____ , succeeded by _____ , before changing its name to the present version on April 12, 2003, as part of the corporation's ending of its bankruptcy status. The company traded on NASDAQ as WCOM and MCIP. The corporation was purchased by Verizon Communications with the deal finalizing on January 6, 2006, and is now identified as that company's Verizon Enterprise Solutions division with the local residential divisions being integrated slowly into local Verizon subsidiaries.

Exam Probability: **Low**

45. *Answer choices:*

(see index for correct answer)

- a. hierarchical
- b. WorldCom
- c. information systems assessment
- d. similarity-attraction theory

Guidance: level 1

:: ::

_____ is a naturally occurring, yellowish-black liquid found in geological formations beneath the Earth's surface. It is commonly refined into various types of fuels. Components of _____ are separated using a technique called fractional distillation, i.e. separation of a liquid mixture into fractions differing in boiling point by means of distillation, typically using a fractionating column.

Exam Probability: **Low**

46. *Answer choices:*

(see index for correct answer)

- a. information systems assessment
- b. Petroleum
- c. Character
- d. hierarchical perspective

Guidance: level 1

:: White-collar criminals ::

_____ refers to financially motivated, nonviolent crime committed by businesses and government professionals. It was first defined by the sociologist Edwin Sutherland in 1939 as "a crime committed by a person of respectability and high social status in the course of their occupation". Typical _____ s could include wage theft, fraud, bribery, Ponzi schemes, insider trading, labor racketeering, embezzlement, cybercrime, copyright infringement, money laundering, identity theft, and forgery. Lawyers can specialize in _____ .

Exam Probability: **High**

47. *Answer choices:*

(see index for correct answer)

- a. White-collar crime
- b. Du Jun

Guidance: level 1

:: Pyramid and Ponzi schemes ::

_____ was an Italian swindler and con artist in the U.S. and Canada. His aliases include Charles Ponci, Carlo, and Charles P. Bianchi. Born and raised in Italy, he became known in the early 1920s as a swindler in North America for his money-making scheme. He promised clients a 50% profit within 45 days or 100% profit within 90 days, by buying discounted postal reply coupons in other countries and redeeming them at face value in the United States as a form of arbitrage. In reality, Ponzi was paying earlier investors using the investments of later investors. While this type of fraudulent investment scheme was not originally invented by Ponzi, it became so identified with him that it now is referred to as a "Ponzi scheme". His scheme ran for over a year before it collapsed, costing his "investors" $20 million.

Exam Probability: **High**

48. *Answer choices:*

(see index for correct answer)

- a. Yilishen Tianxi Group
- b. Charles Ponzi
- c. Aman Futures Group
- d. Donald Anthony Walker Young

Guidance: level 1

:: Organizational structure ::

An _____ defines how activities such as task allocation, coordination, and supervision are directed toward the achievement of organizational aims.

Exam Probability: **Low**

49. *Answer choices:*

(see index for correct answer)

- a. Organizational structure
- b. Blessed Unrest
- c. Organization of the New York City Police Department
- d. Automated Bureaucracy

Guidance: level 1

:: Toxicology ::

_____ or lead-based paint is paint containing lead. As pigment, lead chromate, Lead oxide, , and lead carbonate are the most common forms. Lead is added to paint to accelerate drying, increase durability, maintain a fresh appearance, and resist moisture that causes corrosion. It is one of the main health and environmental hazards associated with paint. In some countries, lead continues to be added to paint intended for domestic use, whereas countries such as the U.S. and the UK have regulations prohibiting this, although _____ may still be found in older properties painted prior to the introduction of such regulations. Although lead has been banned from household paints in the United States since 1978, paint used in road markings may still contain it. Alternatives such as water-based, lead-free traffic paint are readily available, and many states and federal agencies have changed their purchasing contracts to buy these instead.

Exam Probability: **High**

50. *Answer choices:*

(see index for correct answer)

- a. Toxicant
- b. Indian Institute of Toxicology Research
- c. Lead paint
- d. Herbicide

Guidance: level 1

:: Employment compensation ::

A _____ is the minimum income necessary for a worker to meet their basic needs. Needs are defined to include food, housing, and other essential needs such as clothing. The goal of a _____ is to allow a worker to afford a basic but decent standard of living. Due to the flexible nature of the term "needs", there is not one universally accepted measure of what a _____ is and as such it varies by location and household type.

Exam Probability: **Low**

51. *Answer choices:*

(see index for correct answer)

- a. Seasonal bonuses
- b. Salary cap
- c. Living wage
- d. Law Enforcement Availability Pay

Guidance: level 1

:: ::

A _____ is a set of rules, often written, with regards to clothing. _____ s are created out of social perceptions and norms, and vary based on purpose, circumstances and occasions. Different societies and cultures are likely to have different _____ s.

Exam Probability: **High**

52. *Answer choices:*

(see index for correct answer)

- a. Dress code
- b. interpersonal communication
- c. personal values
- d. similarity-attraction theory

Guidance: level 1

:: Industrial ecology ::

_____ is a strategy for reducing the amount of waste created and released into the environment, particularly by industrial facilities, agriculture, or consumers. Many large corporations view P2 as a method of improving the efficiency and profitability of production processes by technology advancements. Legislative bodies have enacted P2 measures, such as the _____ Act of 1990 and the Clean Air Act Amendments of 1990 by the United States Congress.

Exam Probability: **Low**

53. *Answer choices:*

(see index for correct answer)

- a. Pollution Prevention
- b. Biomimetics
- c. Avoided burden

- d. Rebound effect

Guidance: level 1

:: Corporate scandals ::

Exxon Mobil Corporation, doing business as _____, is an American multinational oil and gas corporation headquartered in Irving, Texas. It is the largest direct descendant of John D. Rockefeller's Standard Oil Company, and was formed on November 30, 1999 by the merger of Exxon and Mobil. _____ 's primary brands are Exxon, Mobil, Esso, and _____ Chemical.

Exam Probability: **Low**

54. *Answer choices:*

(see index for correct answer)

- a. Stanford International Bank
- b. ExxonMobil
- c. Great Phenol Plot
- d. YoungStartup Ventures

Guidance: level 1

:: Criminal law ::

_____ is the body of law that relates to crime. It proscribes conduct perceived as threatening, harmful, or otherwise endangering to the property, health, safety, and moral welfare of people inclusive of one's self. Most _____ is established by statute, which is to say that the laws are enacted by a legislature. _____ includes the punishment and rehabilitation of people who violate such laws. _____ varies according to jurisdiction, and differs from civil law, where emphasis is more on dispute resolution and victim compensation, rather than on punishment or rehabilitation. Criminal procedure is a formalized official activity that authenticates the fact of commission of a crime and authorizes punitive or rehabilitative treatment of the offender.

Exam Probability: **Medium**

55. *Answer choices:*

(see index for correct answer)

- a. complicit
- b. Mala in se
- c. Self-incrimination
- d. mitigating factor

Guidance: level 1

:: ::

In regulatory jurisdictions that provide for it, _____ is a group of laws and organizations designed to ensure the rights of consumers as well as fair trade, competition and accurate information in the marketplace. The laws are designed to prevent the businesses that engage in fraud or specified unfair practices from gaining an advantage over competitors. They may also provides additional protection for those most vulnerable in society. _____ laws are a form of government regulation that aim to protect the rights of consumers. For example, a government may require businesses to disclose detailed information about products—particularly in areas where safety or public health is an issue, such as food.

Exam Probability: **High**

56. *Answer choices:*

(see index for correct answer)

- a. deep-level diversity
- b. Consumer Protection
- c. Character
- d. open system

Guidance: level 1

:: Labor rights ::

The _____ is the concept that people have a human _____, or engage in productive employment, and may not be prevented from doing so. The _____ is enshrined in the Universal Declaration of Human Rights and recognized in international human rights law through its inclusion in the International Covenant on Economic, Social and Cultural Rights, where the _____ emphasizes economic, social and cultural development.

Exam Probability: **High**

57. *Answer choices:*

(see index for correct answer)

- a. Right to work
- b. China Labor Watch
- c. China Labour Bulletin
- d. Labor rights

Guidance: level 1

:: ::

_____ or accountancy is the measurement, processing, and communication of financial information about economic entities such as businesses and corporations. The modern field was established by the Italian mathematician Luca Pacioli in 1494. _____, which has been called the "language of business", measures the results of an organization's economic activities and conveys this information to a variety of users, including investors, creditors, management, and regulators. Practitioners of _____ are known as accountants. The terms "_____" and "financial reporting" are often used as synonyms.

Exam Probability: **Medium**

58. *Answer choices:*

(see index for correct answer)

- a. corporate values
- b. Character
- c. functional perspective
- d. deep-level diversity

Guidance: level 1

:: Leadership ::

_____ is leadership that is directed by respect for ethical beliefs and values and for the dignity and rights of others. It is thus related to concepts such as trust, honesty, consideration, charisma, and fairness.

59. *Answer choices:*

(see index for correct answer)

- a. Situational leadership theory
- b. Ethical leadership
- c. Complex adaptive leadership
- d. Trait leadership

Guidance: level 1

Accounting

Accounting or accountancy is the measurement, processing, and communication of financial information about economic entities such as businesses and corporations. The modern field was established by the Italian mathematician Luca Pacioli in 1494. Accounting, which has been called the "language of business", measures the results of an organization's economic activities and conveys this information to a variety of users, including investors, creditors, management, and regulators.

:: Legal terms ::

_____ is a state of prolonged public dispute or debate, usually concerning a matter of conflicting opinion or point of view. The word was coined from the Latin controversia, as a composite of controversus – "turned in an opposite direction," from contra – "against" – and vertere – to turn, or versus , hence, "to turn against."

Exam Probability: **High**

1. *Answer choices:*

(see index for correct answer)

- a. Position of trust
- b. Third party complaint
- c. Demise
- d. Next friend

Guidance: level 1

:: ::

An _____ is a comprehensive report on a company's activities throughout the preceding year. _____ s are intended to give shareholders and other interested people information about the company's activities and financial performance. They may be considered as grey literature. Most jurisdictions require companies to prepare and disclose _____ s, and many require the _____ to be filed at the company's registry. Companies listed on a stock exchange are also required to report at more frequent intervals .

Exam Probability: **Medium**

2. *Answer choices:*

(see index for correct answer)

- a. co-culture
- b. process perspective
- c. interpersonal communication
- d. similarity-attraction theory

Guidance: level 1

:: Stock market ::

_____ is a form of corporate equity ownership, a type of security. The terms voting share and ordinary share are also used frequently in other parts of the world; "_____" being primarily used in the United States. They are known as Equity shares or Ordinary shares in the UK and other Commonwealth realms. This type of share gives the stockholder the right to share in the profits of the company, and to vote on matters of corporate policy and the composition of the members of the board of directors.

Exam Probability: **Low**

3. *Answer choices:*

(see index for correct answer)

- a. Common stock

- b. Book building
- c. Stock exchange
- d. Control premium

Guidance: level 1

:: Costs ::

The _____ is computed by dividing the total cost of goods available for sale by the total units available for sale. This gives a weighted-average unit cost that is applied to the units in the ending inventory.

Exam Probability: **High**

4. *Answer choices:*

(see index for correct answer)

- a. Quality costs
- b. Cost overrun
- c. Average cost
- d. Cost competitiveness of fuel sources

Guidance: level 1

:: Payment systems ::

A _____ is a bond of the redeemable transaction type which is worth a certain monetary value and which may be spent only for specific reasons or on specific goods. Examples include housing, travel, and food _____s. The term _____ is also a synonym for receipt and is often used to refer to receipts used as evidence of, for example, the declaration that a service has been performed or that an expenditure has been made. _____ is a tourist guide for using services with a guarantee of payment by the agency.

Exam Probability: **Low**

5. *Answer choices:*

(see index for correct answer)

- a. Voucher
- b. VocaLink
- c. Certified Payment-Card Industry Security Implementer
- d. Bankgiro

Guidance: level 1

:: Financial ratios ::

_____ or asset turns is a financial ratio that measures the efficiency of a company's use of its assets in generating sales revenue or sales income to the company.

Exam Probability: **Low**

6. *Answer choices:*

(see index for correct answer)

- a. Fixed-asset turnover
- b. Information ratio
- c. Asset turnover
- d. stock turnover

Guidance: level 1

:: Business law ::

A _____ is a business entity created by two or more parties, generally characterized by shared ownership, shared returns and risks, and shared governance. Companies typically pursue _____ s for one of four reasons: to access a new market, particularly emerging markets; to gain scale efficiencies by combining assets and operations; to share risk for major investments or projects; or to access skills and capabilities.

Exam Probability: **Low**

7. *Answer choices:*

(see index for correct answer)

- a. Ordinary course of business
- b. Whitewash waiver
- c. Companies law
- d. Copyright transfer agreement

Guidance: level 1

:: Pricing ::

_____ is the difference between a lower selling price and a higher purchase price, resulting in a financial loss for the seller.

Exam Probability: **High**

8. *Answer choices:*

(see index for correct answer)

- a. Natural gas prices
- b. Capital loss
- c. Cost-plus pricing
- d. Profit maximization

Guidance: level 1

:: Taxation in the United States ::

The Modified Accelerated Cost Recovery System is the current tax depreciation system in the United States. Under this system, the capitalized cost of tangible property is recovered over a specified life by annual deductions for depreciation. The lives are specified broadly in the Internal Revenue Code. The Internal Revenue Service publishes detailed tables of lives by classes of assets. The deduction for depreciation is computed under one of two methods at the election of the taxpayer, with limitations. See IRS Publication 946 for a 120-page guide to _____ .

Exam Probability: **Low**

9. *Answer choices:*

(see index for correct answer)

- a. MACRS
- b. Doctrine of Exchange
- c. BLIPS
- d. Taxpayer Identification Number

Guidance: level 1

:: Budgets ::

_____ is a method of budgeting in which all expenses must be justified and approved for each new period. Developed by Peter Pyhrr in the 1970s, _____ starts from a "zero base" at the beginning of every budget period, analyzing needs and costs of every function within an organization and allocating funds accordingly, regardless of how much money has previously been budgeted to any given line item.

Exam Probability: **Low**

10. *Answer choices:*

(see index for correct answer)

- a. Personal budget
- b. Link budget
- c. Budget set
- d. Programme budgeting

Guidance: level 1

:: Generally Accepted Accounting Principles ::

> Financial statements prepared and presented by a company typically follow an external standard that specifically guides their preparation. These standards vary across the globe and are typically overseen by some combination of the private accounting profession in that specific nation and the various government regulators. Variations across countries may be considerable, making cross-country evaluation of financial data challenging.

Exam Probability: **High**

11. *Answer choices:*

(see index for correct answer)

- a. Operating statement
- b. Net realizable value

- c. Closing entries
- d. Generally Accepted Accounting Principles

Guidance: level 1

:: Accounting in the United States ::

> The _____ is located in Norwalk, Connecticut, United States. It was organized in 1972 as a non-stock, Delaware Corporation. It is an independent organization in the private sector, operating with the goal of ensuring objectivity and integrity in financial reporting standards.

Exam Probability: **Low**

12. *Answer choices:*

(see index for correct answer)

- a. Legal liability of certified public accountants
- b. Other comprehensive income
- c. Financial Accounting Foundation
- d. Variable interest entity

Guidance: level 1

:: International Financial Reporting Standards ::

_____ , usually called IFRS, are standards issued by the IFRS Foundation and the International Accounting Standards Board to provide a common global language for business affairs so that company accounts are understandable and comparable across international boundaries. They are a consequence of growing international shareholding and trade and are particularly important for companies that have dealings in several countries. They are progressively replacing the many different national accounting standards. They are the rules to be followed by accountants to maintain books of accounts which are comparable, understandable, reliable and relevant as per the users internal or external. IFRS, with the exception of IAS 29 Financial Reporting in Hyperinflationary Economies and IFRIC 7 Applying the Restatement Approach under IAS 29, are authorized in terms of the historical cost paradigm. IAS 29 and IFRIC 7 are authorized in terms of the units of constant purchasing power paradigm.IAS 2 is related to inventories in this standard we talk about the stock its production process etcIFRS began as an attempt to harmonize accounting across the European Union but the value of harmonization quickly made the concept attractive around the world. However, it has been debated whether or not de facto harmonization has occurred. Standards that were issued by IASC are still within use today and go by the name International Accounting Standards , while standards issued by IASB are called IFRS. IAS were issued between 1973 and 2001 by the Board of the International Accounting Standards Committee . On 1 April 2001, the new International Accounting Standards Board took over from the IASC the responsibility for setting International Accounting Standards. During its first meeting the new Board adopted existing IAS and Standing Interpretations Committee standards . The IASB has continued to develop standards calling the new standards " _____ ".

Exam Probability: **Low**

13. *Answer choices:*

(see index for correct answer)

- a. IAS 10
- b. International Public Sector Accounting Standards
- c. IFRS 5

- d. International Financial Reporting Standards

Guidance: level 1

:: Legal terms ::

An _____ is an action which is inaccurate or incorrect. In some usages, an _____ is synonymous with a mistake. In statistics, "_____" refers to the difference between the value which has been computed and the correct value. An _____ could result in failure or in a deviation from the intended performance or behaviour.

Exam Probability: **Medium**

14. *Answer choices:*

(see index for correct answer)

- a. Good cause
- b. Deadlock provision
- c. Nonjoinder of party
- d. Parole

Guidance: level 1

:: Management ::

_____ is a style of business management that focuses on identifying and handling cases that deviate from the norm, recommended as best practice by the project management method PRINCE2.

Exam Probability: **Medium**

15. *Answer choices:*

(see index for correct answer)

- a. Event to knowledge
- b. Planning
- c. Management by exception
- d. Automated decision support

Guidance: level 1

:: Accounting software ::

_____ describes a type of application software that records and processes accounting transactions within functional modules such as accounts payable, accounts receivable, journal, general ledger, payroll, and trial balance. It functions as an accounting information system. It may be developed in-house by the organization using it, may be purchased from a third party, or may be a combination of a third-party application software package with local modifications. _____ may be on-line based, accessed anywhere at any time with any device which is Internet enabled, or may be desktop based. It varies greatly in its complexity and cost.

Exam Probability: **High**

16. *Answer choices:*

(see index for correct answer)

- a. Accounting software
- b. Open Systems Accounting Software
- c. Microsoft Money
- d. Personable Inc.

Guidance: level 1

:: Management accounting ::

A _____ is a part of a business which is expected to make an identifiable contribution to the organization's profits.

Exam Probability: **High**

17. *Answer choices:*

(see index for correct answer)

- a. Profit center
- b. Throughput accounting
- c. Overhead
- d. Management control system

Guidance: level 1

:: Data security ::

_____ is the concept of having more than one person required to complete a task. In business the separation by sharing of more than one individual in one single task is an internal control intended to prevent fraud and error. The concept is alternatively called segregation of duties or, in the political realm, separation of powers. In democracies, the separation of legislation from administration serves a similar purpose. The concept is addressed in technical systems and in information technology equivalently and generally addressed as redundancy.

Exam Probability: **High**

18. *Answer choices:*

(see index for correct answer)

- a. Separation of duties
- b. Firewall
- c. Alternative compensation system
- d. Multi-party authorization

Guidance: level 1

:: ::

_____ is a costing method that identifies activities in an organization and assigns the cost of each activity to all products and services according to the actual consumption by each. This model assigns more indirect costs into direct costs compared to conventional costing.

Exam Probability: **Medium**

19. *Answer choices:*

(see index for correct answer)

- a. Sarbanes-Oxley act of 2002
- b. Activity-based costing
- c. imperative
- d. personal values

Guidance: level 1

:: International taxation ::

A _____ tax, or a retention tax, is an income tax to be paid to the government by the payer of the income rather than by the recipient of the income. The tax is thus withheld or deducted from the income due to the recipient. In most jurisdictions, _____ tax applies to employment income. Many jurisdictions also require _____ tax on payments of interest or dividends. In most jurisdictions, there are additional _____ tax obligations if the recipient of the income is resident in a different jurisdiction, and in those circumstances _____ tax sometimes applies to royalties, rent or even the sale of real estate. Governments use _____ tax as a means to combat tax evasion, and sometimes impose additional _____ tax requirements if the recipient has been delinquent in filing tax returns, or in industries where tax evasion is perceived to be common.

Exam Probability: **Medium**

20. *Answer choices:*

(see index for correct answer)

- a. Withholding
- b. Expatriation tax
- c. Controlled foreign corporation
- d. Common Reporting Standard

Guidance: level 1

:: Manufacturing ::

_____ costs are all manufacturing costs that are related to the cost object but cannot be traced to that cost object in an economically feasible way.

Exam Probability: **Medium**

21. *Answer choices:*

(see index for correct answer)

- a. Advanced planning and scheduling
- b. Glass production
- c. Acheson process
- d. Initial Reject

Guidance: level 1

:: Generally Accepted Accounting Principles ::

A _____ , in accrual accounting, is any account where the asset or liability is not realized until a future date , e.g. annuities, charges, taxes, income, etc. The deferred item may be carried, dependent on type of _____ , as either an asset or liability. See also accrual.

Exam Probability: **Low**

22. *Answer choices:*

(see index for correct answer)

- a. Liability
- b. Operating profit
- c. Net profit
- d. Deferral

Guidance: level 1

:: Valuation (finance) ::

The _____ is one of three major groups of methodologies, called valuation approaches, used by appraisers. It is particularly common in commercial real estate appraisal and in business appraisal. The fundamental math is similar to the methods used for financial valuation, securities analysis, or bond pricing. However, there are some significant and important modifications when used in real estate or business valuation.

Exam Probability: **High**

23. *Answer choices:*

(see index for correct answer)

- a. Appraisal Institute
- b. Appraisal value
- c. Value-in-use
- d. International Valuation Standards Council

Guidance: level 1

:: Types of business entity ::

A sole _____, also known as the sole trader, individual entrepreneurship or _____, is a type of enterprise that is owned and run by one person and in which there is no legal distinction between the owner and the business entity. A sole trader does not necessarily work 'alone'—it is possible for the sole trader to employ other people.

Exam Probability: **Medium**

24. *Answer choices:*

(see index for correct answer)

- a. Private company limited by guarantee
- b. Quasi corporation
- c. Proprietorship
- d. Svenskt utlandsregistrerat f%C3%B6retag

Guidance: level 1

:: Accounting software ::

_____ is any item or verifiable record that is generally accepted as payment for goods and services and repayment of debts, such as taxes, in a particular country or socio-economic context. The main functions of _____ are distinguished as: a medium of exchange, a unit of account, a store of value and sometimes, a standard of deferred payment. Any item or verifiable record that fulfils these functions can be considered as _____ .

Exam Probability: **Medium**

25. *Answer choices:*

(see index for correct answer)

- a. Money
- b. Kerridge Commercial Systems
- c. Cheqbook
- d. Teaspiller

Guidance: level 1

:: Accounting source documents ::

_____ is a letter sent by a customer to a supplier to inform the supplier that their invoice has been paid. If the customer is paying by cheque, the _____ often accompanies the cheque. The advice may consist of a literal letter or of a voucher attached to the side or top of the cheque.

Exam Probability: **Low**

26. *Answer choices:*

(see index for correct answer)

- a. Invoice
- b. Credit memorandum
- c. Bank statement
- d. Remittance advice

Guidance: level 1

:: Accounting terminology ::

_____ is money owed by a business to its suppliers shown as a liability on a company's balance sheet. It is distinct from notes payable liabilities, which are debts created by formal legal instrument documents.

Exam Probability: **Medium**

27. *Answer choices:*

(see index for correct answer)

- a. Enterprise liquidity
- b. Capital surplus
- c. Basis of accounting
- d. Accounts payable

Guidance: level 1

:: Debt ::

A _____ is a party that has a claim on the services of a second party. It is a person or institution to whom money is owed. The first party, in general, has provided some property or service to the second party under the assumption that the second party will return an equivalent property and service. The second party is frequently called a debtor or borrower. The first party is called the _____ , which is the lender of property, service, or money.

Exam Probability: **Low**

28. *Answer choices:*

(see index for correct answer)

- a. Creditor
- b. Christians Against Poverty
- c. gearing
- d. Debit note

Guidance: level 1

:: Fraud ::

In law, _____ is intentional deception to secure unfair or unlawful gain, or to deprive a victim of a legal right. _____ can violate civil law, a criminal law, or it may cause no loss of money, property or legal right but still be an element of another civil or criminal wrong. The purpose of _____ may be monetary gain or other benefits, for example by obtaining a passport, travel document, or driver's license, or mortgage _____, where the perpetrator may attempt to qualify for a mortgage by way of false statements.

Exam Probability: **High**

29. *Answer choices:*

(see index for correct answer)

- a. Double billing
- b. SHERIFF
- c. Fraud Squad
- d. Parcel mule scam

Guidance: level 1

:: Accounting terminology ::

_____ is an independent, objective assurance and consulting activity designed to add value to and improve an organization's operations. It helps an organization accomplish its objectives by bringing a systematic, disciplined approach to evaluate and improve the effectiveness of risk management, control and governance processes. _____ achieves this by providing insight and recommendations based on analyses and assessments of data and business processes. With commitment to integrity and accountability, _____ provides value to governing bodies and senior management as an objective source of independent advice. Professionals called internal auditors are employed by organizations to perform the _____ activity.

Exam Probability: **Low**

30. *Answer choices:*

(see index for correct answer)

- a. Accrual
- b. Basis of accounting
- c. Mark-to-market
- d. Internal auditing

Guidance: level 1

:: Management accounting ::

_____ is a professional certification credential in the management accounting and financial management fields. The certification signifies that the person possesses knowledge in the areas of financial planning, analysis, control, decision support, and professional ethics. The CMA is a U.S.-based, globally recognized certification offered by the Institute of Management Accountants.

Exam Probability: **Low**

31. *Answer choices:*

(see index for correct answer)

- a. Financial statement analysis
- b. Operating profit margin
- c. Contribution margin
- d. Investment center

Guidance: level 1

:: Management accounting ::

_____s are costs that change as the quantity of the good or service that a business produces changes. _____s are the sum of marginal costs over all units produced. They can also be considered normal costs. Fixed costs and _____s make up the two components of total cost. Direct costs are costs that can easily be associated with a particular cost object. However, not all _____s are direct costs. For example, variable manufacturing overhead costs are _____s that are indirect costs, not direct costs. _____s are sometimes called unit-level costs as they vary with the number of units produced.

Exam Probability: **Medium**

32. *Answer choices:*

(see index for correct answer)

- a. Constraints accounting
- b. Financial statement analysis
- c. Direct material price variance
- d. Variance

Guidance: level 1

:: Accounting terminology ::

Accounts are typically defined by an identifier and a caption or header and are coded by account type. In computerized accounting systems with computable quantity accounting, the accounts can have a quantity measure definition.

Exam Probability: **Low**

33. *Answer choices:*

(see index for correct answer)

- a. Account
- b. Checkoff
- c. Statement of financial position
- d. Chart of accounts

Guidance: level 1

:: ::

> In accounting, the _____ is a measure of the number of times inventory is sold or used in a time period such as a year. It is calculated to see if a business has an excessive inventory in comparison to its sales level. The equation for _____ equals the cost of goods sold divided by the average inventory. _____ is also known as inventory turns, merchandise turnover, stockturn, stock turns, turns, and stock turnover.

Exam Probability: **Medium**

34. *Answer choices:*

(see index for correct answer)

- a. information systems assessment
- b. levels of analysis

- c. co-culture
- d. Inventory turnover

Guidance: level 1

:: Accounting organizations ::

> The _____ promotes accounting education, research and practice. Founded in 1916 as the American Association of University Instructors in Accounting, its present name was adopted in 1936. The Association is a voluntary group of persons interested in accounting education and research.

Exam Probability: **Low**

35. *Answer choices:*

(see index for correct answer)

- a. American Accounting Association
- b. Professional accounting body
- c. Public Interest Oversight Board
- d. Centre for Social and Environmental Accounting Research

Guidance: level 1

:: Loans ::

In finance, a _____ is the lending of money by one or more individuals, organizations, or other entities to other individuals, organizations etc. The recipient incurs a debt, and is usually liable to pay interest on that debt until it is repaid, and also to repay the principal amount borrowed.

Exam Probability: **Medium**

36. *Answer choices:*

(see index for correct answer)

- a. Loan
- b. Stafford Loan
- c. Mortgage assumption
- d. Federal Perkins Loan

Guidance: level 1

:: Inventory ::

_____ is the amount of inventory a company has in stock at the end of its fiscal year. It is closely related with _____ cost, which is the amount of money spent to get these goods in stock. It should be calculated at the lower of cost or market.

Exam Probability: **Low**

37. *Answer choices:*

(see index for correct answer)

- a. Reorder point
- b. Inventory optimization
- c. Periodic inventory
- d. Order picking

Guidance: level 1

:: Management ::

The _____ is a strategy performance management tool – a semi-standard structured report, that can be used by managers to keep track of the execution of activities by the staff within their control and to monitor the consequences arising from these actions.

Exam Probability: **High**

38. *Answer choices:*
(see index for correct answer)

- a. Omnex
- b. Complementary assets
- c. Behavioral risk management
- d. Remedial action

Guidance: level 1

:: ::

A _____ is an organization, usually a group of people or a company, authorized to act as a single entity and recognized as such in law. Early incorporated entities were established by charter. Most jurisdictions now allow the creation of new _____ s through registration.

Exam Probability: **Low**

39. *Answer choices:*

(see index for correct answer)

- a. cultural
- b. Corporation
- c. similarity-attraction theory
- d. information systems assessment

Guidance: level 1

:: Financial accounting ::

A _____ is an ownership interest in a corporation with enough voting stock shares to prevail in any stockholders' motion. A majority of voting shares is always a _____ . When a party holds less than the majority of the voting shares, other present circumstances can be considered to determine whether that party is still considered to hold a controlling ownership interest.

Exam Probability: **Medium**

40. *Answer choices:*
(see index for correct answer)

- a. Deferred Acquisition Costs
- b. Accelerated depreciation
- c. Controlling interest
- d. Associate company

Guidance: level 1

:: Information systems ::

An accounting as an information system is a system of collecting, storing and processing financial and accounting data that are used by decision makers. An _____ is generally a computer-based method for tracking accounting activity in conjunction with information technology resources. The resulting financial reports can be used internally by management or externally by other interested parties including investors, creditors and tax authorities.

_____ s are designed to support all accounting functions and activities including auditing, financial accounting & reporting, managerial/ management accounting and tax. The most widely adopted accounting information systems are auditing and financial reporting modules.

Exam Probability: **High**

41. *Answer choices:*

(see index for correct answer)

- a. Work systems
- b. Social Study of Information Systems
- c. Shadow IT
- d. Accounting information system

Guidance: level 1

:: Accounting in the United States ::

Founded in 1887, the _____ is the national professional organization of Certified Public Accountants in the United States, with more than 418,000 members in 143 countries in business and industry, public practice, government, education, student affiliates and international associates. It sets ethical standards for the profession and U.S. auditing standards for audits of private companies, non-profit organizations, federal, state and local governments. It also develops and grades the Uniform CPA Examination. The AICPA maintains offices in New York City; Washington, DC; Durham, NC; and Ewing, NJ. The AICPA celebrated the 125th anniversary of its founding in 2012.

Exam Probability: **High**

42. *Answer choices:*

(see index for correct answer)

- a. Certified Government Financial Manager
- b. Other comprehensive income
- c. American Institute of Certified Public Accountants
- d. Accounting Today

Guidance: level 1

:: Expense ::

A company's _____, or As a result, the computation of the _____ is considerably more complex. Tax law may provide for different treatment of items of income and expenses as a result of tax policy. The differences may be of permanent or temporary nature. Permanent items are in the form of non taxable income and non taxable expenses. Things such as expenses considered not deductible by taxing authorities , the range of tax rates applicable to various levels of income, different tax rates in different jurisdictions, multiple layers of tax on income, and other issues.

Exam Probability: **High**

43. *Answer choices:*

(see index for correct answer)

- a. Expense account
- b. Stock option expensing
- c. Tax expense
- d. Freight expense

Guidance: level 1

:: United States federal income tax ::

Under United States tax law, the _____ is a dollar amount that non-itemizers may subtract from their income before income tax is applied. Taxpayers may choose either itemized deductions or the _____ , but usually choose whichever results in the lesser amount of tax payable. The _____ is available to US citizens and aliens who are resident for tax purposes and who are individuals, married persons, and heads of household. The _____ is based on filing status and typically increases each year. It is not available to nonresident aliens residing in the United States. Additional amounts are available for persons who are blind and/or are at least 65 years of age.

Exam Probability: **Low**

44. *Answer choices:*

(see index for correct answer)

- a. Dealer equity option
- b. Standard deduction
- c. Stepped-up basis
- d. Philippines Charitable Giving Assistance Act

Guidance: level 1

:: Inventory ::

It requires a detailed physical count, so that the company knows exactly how many of each goods brought on specific dates remained at year end inventory. When this information is found, the amount of goods are multiplied by their purchase cost at their purchase date, to get a number for the ending inventory cost.

Exam Probability: **Medium**

45. *Answer choices:*

(see index for correct answer)

- a. Specific identification
- b. Consignment stock
- c. Stock-taking
- d. Stock obsolescence

Guidance: level 1

:: Generally Accepted Accounting Principles ::

In accrual accounting, the revenue recognition principle states that expenses should be recorded during the period in which they are incurred, regardless of when the transfer of cash occurs. Conversely, cash basis accounting calls for the recognition of an expense when the cash is paid, regardless of when the expense was actually incurred.

Exam Probability: **Low**

46. *Answer choices:*

(see index for correct answer)

- a. Depreciation
- b. Matching principle
- c. net realisable value
- d. Standard Business Reporting

Guidance: level 1

:: Television terminology ::

> A nonprofit organization, also known as a non-business entity, _____ organization, or nonprofit institution, is dedicated to furthering a particular social cause or advocating for a shared point of view. In economic terms, it is an organization that uses its surplus of the revenues to further achieve its ultimate objective, rather than distributing its income to the organization's shareholders, leaders, or members. Nonprofits are tax exempt or charitable, meaning they do not pay income tax on the money that they receive for their organization. They can operate in religious, scientific, research, or educational settings.

Exam Probability: **Low**

47. *Answer choices:*

(see index for correct answer)

- a. multiplexing
- b. distance learning

- c. Satellite television
- d. Not-for-profit

Guidance: level 1

:: Financial ratios ::

_____ is the difference between revenue and cost of goods sold divided by revenue. _____ is expressed as a percentage. Generally, it is calculated as the selling price of an item, less the cost of goods sold. _____ is often used interchangeably with Gross Profit, but the terms are different. When speaking about a monetary amount, it is technically correct to use the term Gross Profit; when referring to a percentage or ratio, it is correct to use _____. In other words, _____ is a percentage value, while Gross Profit is a monetary value.

Exam Probability: **Medium**

48. *Answer choices:*

(see index for correct answer)

- a. Gross margin
- b. Net profit margin
- c. Quick ratio
- d. Return on tangible equity

Guidance: level 1

:: Banking ::

A _____ is a financial institution that accepts deposits from the public and creates credit. Lending activities can be performed either directly or indirectly through capital markets. Due to their importance in the financial stability of a country, _____ s are highly regulated in most countries. Most nations have institutionalized a system known as fractional reserve _____ ing under which _____ s hold liquid assets equal to only a portion of their current liabilities. In addition to other regulations intended to ensure liquidity, _____ s are generally subject to minimum capital requirements based on an international set of capital standards, known as the Basel Accords.

Exam Probability: **High**

49. *Answer choices:*

(see index for correct answer)

- a. Overnight market
- b. Numbered bank account
- c. Variance swap
- d. Bank

Guidance: level 1

:: Asset ::

In accounting, a _____ is any asset which can reasonably be expected to be sold, consumed, or exhausted through the normal operations of a business within the current fiscal year or operating cycle . Typical _____ s include cash, cash equivalents, short-term investments , accounts receivable, stock inventory, supplies, and the portion of prepaid liabilities which will be paid within a year.In simple words, assets which are held for a short period are known as _____ s. Such assets are expected to be realised in cash or consumed during the normal operating cycle of the business.

Exam Probability: **Low**

50. *Answer choices:*

(see index for correct answer)

- a. Current asset
- b. Asset

Guidance: level 1

:: Business ethics ::

In accounting and in most Schools of economic thought, _____ is a rational and unbiased estimate of the potential market price of a good, service, or asset. It takes into account such objectivity factors as.

Exam Probability: **Low**

51. *Answer choices:*

(see index for correct answer)

- a. Workplace bullying
- b. Anti-sweatshop movement
- c. Bribery Act 2010
- d. Anatomy of Greed

Guidance: level 1

:: Financial statements ::

A Statement of changes in equity and similarly the statement of changes in owner's equity for a sole trader, statement of changes in partners' equity for a partnership, statement of changes in Shareholders' equity for a Company or statement of changes in Taxpayers' equity for Government financial statements is one of the four basic financial statements.

Exam Probability: **Medium**

52. *Answer choices:*
(see index for correct answer)

- a. Statement on Auditing Standards No. 70: Service Organizations
- b. Statement of retained earnings
- c. Emphasis of matter
- d. Balance sheet

Guidance: level 1

:: Management accounting ::

_____ accounting is a traditional cost accounting method introduced in the 1920s, as an alternative for the traditional cost accounting method based on historical costs.

Exam Probability: **Low**

53. *Answer choices:*

(see index for correct answer)

- a. Institute of Certified Management Accountants
- b. Institute of Cost and Management Accountants of Bangladesh
- c. Standard cost
- d. Management accounting

Guidance: level 1

:: Taxation in the United States ::

Basis, as used in United States tax law, is the original cost of property, adjusted for factors such as depreciation. When property is sold, the taxpayer pays/ taxes on a capital gain/ that equals the amount realized on the sale minus the sold property's basis.

Exam Probability: **High**

54. *Answer choices:*

(see index for correct answer)

- a. Conscience Fund
- b. Tax ladder
- c. Cost basis
- d. Treasury Inspector General for Tax Administration

Guidance: level 1

:: ::

A _____, in the word's original meaning, is a sheet of paper on which one performs work. They come in many forms, most commonly associated with children's school work assignments, tax forms, and accounting or other business environments. Software is increasingly taking over the paper-based _____.

Exam Probability: **High**

55. *Answer choices:*

(see index for correct answer)

- a. hierarchical
- b. imperative
- c. Worksheet
- d. process perspective

Guidance: level 1

:: Generally Accepted Accounting Principles ::

> In business and accounting, _____ is an entity's income minus cost of goods sold, expenses and taxes for an accounting period. It is computed as the residual of all revenues and gains over all expenses and losses for the period, and has also been defined as the net increase in shareholders' equity that results from a company's operations. In the context of the presentation of financial statements, the IFRS Foundation defines _____ as synonymous with profit and loss. The difference between revenue and the cost of making a product or providing a service, before deducting overheads, payroll, taxation, and interest payments. This is different from operating income.

Exam Probability: **High**

56. *Answer choices:*

(see index for correct answer)

- a. Closing entries
- b. Gross income
- c. Net income

- d. Generally accepted accounting principles

Guidance: level 1

:: Mathematical finance ::

In economics and finance, _____, also known as present discounted value, is the value of an expected income stream determined as of the date of valuation. The _____ is always less than or equal to the future value because money has interest-earning potential, a characteristic referred to as the time value of money, except during times of negative interest rates, when the _____ will be more than the future value. Time value can be described with the simplified phrase, "A dollar today is worth more than a dollar tomorrow". Here, `worth more` means that its value is greater. A dollar today is worth more than a dollar tomorrow because the dollar can be invested and earn a day`s worth of interest, making the total accumulate to a value more than a dollar by tomorrow. Interest can be compared to rent. Just as rent is paid to a landlord by a tenant without the ownership of the asset being transferred, interest is paid to a lender by a borrower who gains access to the money for a time before paying it back. By letting the borrower have access to the money, the lender has sacrificed the exchange value of this money, and is compensated for it in the form of interest. The initial amount of the borrowed funds is less than the total amount of money paid to the lender.

Exam Probability: **Medium**

57. *Answer choices:*

(see index for correct answer)

- a. Present value
- b. No-arbitrage bounds

- c. Black swan theory
- d. No free lunch with vanishing risk

Guidance: level 1

:: Legal terms ::

A _____ is a gathering of people who have been invited by a host for the purposes of socializing, conversation, recreation, or as part of a festival or other commemoration of a special occasion. A _____ will typically feature food and beverages, and often music and dancing or other forms of entertainment. In many Western countries, parties for teens and adults are associated with drinking alcohol such as beer, wine, or distilled spirits.

Exam Probability: **Low**

58. *Answer choices:*

(see index for correct answer)

- a. Adverse party
- b. Party
- c. Argumentative
- d. Grievous bodily harm

Guidance: level 1

:: Inventory ::

Costs are associated with particular goods using one of the several formulas, including specific identification, first-in first-out, or average cost. Costs include all costs of purchase, costs of conversion and other costs that are incurred in bringing the inventories to their present location and condition. Costs of goods made by the businesses include material, labor, and allocated overhead. The costs of those goods which are not yet sold are deferred as costs of inventory until the inventory is sold or written down in value.

Exam Probability: **Medium**

59. *Answer choices:*

(see index for correct answer)

- a. Cost of goods available for sale
- b. Safety stock
- c. Cost of goods sold
- d. Stock control

Guidance: level 1

INDEX: Correct Answers

Foundations of Business

1. d: Planning

2. b: Firm

3. a: Negotiation

4. d: Cooperative

5. c: Marketing

6. c: Information systems

7. b: Strategic planning

8. b: Competitor

9. c: Foreign direct investment

10. d: Strategy

11. c: Health

12. a: Cash flow

13. b: Life

14. a: Building

15. d: Affirmative action

16. a: Management

17. a: Explanation

18. : Credit

19. d: Policy

20. b: Number

21. a: Limited liability

22. b: Finance

23. : Error

24. b: Threat

25. b: Manufacturing

26. : Stock

27. b: Economies of scale

28. : Internal control

29. : Contract

30. c: Empowerment

31. a: Cooperation

32. c: Stock market

33. b: Analysis

34. d: Copyright

35. a: Risk

36. c: Law

37. b: Opportunity cost

38. b: Brainstorming

39. c: Comparative advantage

40. a: Scheduling

41. b: Working capital

42. a: Perception

43. b: Question

44. d: Competitive advantage

45. : Privacy

46. d: Human resources

47. b: Economy

48. : Patent

49. a: Buyer

50. d: Net income

51. : Price

52. c: Outsourcing

53. : Sales

54. d: Resource management

55. d: Organizational structure

56. c: Pattern

57. a: Loan

58. : Entrepreneur

59. : Currency

Management

1. : North American Free Trade Agreement

2. : Myers-Briggs type

3. : Management process

4. b: Bias

5. b: Reputation

6. b: Cost leadership

7. a: Enron

8. d: Simulation

9. b: General manager

10. d: Partnership

11. d: Property

12. a: Competitive advantage

13. a: Risk management

14. d: Economies of scale

15. b: Kaizen

16. c: Bottom line

17. b: Decision-making

18. : Assessment center

19. c: Return on investment

20. d: Project manager

21. d: Situational leadership

22. a: Outsourcing

23. : Telecommuting

24. a: Income

25. : Employment

26. c: Goal setting

27. a: Corporate governance

28. b: Continuous improvement

29. : Training and development

30. b: Environmental scanning

31. : Revenue

32. : Supervisor

33. : Decision tree

34. b: Asset

35. d: Discipline

36. : Board of directors

37. b: Leadership development

38. d: Job enlargement

39. c: Research and development

40. c: Market share

41. b: Performance appraisal

42. d: Interaction

43. a: Job design

44. b: Initiative

45. : Overtime

46. c: Recruitment

47. a: Bounded rationality

48. b: Intellectual property

49. d: Operations management

50. a: Inventory control

51. a: Philosophy

52. d: Offshoring

53. : Tariff

54. c: Enabling

55. a: Product design

56. d: Organizational structure

57. b: Labor relations

58. : Industrial Revolution

59. b: Merger

Business law

1. b: Money laundering

2. d: Reasonable person

3. : Tangible

4. a: Operation of law

5. b: Competitor

6. c: Real property

7. d: Oral contract

8. c: Lanham Act

9. d: Contract

10. : Subsidiary

11. d: Issuer

12. b: Clayton Act

13. c: Asset

14. b: Creditor

15. b: Presumption

16. b: Implied warranty

17. b: Res ipsa

18. b: Investment

19. d: Trial

20. c: Breach of contract

21. : Contract law

22. : Plaintiff

23. : Consideration

24. b: Restraint of trade

25. c: Mediation

26. a: Public policy

27. a: Complaint

28. : Exclusionary rule

29. c: Criminal procedure

30. a: Bankruptcy

31. d: Charter

32. : Private law

33. d: Garnishment

34. b: Categorical imperative

35. b: Auction

36. c: Requirements contract

37. : S corporation

38. b: Offeree

39. d: Certiorari

40. : Statute of limitations

41. : Treaty

42. : Insurable interest

43. c: Lease

44. : Appellate Court

45. c: Interest

46. a: Economic Espionage Act

47. b: Service mark

48. : Limited partnership

49. : Operating agreement

50. c: Joint venture

51. c: Amendment

52. b: Committee

53. d: Authority

54. a: Prohibition

55. : Implied authority

56. a: Free trade

57. : Insurance

58. b: Constitutional law

59. c: Ford

Finance

1. b: Return on assets

2. c: Accelerated depreciation

3. a: Financial risk

4. : Treasury stock

5. a: Amortization

6. : General ledger

7. b: Historical cost

8. d: Risk premium

9. b: Land

10. c: Investment

11. b: Capital gain

12. a: Annuity

13. b: Rate risk

14. d: Government bond

15. a: Time value of money

16. c: Market value

17. c: Subsidiary ledger

18. c: Risk

19. : Write-off

20. c: Goldman Sachs

21. : Net present value

22. d: Cash flow

23. d: Equity method

24. d: Economy

25. d: Income

26. : Convertible bond

27. : Pension

28. d: Financial analysis

29. a: Source document

30. a: Interest

31. d: Yield to maturity

32. c: Purchasing

33. a: Fiscal year

34. d: Derivative

35. d: Debit card

36. c: Financial crisis

37. c: Periodic inventory

38. d: Discounting

39. d: Customer

40. a: Value Line

41. c: Relevance

42. c: Stock

43. : Management accounting

44. b: Asset

45. c: Board of directors

46. c: Credit

47. c: Internal rate of return

48. : Accountant

49. c: Payback period

50. : Long-term liabilities

51. d: Current ratio

52. a: Commercial bank

53. a: Gross margin

54. : Capital asset

55. a: WorldCom

56. a: Income tax

57. c: Public Company Accounting Oversight Board

58. : Vacation

59. d: Annual report

Human resource management

1. a: Labor relations

2. b: Internship

3. c: Intuition

4. d: Workforce planning

5. d: Union shop

6. b: Trainee

7. : Executive search

8. b: Theory Z

9. c: Interview

10. : Meeting

11. d: Centralization

12. d: Expatriate

13. c: Resource management

14. : Halo effect

15. c: Employee stock

16. d: Seniority

17. : Global workforce

18. c: Succession planning

19. d: Career development

20. b: Predictive validity

21. : McDonnell Douglas Corp. v. Green

22. b: Performance management

23. d: Glass ceiling

24. a: Proactive

25. c: Cross-functional team

26. : Strategic planning

27. c: Officer

28. : Organizational socialization

29. d: Enforcement

30. a: Ricci v. DeStefano

31. b: Goal setting

32. : Criterion validity

33. b: Substance abuse

34. d: Background check

35. : Restructuring

36. a: On-the-job training

37. a: Social contract

38. c: Employee engagement

39. b: Profession

40. : Health Reimbursement Account

41. d: Applicant tracking system

42. a: Congress

43. c: Assessment center

44. d: Job fair

45. c: Management by objectives

46. c: International Brotherhood of Teamsters

47. b: Age Discrimination in Employment Act

48. d: Minimum wage

49. a: Expert power

50. a: Behavior modification

51. b: Career management

52. a: Cost leadership

53. d: Socialization

54. b: Telecommuting

55. : Closed shop

56. a: Trade union

57. b: Cafeteria plan

58. c: Flexible spending account

59. b: Census

Information systems

1. c: Business process

2. d: Statistics

3. : Security controls

4. c: Business process management

5. c: Mozy

6. : Software as a service

7. b: Word

8. d: Competitive intelligence

9. d: Data element

10. d: Online analytical processing

11. c: Payment system

12. c: Blogger

13. b: PayPal

14. d: Authentication

15. d: Cybersquatting

16. a: Vulnerability

17. d: Documentation

18. b: Resource management

19. b: Master data

20. : Supply chain management

21. a: Google

22. c: Automation

23. a: Random access

24. d: Consumerization

25. a: Digital rights management

26. d: Click-through

27. b: Service-oriented architecture

28. a: Information systems

29. : Structured query language

30. a: Web page

31. d: Information technology

32. b: M-Pesa

33. a: Google Calendar

34. c: Change management

35. c: Social shopping

36. a: Commercial off-the-shelf

37. a: Read-only memory

38. d: Social network

39. d: BitTorrent

40. : Authentication protocol

41. b: Password

42. a: Wide Area Network

43. c: Availability

44. d: Computer security

45. a: American Express

46. b: Data center

47. b: Global Positioning System

48. a: Telnet

49. b: Information literacy

50. : Data integration

51. : Netflix

52. a: Semantic Web

53. b: Expert system

54. d: Electronic funds transfer

55. : Health Insurance Portability and Accountability Act

56. c: Authorization

57. d: Domain name

58. c: Business process reengineering

59. : Carnivore

Marketing

1. b: Market share

2. c: Warehouse

3. c: Incentive

4. : Merchant

5. d: Mass marketing

6. d: Cost

7. : Competitor

8. b: Noise

9. b: North American Free Trade Agreement

10. d: Reseller

11. : Customer retention

12. b: Loyalty program

13. c: Corporation

14. : Intranet

15. c: Business marketing

16. b: Electronic data interchange

17. a: Supermarket

18. c: Market development

19. b: Cognitive dissonance

20. : Productivity

21. : Resource

22. c: Public

23. d: Inflation

24. c: Aid

25. c: Early adopter

26. d: Consideration

27. b: Product differentiation

28. d: Evolution

29. a: Psychographic

30. : Brand equity

31. c: Testimonial

32. c: Blog

33. : Creative brief

34. a: Information system

35. b: Wall Street Journal

36. d: Gross domestic product

37. c: Sales promotion

38. c: Interactive marketing

39. b: Communication

40. a: Raw material

41. d: Social networking

42. d: Statistic

43. d: Retailing

44. : Health

45. d: Brand loyalty

46. a: Credit

47. b: Fixed cost

48. d: Market segments

49. d: Expense

50. a: Supply chain management

51. c: Billboard

52. c: Clayton Act

53. : Industry

54. c: Quantitative research

55. : Exchange rate

56. b: American Express

57. d: Life

58. : Global marketing

59. b: INDEX

Manufacturing

1. b: Management process

2. c: Quality costs

3. c: Supplier relationship management

4. b: Pareto analysis

5. b: Technical support

6. d: Knowledge management

7. d: Dimension

8. c: Six Sigma

9. c: Pattern

10. b: Process capital

11. c: Synergy

12. b: Scientific management

13. : Transaction cost

14. b: Gantt chart

15. d: Paper

16. d: ROOT

17. c: Asset

18. c: Quality control

19. b: Reflux

20. a: Purchasing process

21. a: Rolling Wave planning

22. d: Clay

23. a: Resource

24. b: Heat transfer

25. a: Opportunity cost

26. d: Prize

27. d: Elastomer

28. : Economic order quantity

29. a: Rolling

30. : Third-party logistics

31. : Aggregate planning

32. d: Malcolm Baldrige National Quality Award

33. b: Coating

34. a: Process management

35. c: Blanket

36. c: Change management

37. b: Mary Kay

38. d: Concurrent engineering

39. d: Inventory

40. d: Poka-yoke

41. : Toshiba

42. : Good

43. : Zero Defects

44. d: METRIC

45. b: New product development

46. : Control chart

47. d: Perfect competition

48. d: Cost

49. b: Ball

50. c: Licensed production

51. b: Strategic sourcing

52. d: Request for quotation

53. b: Retail

54. c: Process engineering

55. b: Total quality management

56. b: Process flow diagram

57. b: Purchasing manager

58. c: Solution

59. c: Quality management

Commerce

1. c: Technology

2. b: Walt Disney

3. : Evaluation

4. d: Import

5. d: Automation

6. b: Wall Street Journal

7. c: Bankruptcy

8. c: Silver

9. a: Credit card

10. d: Value-added network

11. d: Investment

12. b: Customs

13. d: Committee

14. c: Phishing

15. a: Total cost

16. b: Welfare

17. c: Initiative

18. d: Competitive advantage

19. c: Competitor

20. c: Overtime

21. : Recruitment

22. d: Shares

23. a: Cost structure

24. b: WebSphere Commerce

25. d: Payment card

26. a: Organization chart

27. b: Credit

28. c: Quality assurance

29. : Standing

30. : Online advertising

31. a: Antitrust

32. a: Planning

33. : Encryption

34. : Minimum wage

35. c: Utility

36. b: Micropayment

37. d: Revenue

38. d: Lease

39. c: Return on investment

40. a: Goal

41. d: Trade show

42. a: Stock

43. d: Brand

44. b: Dutch auction

45. d: Lycos

46. a: Publicity

47. d: Americans with Disabilities Act

48. b: Reverse auction

49. : Hearing

50. : Tariff

51. c: Boot

52. b: Market research

53. a: International trade

54. a: Free market

55. c: Subsidy

56. a: Advertisement

57. a: Land

58. b: Industry

59. d: Merchandising

Business ethics

1. b: Martin Luther

2. a: Collusion

3. b: Lead

4. b: Volcker Rule

5. d: Clayton Act

6. : New York Stock Exchange

7. d: Recovery Act

8. b: Minimum wage

9. c: Electronic waste

10. a: Natural gas

11. : Principal Financial

12. a: Community development financial institution

13. c: Partnership

14. : Internal control

15. a: Energy policy

16. c: Employee Polygraph Protection Act

17. b: Pollution

18. d: Protestant work ethic

19. d: Lawsuit

20. d: Foreign Corrupt Practices Act

21. c: Risk assessment

22. d: Trade

23. : Hedonism

24. d: Biofuel

25. b: Supply Chain

26. b: Corporation

27. b: Greenwashing

28. : Sexual harassment

29. d: Cause-related marketing

30. a: Financial Stability Oversight Council

31. c: Public relations

32. d: Catholicism

33. c: Sullivan principles

34. d: Edgewood College

35. b: Executive compensation

36. : Dilemma

37. b: Green marketing

38. c: Ponzi scheme

39. a: Pure Food and Drug Act

40. d: Social responsibility

41. a: Coal

42. a: Sustainability

43. d: Real estate

44. a: Skill

45. b: WorldCom

46. b: Petroleum

47. a: White-collar crime

48. b: Charles Ponzi

49. a: Organizational structure

50. c: Lead paint

51. c: Living wage

52. a: Dress code

53. a: Pollution Prevention

54. b: ExxonMobil

55. : Criminal law

56. b: Consumer Protection

57. a: Right to work

58. : Accounting

59. b: Ethical leadership

Accounting

1. : Controversy

2. : Annual report

3. a: Common stock

4. c: Average cost

5. a: Voucher

6. c: Asset turnover

7. : Joint venture

8. b: Capital loss

9. a: MACRS

10. : Zero-based budgeting

11. d: Generally Accepted Accounting Principles

12. c: Financial Accounting Foundation

13. d: International Financial Reporting Standards

14. : Error

15. c: Management by exception

16. a: Accounting software

17. a: Profit center

18. a: Separation of duties

19. b: Activity-based costing

20. a: Withholding

21. : Manufacturing overhead

22. d: Deferral

23. : Income approach

24. c: Proprietorship

25. a: Money

26. d: Remittance advice

27. d: Accounts payable

28. a: Creditor

29. : Fraud

30. d: Internal auditing

31. : Certified Management Accountant

32. : Variable cost

33. d: Chart of accounts

34. d: Inventory turnover

35. a: American Accounting Association

36. a: Loan

37. : Ending inventory

38. : Balanced scorecard

39. b: Corporation

40. c: Controlling interest

41. d: Accounting information system